IT'S ALL IN THE
Delivery

THE WILLIAM & BETTYE NOWLIN SERIES
in Art, History, and Culture of the Western Hemisphere

IT'S ALL IN THE
Delivery

PREGNANCY
in AMERICAN
FILM
and
TELEVISION
COMEDY

VICTORIA STURTEVANT

University of Texas Press *Austin*

Copyright © 2024 by the University of Texas Press
All rights reserved
Printed in the United States of America
First edition, 2024

Requests for permission to reproduce material from this work should be sent to
permissions@utpress.utexas.edu.

♾ The paper used in this book meets the minimum requirements of ANSI/NISO
Z39.48-1992 (R1997) (Permanence of Paper).

Library of Congress Cataloging-in-Publication Data

Names: Sturtevant, Victoria, 1973– author.
Title: It's all in the delivery : pregnancy in American film and television comedy /
    Victoria Sturtevant.
Other titles: It is all in the delivery : pregnancy in American film and television
    comedy | William & Bettye Nowlin series in art, history, and culture of the Western
    Hemisphere.
Description: First edition. | Austin : University of Texas Press, 2024. | Series: The William
    & Bettye Nowlin series in art, history, and culture of the Western Hemisphere |
    Includes index.
Identifiers: LCCN 2024009758
    ISBN 978-1-4773-3043-2 (hardcover)
    ISBN 978-1-4773-3044-9 (paperback)
    ISBN 978-1-4773-3045-6 (pdf)
    ISBN 978-1-4773-3046-3 (epub)
Subjects: LCSH: Pregnancy in motion pictures—History. | Pregnancy in motion
    pictures—Social aspects—History. | Pregnancy in motion pictures—Censorship—
    History. | Pregnancy in popular culture—United States—History. | Pregnancy—
    United States—Public opinion—History. | Pregnancy—United States—Humor—
    History. | Television comedies—United States—Themes, motives—History. | Motion
    pictures—United States—Themes, motives—History.
Classification: LCC PN1995.9.P66 S78 2024 | DDC 791.43/6561—dc23/
    eng/20240329
LC record available at https://lccn.loc.gov/2024009758

doi:10.7560/330432

CONTENTS

Introduction.
What to Expect When You're Expecting
(to Read This Book) *1*

Chapter 1. **CONFINEMENTS**
Enter the Stork *29*

Chapter 2. **HYSTERICAL FATHERHOOD**
Male Pregnancy On-Screen *61*

Chapter 3. **BAD PREGNANCIES**
Social Problems and Bad Seeds *93*

Chapter 4. **BABY BUST**
Infertility and Its Discontents *119*

Chapter 5. **SHMASHMORTION**
Terminating Abortion Stigma through Comedy *153*

Conclusion.
It's All in the Delivery *187*

Acknowledgments *199*
Notes *201*
Index *215*

IT'S ALL IN THE
Delivery

FIGURE 0.1. Blondie's Blessed Event *(1942). Hollywood movies before about 1949 never showed a "baby bump," even when characters were in advanced stages of pregnancy. Here, the character Blondie (Penny Singleton) is expecting a baby quite soon but shows no sign of a bump beneath her form-fitting dress. Credit: Everett Collection.*

Introduction
WHAT TO EXPECT WHEN YOU'RE EXPECTING (TO READ THIS BOOK)

IN THE 1942 COMEDY *Blondie's Blessed Event*, Blondie Bumstead (Penny Singleton) is expecting a child at any moment—in fact, her husband has just rushed home from work, mistaking news of his dog having puppies for the beginning of his wife's labor (figure 0.1). Viewers do not need any special powers of discernment to notice that Blondie does not look the slightest bit pregnant. The big bow over the actress's belly may have been designed to disguise the lack of a "baby bump," but in fact it does the opposite, drawing attention to her slim waist. No wonder her son is building a large net to catch the stork when it visits their house—his mother shows no signs of carrying the baby in her body. In deference to midcentury rules of good taste and sexless morality, codified in the Motion Picture Production Code of 1930, physical evidence of human reproduction is simply absent from this scene.

Compare Blondie's figure with those of the women profiled in the publicity posters for the 2012 ensemble comedy *What to Expect When You're Expecting*, which celebrated a loosely connected social network of expectant mothers (see figure 0.2). The carefully styled blonde women cradle their baby bumps, stand in profile to the camera, and lean back to make their pregnant figures

1

FIGURE 0.2. *Publicity posters for* What to Expect When You're Expecting *(2012). Hollywood movies of the early twenty-first century featured baby bumps as fashionable lifestyle accessories.*

more visible. Named after a popular medical guide to pregnancy, *What to Expect* promises to immerse viewers in the nitty-gritty details behind a pastel world of glowing and very visible maternity.

A lot has changed in the years that passed between these two movies, from euphemistic erasure of the physiology of pregnancy to its unabashed proliferation. The link between sexuality and reproduction is no longer a source of shame for these women, who display their bumps like a postfeminist lifestyle accessory, marking their success in the game of acquiring it "all": financial security, heterosexual desirability, and children. The variations in the images and the accompanying pull quotes (ranging from "I just have all this extra energy" to "Pregnancy sucks") are meant to suggest a range of experiences, but that range is vanishingly narrow, as the women are still all white, middle-class, slender in the arms and face, glamorous, heterosexually coupled, and approximately in their thirties. As far as movies have come in the years since Blondie relied on the stork, a lot has also stayed the same, as popular celebrations of impending motherhood still default to blonde archetypes and still contain pregnant women in tightly structured social frames.

It's All in the Delivery: Pregnancy in American Film and Television Comedy looks at the decades connecting these two films and links the social evolution of attitudes toward pregnancy in the United States with representational strategies that transformed social discomforts into comedy. The history of on-screen pregnancy in the United States provides a fascinating lens through which to understand how reproductive biology has defined women's roles across the twentieth century and into the present, beginning with studio-era prohibitions on using the word "pregnant" or showing a visible baby bump. The book examines the baby boom–era fetishization of sentimental pregnancy, how the sexual revolution and the birth control pill ushered in new interest in nonmarital pregnancy in the 1960s and 1970s, and the emphasis on biological clocks and infertility in the 1980s and 1990s. It concludes with the millennial move toward more medically and socially candid representations of pregnancy. Throughout the book, I also reflect on the overwhelming whiteness of most of this history and the additional barriers and stigmas against non-white reproduction that have led to its shocking underrepresentation in popular media.

I define "pregnancy" broadly for this project, including issues in the interconnected spectrum of reproductive biology and family formation such as infertility, birth control, abortion, miscarriage, assisted reproductive technology, and adoption. Thinking of pregnancy broadly like this centers the diverse experiences of reproductive-age women rather than an imagined fetal trajectory from conception to birth. And while I am defining terms, I note that I use "pregnant woman" more often than the preferred "pregnant person" for much of this project because I am focusing on a specific history of how reproductive capacity has anchored a binary and asymmetrical system of gender roles. This history has always obscured the ways trans, nonbinary, and queer individuals may experience pregnancy, and it is my hope that by revealing the assumptions underscoring conventionally gendered representations of pregnancy, this book can help clear the way for more inclusive and imaginative understandings of the pregnant body. So let's get to work.

LADY PARTS

Much of this book traces a history in which pregnancy has been taboo, distorted, filtered through multiple social frames, or politicized, so I want to take a moment here to note what is at stake when popular media fall short of real candor in narratives about childbearing. Understanding the public discourse and biological facts around pregnancy and nonpregnancy is of the utmost importance at this historic moment in the United States of America. As I am writing this introduction in early 2023, less than a year has passed since the US Supreme Court's *Dobbs v. Jackson Women's Health Organization* decision ended constitutional protection of the right to abortion across all fifty states. The complex assumptions underpinning this decision emerge from decades of anti-abortion organizing that emphasized a specific view of pregnancy.

The ideas that pregnancy is easy and uncomplicated, that it is a women's issue that does not merit male attention, that the biological complexities of

Introduction · 3

the condition are shameful and taboo, and that the generic "happy ending" of new parenthood always erases maternal ambivalence about childbearing all have direct corollaries in the ways pregnancy is regulated, socially managed, insured, medicated, and economically structured in the United States. None of these familiar tropes necessarily represents the natural or inevitable way to understand pregnancy, but they have been highly influential ideological gestures specifically designed to justify a restriction on the right to abortion, as well as to gin up hostility toward other measures that enable reproductive choice, such as birth control or assisted reproductive technology. This book documents how the euphemisms, myths, and falsehoods about pregnancy that have historically circulated in American film and television implicitly support the narrowing of reproductive choices by oversimplifying a complex physical, emotional, and social experience into a set of sentimental or sexual tropes.

So why tackle this serious topic through the lens of comedy? Comedy and satire have long played an important role in making visible the blind spots in sanitized political discourse. For instance, in 2012, a number of American newspapers refused to publish a week's worth of *Doonesbury* comic strips satirizing Texas's law requiring individuals seeking an abortion to first receive and pay for a transvaginal ultrasound. In one strip (figure 0.3), a woman explains to her doctor in the first panel that she doesn't want an ultrasound in advance of the procedure. In the second and third panels, he insists that the law requires one and calls the instrument a "shaming wand." In the final panel, the doctor intones, "By the authority vested in me by the GOP base, I thee rape." David Averill, editorial page editor for the *Tulsa World* (which ran the strip on its editorial page, not the funny pages), was quoted in the *New York Times* explaining, "Many of our readers will be offended by the political stance the series takes, and some will be offended by the clinical language."[1]

It is striking that the word "clinical," often used as a synonym for clean or rigorous, here denotes obscenity because of the context of reproductive medicine. The public is understood to have a right *not* to have to encounter the details of childbearing in any but the most sanitized forms. The problem with this stance is that the public is *also* understood to have the right to weigh in on the ethics, medical care, and social behavior of pregnant women at every stage. If the public simultaneously has the right to remain ignorant of the physiology of pregnancy *and* the right to regulate its social and physical features, we have a situation that can produce effects like the Texas ultrasound law that *Doonesbury* satirizes, whose interest in the embryo imposes unexamined costs on the body of the pregnant person.

Turning from the news to the multiplex, this book argues that the increasing candor developing in cinematic representations of pregnancy is laying

FIGURE 0.3. Doonesbury *(2012)*. *This comic strip satirizing Texas ultrasound law was censored from the funny pages of some newspapers.*

important groundwork for more frank and informed public conversations about how pregnancy is a mature embodied experience, not just a fetal one. As American film comedy has gradually shed old prohibitions on the representation of bodily life in general, film and television have pushed new boundaries, mining both the clinical and the grotesque and opening up a larger zone of discourse around pregnancy as a lived experience rather than a blank space of time from which a baby will eventually emerge.

For instance, in *The Back-Up Plan* (2010), Zoe (Jennifer Lopez) invites her boyfriend Stan (Alex O'Loughlin) to accompany her to the first ultrasound of her pregnancy, achieved through donor sperm before the two met. The scene builds its comedy from Stan's surprise at the intrusiveness of the procedure. First he recoils at the wand, while the doctor provides a brief tutorial:

> DOCTOR: Now I'm going to do an ultrasound. This is how we view the fetus.
> STAN: Oh, I see, you rub it on her stomach. For a minute I thought you were going to put that huge thing . . .
> DOCTOR: In her vagina? I am. It's too early to go through the abdomen, you see, so we have to go through the vagina. Vagina. Vagina. Vagina. Vagina. . . . Maybe if I say it enough, you'll feel a little more comfortable. Vagina.
> STAN: Not working.
> DOCTOR: OK.

Zoe watches with slight trepidation as the doctor puts a condom on the ultrasound wand, and then she winces as he inserts it. After the procedure, the camera's gaze again focuses on the doctor, so the viewer can clearly see the wand covered with lubricant and a little bit of blood after he removes it from Zoe's vagina (figure 0.4). A shocked Stan passes out, traumatized by the sight.

FIGURE 0.4. *The Back-Up Plan (2010). Following a transvaginal sonogram, Doctor Harris (Robert Klein) holds up the bloodied wand.*

While this moment has no obvious political intent, it certainly pioneers a new version of the warm and fuzzy ultrasound scene conventional in these comedies.

The suppression of clinical language and images of childbearing is a political project closely linked with anti-choice figures and policies. In 2012, Michigan state representative Lisa Brown was barred from the house floor after using the word "vagina" in her arguments against an abortion regulation. One of her colleagues insisted, "It was so offensive, I wouldn't even want to say it in front of women. I would not say that in mixed company."[2] When asked what a more appropriate term for the female anatomy would be, the Speaker of the state house suggested "lady parts."[3] In a national context in which even saying the word "vagina" in public offends officials who would regulate women's healthcare (and incidents like this one emerge in every news cycle), it is more important than ever that cinematic representations of pregnancy be audaciously candid about where babies come from. In each chapter of this book, I have tried to articulate how the culture of euphemism around pregnancy—its sentimentalization and stigmatization, as well as the lingering clichés and gaps that define its on-screen representation—has directly reflected and reified the public conversation around issues of reproductive healthcare.

Stand-up comedian Michelle Wolf makes my point more succinctly in her 2019 special, *Joke Show*:

> Women, we're still too cute about all the stuff that happens to our bodies. We've got to stop being cute! Like, when we have a baby, we say it's a miracle. Stop it! These men hear "miracle," and they say, "Yeah, so why do you need healthcare? It's a miracle."

Through this joke, Wolf articulates a very real problem. Film and television have often been all-in on the "cute" and "miracle" discourses, showing a sanitized and sentimentalized vision of pregnancy and childbirth (or the inverse, portraying pregnancy as a punishment for sexual irresponsibility) and failing to dramatize the real physical rigors and emotional complexity of the process. For better or for worse, popular culture still serves as a major source of information and misinformation about reproductive biology, particularly as book bans, abstinence-only sex education, gag rules, and a new puritanism grip schools and influence other "official" sources where individuals might go for further details about reproductive biology. While most of the films and shows featured in this volume are not didactic or explicitly political in intention, they are political in effect: they have the power to shrink or expand public knowledge about reproductive biology. Throughout the history covered here, such knowledge has been profoundly limited.

No doubt the films and shows discussed in this book often hew closely to conventional romantic comedy or sitcom plots that are not exactly revolutionary. Romantic comedy pregnancies often yoke women with problematic partners and get lost in euphoric endings that celebrate new parenthood without representing its personal, financial, and health costs. But even in the midst of an imperfect framing narrative, little moments of candor can signal powerfully to audiences hungry for some recognition of the bodily experience of pregnancy. Film critic Amy Biancolli of the *Houston Chronicle* speaks of one such moment of recognition in her review of *The Back-Up Plan*: "And if Robert Klein does nothing else for the rest of his life, I will always love him for the way he shouts a single noun—four times, with zest—as Zoe's obstetrician. It's a few brief seconds of chick-flick nirvana."[4]

Those "few brief seconds" are a moment of laughter, an example of how comedy can break through a set of stale representational norms and create a shock of recognition. *It's All in the Delivery* centers comedy for precisely the reason that it can challenge narrative conventions, often leading to new insights and recognitions that can move the needle on social change—if only one joke at a time.

GENRE TROUBLE

I define "comedy" broadly here, both as a narrative genre of playful plot events and happy endings (as in romantic comedy or situation comedy) and as an effect produced by isolated jokes and gags, which may exist within other genres or even entirely outside of narrative genre fiction in the form of stand-up comedy, post-credit sequences, sketch comedy, and so forth. Some of the feature films mentioned in this volume are cataloged in IMDb and similar databases as comedy dramas or dramedy, usually meaning family melodramas with moments of lightness and happy endings. These films are relevant for this study as well because comedy, while a genre unto itself, is also a mode of storytelling that exists in close or hybridized relationship to nearly any genre, all of which rely on some use of wit or emotional release to produce their own effects.

In particular, melodrama recurs frequently in this volume, often as a foil to comedy but also as its closest cousin. Kathleen Rowe Karlyn argues that the genres of romantic comedy and melodrama overlap and complement each other in being feminine and family genres, debased cousins of prestige drama and tragedy. Similarly, a push-pull between possible happy endings and sad ones, laughter and tears, animates both genres. As Karlyn explains, "Romantic comedy usually contains a potential melodrama, and melodrama . . . contains a potential romantic comedy."[5] This is particularly true of pregnancy comedy, as melodrama nearly always haunts these texts in the high emotional stakes and psychological intensity of the experience.

Melodrama is far more closely associated with motherhood in general than comedy is, a fact visible in the many groundbreaking considerations of "maternal melodrama" that populate feminist film scholarship of the 1980s and 1990s. Essential work by Ann Kaplan, Mary Ann Doane, Linda Williams, Tania Modleski, and many others built on feminist psychoanalytic theories to explore the figure of the self-sacrificing mother in melodramas such as *Stella Dallas* (1937), *Imitation of Life* (1934 and 1959), and *Mildred Pierce* (1945).[6] As Williams notes, "The device of devaluing and debasing the actual figure of the mother while sanctifying the institution of motherhood is typical of 'the woman's film' in general and the sub-genre of the maternal melodrama in particular."[7] The mother's tears are often proof of her virtue: in these films, she must perform an act of self-sacrifice that clears her of sexual guilt over the child's conception or of her controlling maternal excess.

And while mothers are ubiquitous in melodrama studies, they have long presented a problem for scholarship on comedy. In her 1974 book, Molly Haskell argues that rambunctious physical comedy, by its very nature, represents masculine resentment of feminine civility: "[Comedy] instinctively sets out to destroy, through ridicule or physical assault, the props of an orderly society over which woman presides."[8] This dynamic is responsible for the pattern Lucy Fischer identifies in her book *Cinematernity*: when popular comedies of the twentieth century were built around the perspective of adolescent masculinity, they reduced the mother to a figure of family authority. If Mom is the obstacle to fun, then the only answer is to remove her from the comic film so the boys can enjoy themselves: "The figure of the mother is largely suppressed, absent, violated, or replaced."[9] Sitcom mothers, for instance, have often served as "straight men" for the antics of the established comedians playing sitcom dads (e.g., Bill Cosby, Tim Allen, Ray Romano, and Anthony Anderson). While important exceptions to this pattern have always existed and continue to emerge—for instance, in sitcoms that feature established women comics as mothers, such as *Mama's Family* (1983–1990) and *Roseanne* (1988–1997)— the association between mothers and the role of killjoy is well established in the popular imagination and has dominated feminist examinations of the role of mother in comic genres.

I hope that this book provides new and useful models for how pregnancy comedies can break through some of the problematic associations of motherhood with melodrama by examining concepts that limit "motherhood" to a position of either sacrifice or sanction. Pregnancy comedies occupy a peculiar generic space, poised between the woman's role as sexual partner (possessed of comic spark) and her role as mother (a figure of sentiment). The films and shows examined in this volume often struggle with the liminality of the pregnant person's role, expressed in wild tonal shifts between comic spectacle and sentimental family comedy narrative.[10] At its best, this liminality helps open up space to imagine comic motherhood, to locate the origins of the future mother in the absurdities of pregnancy, with all its out-of-control physical indignities and social ambiguity.

And while pregnancy is closely related to motherhood, it is also useful to examine the ways they are not really the same. A mother and child are two separate entities, with individual identities and histories. A pregnant person has a complexly intermingled identity and indeed may not become a parent at all, particularly if the pregnancy ends in miscarriage or abortion. Often the best films about pregnancy exploit the condition's liminality specifically to break the frame of sentimental motherhood. The pregnant person retains her own identity and bodily integrity rather than being represented as the vessel for a future citizen whose importance eclipses her own. The comic reframing of pregnancy as something other than a serene period of self-effacement can help create the conditions to understand motherhood as something else as well.

I've used the term "the best films" in this genre, so I should explain what I mean by that judgment. At its best, comedy as a genre and a mode has the potential to offer satiric critiques, push against social boundaries, challenge stigmas, and create affective experiences of release. At its worst, it reinforces clichés and flattens representational norms, centers a masculine comic sensibility that treats the pregnant body as alien, and "punches down," aiming its humor at already-marginalized groups or individuals. I explore each of these strengths and weaknesses multiple times throughout the volume, as they form a recurring pattern with roots in the earliest days of the production code. The studio-era taboo against showing pregnant bodies or using the word "pregnant" helped create a set of representational norms that decentered the experience of pregnant women in favor of two elements that could be shown and heard without restriction: the father and the baby. These tropes of maternal invisibility so perfectly captured the ideological logic of patriarchy that—although pregnant bodies are now hypervisible in popular media—the subordination of the pregnancy experience to both fathers and infants lingers on large and small screens.

Comedy's weaknesses (particularly its tendency to recycle stale jokes about hysterical women) have helped perpetuate these problems, but comedy's strengths have played an important role in challenging these inherited taboos and stigmas around the pregnant body. Comedy has provided the generic context for some of the most groundbreaking moments in pregnant representation in the United States, including the outrageous sextuplets of the screwball comedy *The Miracle of Morgan's Creek* (1944); Lucille Ball's real-life pregnancy on *I Love Lucy* (1951–1957); Maude's abortion on *Maude* (1972–1978); Murphy Brown's controversial single motherhood on *Murphy Brown* (1988–1998); Arnold Schwarzenegger's medically improbable pregnancy in *Junior* (1994); the use of abortion as a romantic comedy plot in *Obvious Child* (2014); and the spectacle of a stand-up comic's own pregnancy as a performance prop in *Ali Wong: Baby Cobra* (2016). In each case, these breakthroughs were enabled by the "strengths" of comedy, which sanction the violation of earlier, more restrictive norms of pregnant representation.

In the spirit of those strengths, here are four specific ways to understand comedy's potential to support social change:

Comedy enables satiric critiques that reframe entrenched social and political issues.

A handful of the films and shows mentioned in this volume, such as *Citizen Ruth* (1996) and *Saved!* (2004), could be defined as true satires, making a didactic point about the social features of reproduction through the mechanism of comedy. Similarly, sketch comedy from *Saturday Night Live* or *Inside Amy Schumer* nearly always incorporates a satiric point, as when Schumer stars in a parodic commercial for a fictional brand of birth control, the narrator intoning, "Ask your doctor if birth control is right for you. Then ask your boss if birth control is right for you. Ask your boss to ask his priest" ("Last F——Able Day," S3E2, April 21, 2015). The sketch goes on to add multiple layers of absurdity to the list, making a sharp point about patriarchal overreach into reproductive healthcare.

But more commonly, popular media incorporate moments of satire into family comedy structures that are not explicitly political. For instance, recent pregnancy comedies often poke fun at the culture of surveillance around pregnancy, in which medical professionals, friends, family, partners, acquaintances, bosses, authors of books, and even complete strangers are socially empowered to pass judgment on a pregnant person's appearance and lifestyle choices. For instance, in *Tully* (2018), a weary and pregnant Marlo (Charlize Theron) orders a decaf skim latte at a coffee shop and is immediately reprimanded by another customer: "You know there are trace amounts of caffeine even in decaf, right?" Jokes like this one are designed to hold a real social attitude up for ridicule: the idea that a pregnant person is continually under surveillance by strangers and that every scrap of comfort or pleasure she takes will be treated as a danger to the fetus, no matter how remote the possibility of harm. Comedy provides the tools to drive these points home with special force.

Comedy can activate social bonds, creating a common language of shared experiences cemented by the affective bond of laughter.

Henri Bergson describes comedy's role in building social bonds as a kind of "complicity": "However spontaneous it seems, laughter always implies a secret freemasonry, or even complicity, with other laughers, real or imaginary."[11] I find this idea of complicity richly ambivalent, as it captures the affective nature of healthy group bonding but also perfectly describes the bully's laughter, the type of humor that draws boundaries between "us" and "them" while increasing stigma and marginalizing outgroups. Sara Ahmed's work on an "affective economy" of emotions that produce group identity and Raul Perez's work on how racist humor "align[s] and bind[s] some bodies against others in a white-dominated society" have demonstrated how the social bonds created by humor can serve as a tool of oppression.[12] Comedy films have been most guilty of this negative use of humor in their presentation of pregnancy through the perspective of a male partner who finds his pregnant wife's behavior alien and inscrutable. The stereotypes of pregnant women as hysterical, emotional, controlling, needy, or just weird all use this problematic element of humor to "bind" the spectator to an anti-feminist subject position through laughter.

At the same time, the use of laughter to create identification and social bonds is an equally powerful tool for liberation. Sharing a laugh over the physical indignities of pregnancy, the shocking norms that govern its embodiment, or the political debates that dictate the terms of its medical management can be particularly effective forms of community building and release.

There is a quick but powerful moment in *Bad Moms* (2016) when the titular moms throw a PTA meeting that turns into a wild party. A brief montage shows a range of un-mom-like behavior, including Jell-O shots, drinking games, and wild dancing. At one point, a ring of dancing women breaks apart to reveal a very pregnant woman at the center, bumping her belly up and down in time to the music. The impact of this moment is more impressionistic than intellectual: watching it, I immediately remembered the weight and physicality of being pregnant and laughed at the rebellious phantom sensation of a belly bouncing to the beat. The scene is a wonderful literalization of complicity as a little bit transgressive, as the bad moms refuse the position of sentimental authority figures in the dreaded PTA and instead seek the affective release of a wild party. By placing pregnant embodiment at the center of the party, the film invites the viewer to think of and feel the baby bump as a ludicrous physical weight, not as an idealized or shameful symbol of human fecundity. I would even argue that this moment invites the spectator to imagine the physicality of pregnancy regardless of their own history, sex, or gender, opening up pregnant embodiment as an area of identification rather than objectification.

Finally, the idea of community building through laughter is particularly important when applied to stigmatized reproductive experiences like unpartnered pregnancy, miscarriage, infertility, and abortion. As this book shows, the code of silence around these experiences can contribute to feelings of isolation and even shame. In defiance of that shame, shared laughter provides powerful affective solidarity. Ahmed argues that shared laughter is an essential feature of activism, because "when we catch with words a logic that is often reproduced by not being put into words, it can be such a relief. . . . Laughter, peals of it; our bodies catching that logic, too."[13] Laughter as a physical manifestation of shared logic points to the power and promise of comedy as a tool of liberation.

Comedy is a genre of disorder and resists simple or dogmatic ways of thinking.

Comedy provides an ideal framework to explode a tremendous range of bad ideas about gender and identity. Literary scholar Arthur Koestler has advanced a theory of comedy that he calls "bisociation," arguing that humor occurs at the intersection of "two self-consistent but habitually incompatible frames of reference," creating a flash of insight in the mind of the viewer, reader, or listener.[14] This is a fruitful model for understanding comedy's dynamic potential to explore the competing narratives of pregnancy visible in American popular culture. One narrative treats the condition as sacred, bourgeois, familial, and wholesome, or what Luce Irigaray calls "some weird kind of holiness."[15] This perspective insists that pregnant women "glow" or resemble the sacred Madonna, and it suppresses the clinical facts of the condition beneath a facade of ease or martyrdom. The second logical chain treats pregnancy as profane or grotesque, focusing on its connection to sexuality, abject physical symptoms like vomiting and hemorrhoids, uncontrolled emotional outbursts, and the pain and messiness of childbirth. This perspective treats the pregnant body as a monstrous Other, not only in the sense of sexual excess or fatness but also in the uncanny doubleness of two beings in one body.

Neither of these frames is especially good for women, as both lock them into narrow categories of identity, and both represent justifications to restrict women's social and professional choices and reproductive rights. Good pregnancy comedies use the fundamental incompatibility of these two frames to create the tension that generates laughter, effectively exploding them both. Because comedy enjoys a unique capacity to bring to light the contradictory and hypocritical ways women's pregnant bodies are disciplined by the logic of American cultural attitudes, pregnancy represents fertile ground for comedy.

At its best, comedy opens space for a greater frankness and irreverence about reproductive biology and moves the discourse toward treating the womb as, in Angela Carter's words, "an organ like any other organ," one that can be experienced, examined, and considered without the weight of the entire Madonna/whore binary coming into play each time a pink plus sign does or doesn't appear on a drugstore test.[16] The feature film *Waitress* (2007), for instance, sees a working-class white character, Jenna (Keri Russell), trapped in a bad marriage to a financially controlling abuser. Her unplanned pregnancy, which she rationally fears will further entrench her in poverty and dependence, instead brings sexual fulfillment (through an affair with her obstetrician), creative fulfillment (first through pies, then through parenting), and freedom (as the birth of her daughter produces instant resolve to leave both her husband and her lover). By mixing up the conventional order of operations in the formula for women's happiness (love, marriage, baby), *Waitress* explores ways of experiencing pregnancy outside the good/bad binary, creating space for Jenna's unexpected experience of childbearing as self-creation, not self-sacrifice.

Comedy refuses a discourse of shame, providing a frame for breaking social taboos and censures, particularly as regards the body.

Finally, perhaps the greatest strength that comedy brings to the subject of childbearing in popular cinema in the United States is its license to be forthright, impolite, and even crude. This book chronicles a century plus of euphemisms, evasions, clichés, misrepresentations, and lazy tropes, which have often been structured to avoid the possibility of offending the audience's "good taste." Comedy often pushes the boundaries of taste in pursuit of a joke and has helped break down the taboos of pregnancy and childbirth in large and small ways over the course of this history. The literary concepts of the grotesque and the carnivalesque provide a theoretical frame for understanding how comedy is often a joyful celebration of bad taste.

By accessing the logic of the grotesque, comedy taps into a long comic tradition born of folk carnival, a ritual with deep roots in the feminine and in reproduction itself. Mikhail Bakhtin's *Rabelais and His World* documents a tendency in literary scholarship to value the official and serious over the chaotic folk tradition known as "carnival." Carnival refers to a series of medieval holiday traditions (with roots in the ancient world) that release both high- and low-status subjects into a chaotic celebration of common features of bodily life.[17]

Describing the literary aesthetic derived from this social ritual, Bakhtin introduced the use of the term "carnivalesque" to denote the low humor of jokes and folk comedy. Like carnival itself, the carnivalesque uses the unruly logic of bodily life to undermine social hierarchies and pieties. Bakhtin argues that cultural taboos (the rules of "good taste") exist to separate the classical, well-regulated body (represented by the head, torso, eyes, and faculties of reason) from the grotesque, unruly body (which draws attention to the "lower bodily stratum," responsible for sex and defecation and in closer contact with the dirt of the ground).[18] Kathleen Rowe argues that "the grotesque body breaks down the boundaries between itself and the world outside it, while the classical body, consistent with the ideology of the bourgeois individual, shores them up."[19]

This dichotomy between the coherent, spiritual classical body and the unruly grotesque body becomes particularly sharp in its focus on the bodies of women. While male bodies are culturally understood to be stable from the time of puberty until advanced age, women's reproductive physiology makes them changeable in ways that are threatening to the idea of a closed, coherent, spiritual physicality. Menstruation, hormonal changes, lactation, menopause, and especially pregnancy open the body's boundaries, even challenge the notion of a coherent individual self in favor of a reproductive doubled body. Mary Russo points out that the word "grotesque" is a reference to the threatening and debased qualities of female physicality: "The word itself . . . evokes the cave—the grotto-esque. . . . As bodily metaphor, the grotesque cave tends to look like (and in the most gross metaphorical sense be identified with) the cavernous anatomical female body."[20] As the carnivalesque is nearly always the dark shadow of the sacred, the womb always takes part in a double meaning, as the point of origin for life and also the unknowable, unclosed space of the grotesque.

Because the bourgeois logic of taste privileges the upper bodily stratum, it relies heavily on the performative management of pregnancy—which not only must be regulated within a traditional marriage structure but also must be concealed through appropriate clothing, language, and behavior. Any move to refuse that concealment, to claim the "grotto-esque" and its radical ambivalence, helps disrupt the narrative of the classical body that has long been used to shame women.

In the grotesque anti-sitcom *Married . . . with Children* (1987–1997), for instance, Peg Bundy's pregnancy is frequently represented through her excessive consumption of food. At one point, Peg (Katey Sagal) and her also pregnant neighbor Marcy (Amanda Bearse) gulp down mouthfuls of food and chew with their mouths open. Marcy brings Peg a giant bottle of gas tablets, which she dumps on her spaghetti like a condiment; Marcy gnaws all the chicken off a bone and tosses the bone behind her, where it lands on the floor. The two women are demanding, emotional, and voracious in pregnancy, presenting a woman-on-top comic alternative to the serene little mother of earlier sitcoms. They are what Russo and Rowe have labeled "unruly women," a style of female embodiment focused on bodily excess. Rowe argues that the unruly woman archetype "reverberates whenever women disrupt the norms of femininity and the social hierarchy of male over female through excess and outrageousness."[21]

Unruly women often break the rules women are asked to follow in order to be pleasing to potential mates. An unruly woman may be too fat, too talkative, too androgynous, or too dirty, or she may laugh too loudly. Rowe also includes pregnancy among these rule-breaking behaviors ("She may be pregnant") for the ways that it often taps into notions of fatness, loudness, or unrestrained sexuality, as well as for the ways it is an expression of the female body's openness and potential doubleness, its violation of the closed logic of the classical body. Although unruly women may provoke "unease, derision, or fear," that reaction need not be privileged over the sheer pleasure and freedom to be found in the representation of women cutting loose and being gross.[22] Pregnancy for the unruly woman becomes a carnival time, when bodily license, including the license to be fat, creates new frames for female pleasure.

PREGNANCY IN IDEOLOGY

This introduction has focused so far on how comedy as a genre and a mode has enabled a pattern of increasing candor about the physical details of pregnancy, one that is disruptive and physical but not always progressive in a linear way. This pattern is complicated by three specific subthreads that are woven into

FIGURE 0.5. Away We Go *(2009)*. *Verona (Maya Rudolph) with her mother-in-law (Catherine O'Hara) putting an ear against her belly bump. Other characters continually touch and comment on Verona's pregnant body.*

the social history of pregnancy over the century plus covered in this book: surveillance culture, whiteness, and the free-range fetus. These themes recur frequently in the chapters to come.

Surveillance culture

The following chapters chronicle, alongside the films themselves, the various legal and social changes that have regulated pregnancy over the period of history represented here: the relaxation of sanctions on birth control, changes in adoption practices, the mainstreaming of fertility treatments, cultural debates about pain management and hospital labor, and the still-volatile landscape of abortion. The thread that connects these disparate conversations is the basic assumption that reproductive biology and American family formation are matters of public scrutiny and interest, shaped by institutions, laws, and pressures that surround the pregnant individual.

To take an extended example, *Away We Go* (2009) shows pregnant Verona (Maya Rudolph) on a cross-country road trip with her partner Burt (John Krasinski) to visit family and friends. At each stop along their journey, someone touches her belly. The film makes a joke of their loved ones' well-meaning but intrusive comments and gestures. Burt's father (Jeff Daniels) asks, "Verona, are you on schedule?" and his wife (Catherine O'Hara) immediately interjects, "Oh, Jerry, you don't ask her that!" The visual joke of this moment is that she scolds her husband for his intrusive question while she herself is lying down on the couch, her ear on Verona's belly bump, listening for movement inside her daughter-in-law's body (figure 0.5).

Other friends are equally intrusive and awkward. Brash work acquaintance

Lily (Alison Janney) is irreverent: "Oh, God, look at you! You're only six months in, Jesus, you're huge. And your face is so fat!" Burt's sanctimonious childhood friend LN (pronounced like Ellen, played by Maggie Gyllenhaal) provides intrusive commentary under the cover of a compliment:

> LN: Oh, Verona, you just look beautiful. Look at your hair.
> VERONA (uncomfortable): Yeah.
> LN: And, well, it's a boy.
> VERONA: Oh, a girl.
> LN: No. Really? With those hips and that shape? Who told you it was a girl?
> VERONA: Well, the doctor. And the sonogram.
> LN: Well, we'll see.

These encounters, ranging from the awkward to the painful, drive Verona and Burt from city to city, until they end their road trip by moving into Verona's idyllic childhood home in Florida, with no neighbors for miles around. Buffeted by the ways friends and family project their own hopes, desires, and pain onto Verona's pregnancy, the couple retreat from everyone except each other, choosing to raise their new child in a remote and nostalgic paradise. The title *Away We Go* comes to stand for both launch and retreat. Verona and Burt find no solution to the competing cultural narratives of their pregnancy, which drive them away from social contact entirely.

Away We Go follows the experiences of a relatively privileged, geographically mobile, middle-class couple in their thirties with a partnered pregnancy. Often issues of surveillance, judgment, and regulation are compounded by any deviations from this ideal, many of which are absent from the screen entirely. In each chapter of this volume, I have tried to engage these questions of social surveillance with a critical eye, tracking the narrow range of "good" pregnancy across the twentieth century and into the present, with special attention to which experiences are stigmatized or erased in each generation's evolving ideals of pregnancy, as well as to eugenic formulations about who does or does not deserve to have children.

Whiteness

Most of the fictional pregnancies chronicled in this volume are experienced by white women; these films are the products of white creators and white imaginations. While the films and shows in question generally treat their characters as simply neutral or unmarked by race, I have worked hard in the pages that follow to surface the ways that these characters' experiences are enabled by their whiteness, as well as other factors like class privilege and heteronormativity. For many decades, American film and television could see the funny side of pregnancy only when it was experienced by white, able-bodied, coupled women; deviations from that standard are so charged by unresolved social stigma and condemnation that they were rarely the site of social play. Alongside the ensemble of white mothers-to-be in *What to Expect When You're Expecting*, Jennifer Lopez and Rodrigo Santoro play a Latino couple who are adopting, while Chris Rock plays a father whose wife is never actually shown in the movie. In *The Back-Up Plan*, Jennifer Lopez does play a pregnant woman, but her character is isolated from any kind of Latino family, choosing a white sperm donor for her twins and a white romantic partner; her only living relative is a white Jewish grandmother played by Linda Lavin. Though these may seem like small omissions, they are not random but rather reflect a long eugenic history of celebrating white reproduction while seeking to limit or control non-white childbearing.

American racial stereotypes can be ugly in general, but particularly so regarding childbearing. Inequality of resources, social stigmas, and the rhetorical dehumanization of the marginalized all converge on the issue of reproduction. The idea that Black and Brown women are irresponsible, hypersexual, hyperfertile, and unworthy parents has been used to justify a host of abuses, from forced sterilization to family separation and incarceration of women for crimes against their own fetus. Dorothy Roberts notes:

> White childbearing is generally thought to be a beneficial activity: it brings personal joy and allows the nation to flourish. Black reproduction, on the other hand, is treated as a form of *degeneracy*. Black mothers are seen to corrupt the reproduction process at every stage. Black mothers, it is believed, transmit inferior physical traits to the product of conception through their genes. They damage their babies in the womb through their bad habits during pregnancy. Then they impart a deviant lifestyle to their children through example.[23]

The slurs "welfare baby," "crack baby," and "anchor baby" are designed to be hurled at non-white pregnant women and mothers, implying a close connection between non-white parenthood and unfitness or even criminality.

Comedies dealing with reproduction without the protection of whiteness bear an implicit burden to deal with this ideological framing, textually or subtextually. For instance, two white-produced texts that deal with unpartnered pregnancy in Latina families bend over backward to avoid activating social stigmas of non-white hypersexuality by making their heroines actual virgins: *Quinceañera's* (2006) Magdalena (Emily Rios) becomes pregnant when her boyfriend ejaculates on her leg, while in *Jane the Virgin* (2014–2019), Jane Villanueva (Gina Rodriguez) is impregnated through a medical error during an ob-gyn visit. Let me be clear that non-white women should not have to be absolved of sexual guilt to be worthy of care or narrative interest during pregnancy. Similarly, Black pregnancies on-screen are often scrubbed of recognizably Black social and economic contexts in an attempt to sidestep ugly stereotypes, as when the Black family in *Are We Done Yet?* (Ice Cube and Nia Long plus kids) moves to a majority-white neighborhood in the country to prepare for the birth of twins. The white contractor (John C. McGinley) they hire to fix their ramshackle house turns out to possess an assortment of improbable skills, including obstetrics, and he delivers the twins inside the house he has been repairing. The growing Black family is thus entirely framed by a kind of white exurban mastermind whose overbearing presence erases any other character or community that might signify Black history or context.

Many other shows and films choose not to bother with the complicated task of trying to make white audiences comfortable with Black and Brown women's childbearing, eliminating non-white pregnancies altogether. Even so, the specter of race is always present in pregnancy comedy, in the whiteness of its major texts, in the delicacy with which those texts tiptoe around the experiences of non-white women, in the ways that infertility treatment, abortion, and adoption are all available to white characters who seek to access them. It is my hope to make clear in this book how race always and persistently structures childbearing in the popular imagination.

The free-range fetus

The third ideological thread that runs through this book has to do with the rhetorical separation of the fetus from the pregnant person in words and images. The idea that the embryo or fetus is a full person separate from the pregnant person rather than something that is part of her and can be understood or measured only in relation to her body is of relatively modern vintage. Susan Klepp traces a shift in the language of pregnancy in the United States during the revolutionary era (1760–1820), when terms like "breeding" and "great with child" gave way to terms like "little stranger" and "the beloved object." Klepp argues that this shift was a symptom of American aversion to luxury and materiality "in favor of a language of reason, foresight, constraint, and sensibility."[24] But they are also terms that separate maternal body from fetal body: both "an addition to our home" and "a little stranger" skip the process of gestation in a willful social agreement to pretend that a child has suddenly arrived, as if by magic. These treatments of childbirth as a visitation essentially replace pregnancy with a figurative adoption, a concept that was

Introduction • 19

literalized in the figure of the stork, who delivers the child from a mysterious elsewhere into the home of the parents-to-be.

Following this same logic, the rhetorical separation of mother and fetus propelled nearly all the euphemisms for pregnancy that populated the English language in the twentieth century, including cabbage patches, storks, knitted booties, and a host of others detailed in chapter 1. By choosing this mode of euphemism, visually and verbally, film texts across the first half of the twentieth century, as well as the early years of television, transformed the heavy, messy work of bringing a new human into the world into a series of blushing clichés that sanitized female bodies by focusing instead on the imagined future child, the "blessed event" that would restore the proper separation of mother from baby.

The development of ultrasound technology in the 1950s only widened this gulf. In the days before ultrasound, any understanding of the fetus could only be obtained through the mediating body of the woman: her shape, her sensations, her well-being. Since the ultrasound, it is possible for medical professionals, expectant parents, and media consumers to perceive the fetus as something visually separate from the pregnant woman, removed from her on a screen. Jennifer Ellis West notes that "feminists have long been critical of the use of ultrasound imagery by the anti-abortion movement because a sonographic image, standing alone, separates the fetus from its place within the mother's body."[25] The fetus on ultrasound looks like a (somewhat fuzzy) baby in a box, while the pregnant person's body must literally be dissolved out of frame to produce this effect. The psychological effect of this visual isolation of the fetus is the false impression that it exists somehow outside of the body of the gestating woman and can be meaningfully separated from her even before birth.

There are many problems with this elision of the complex interdependency of pregnant person and fetus, most obviously some of the ways pregnancy and abortion are regulated in American communities, medical practices, and courtrooms. In fact, the anti-abortion movement has focused its rhetoric on "fetal life" precisely because being explicit about the experiences, moral status, or rights of the abortion-seeking woman is a far more complicated and less clean moral field than defending the rights of "the unborn." In 2022, anti-abortion senator James Lankford tweeted, "The only difference between a baby at conception or a baby held in your arms is time."[26] The quote, typical of anti-choice rhetoric, is a near-literal parallel to the visual rhetoric of the independent fetus, simply erasing the fertilized embryo's dependency on the person in whose womb it has implanted.

But anti-choice rhetoric stumbles when the figure of the pregnant person is restored to the frame. Jennifer Holland argues, "Women seeking abortions were a perpetual thorn in the side of the [anti-abortion] movement. Were they murderers, Jezebels, dupes, or trauma survivors? The movement easily named the victims, but the transgressors were harder to pin down."[27] Popular media have the potential to restore the centrality of the pregnant person in discussions of pregnancy, an essential tactic toward correcting the inaccuracy of ultrasound's visually isolated fetus, which has been co-opted as a tool of anti-abortion opportunism.

KNOCKED UP AND THE LIMITS OF THE GROTESQUE

To provide a more concrete example of how comedy as a genre can push the boundaries of representational norms around pregnancy, I offer a close reading of *Knocked Up* (2007), the highest-grossing film in the mid-2000s cycle of pregnancy romantic comedies. The film draws heavily from the culture of masculine gross-out comedy, which provides a launchpad for the film's exploration of pregnancy as something intriguingly gross. As with the ultrasound scene in *The Back-Up Plan*, these grotesque moments are usually still contained by a sentimental discourse of bourgeois reproduction. And yet even isolated moments of transgressive attention to bodily functions on-screen portend a consequential shift in the representational norms associated with pregnancy.

Knocked Up is the story of a successful and beautiful young woman, Alison (Katherine Heigl), who finds herself pregnant after a drunken hookup with unemployed stoner Ben (Seth Rogen). The pair form an improbably romantic relationship and, after several challenges, decide to raise their baby daughter together. The film received overwhelmingly positive reviews and accolades for its director, Judd Apatow, who was amassing a reputation for making films that combined male raunch with an unexpected family sentimentality—a combination that seemed to defy easy categorization. Over the summer of 2007, thoughtful essays popped up in dozens of publications debating the film's take on gender, reproduction, maturity, generational difference, and the politics of reproductive choice.[28]

These debates suggested that American audiences were already wary of the formula that insists that women behave like adults—stable, rule-bearing, frequently humorless—while men remain ever more childlike in what can easily be read as passive resistance to feminism. Katherine Heigl acknowledged to *Vanity Fair* that the movie was "a little bit sexist," a remark that seems to have gotten her branded as "difficult" in the industry.[29] Though its sexism is easy and infuriating, *Knocked Up* is a complex enough film to contain multiple strands at once. As a film, it is interested in reconciling adolescent males' experiences of their own grossness with women's experiences in pregnancy. By doing so, it begins—haltingly and with only partial success—to integrate pregnancy into a larger, productive discourse of the ambivalent and the grotesque.

The movie opens with a montage showing the main character Ben engaged in a variety of leisure activities with his housemates, including boxing with gloves that are on fire and mock-heroic jousting over a dirty swimming pool. These sensation-seeking activities are a form of bonding for the mostly male housemates, one that transposes masculine virtues of endurance and aggression onto a context of permanent adolescent homosociality set in a decaying parody of a suburban home. The house they share is always dirty and cluttered with bongs, beer bottles, and assorted debris on every available surface. The guys amuse themselves with jokes about bodily functions, dirt, and sex, and their incomeless occupation is to maintain a website dedicated to documenting nude scenes performed by women in the movies. They prank their housemates by farting into one another's pillows, which causes a pink-eye outbreak in the household. The grotesque features of the housemates' lifestyle represent unbroken carnival, rule-breaking leisure time.

Apatow once described his intention for the house full of young men to be "soft and childlike," which is to say different from the toxic masculinity associated with films like *The Hangover*.[30] As a "soft and childlike" man, Ben's understanding of reproduction is also childish but defined by benign curiosity. With Seth Rogen's round face and slack figure, Ben is easily understood as a big baby himself, an idea the film emphasizes many times, as when he gets stuck in a children's playhouse, his large frame caught in the tiny door, or when he holds baby clothes up to his chin and tells Alison, "Get ready. This will be coming out of you in seven months." Even in self-deprecation, Ben projects his grotesque infantile qualities onto Alison, making her pregnancy monstrous, as if she is taking on the responsibility of giving birth to him as an adult partner for herself.

It takes the whole film for Ben to shed this identity, which doesn't happen until he sees his own grotesqueness mirrored back. In a late sequence where Ben attends a Cirque du Soleil show while high on hallucinatory mushrooms, he reacts with horror at the sight of a middle-aged clown dressed as a baby, in clothing strikingly similar to what Ben had put on in the earlier scene. This specter of the hideous clown-baby shocks Ben to such a degree that he races out of the show. Upon his return to Los Angeles, he moves out of his grubby communal home, gets a job, and generally begins to assume the trappings of a bourgeois adult.

The representative of order, ambition, and middle-class values, Alison is certainly the least gross thing for most of the movie, even as her pregnancy is one of the few things that can disrupt the composure of the housemates. When she enters the house, she gamely sits on the cluttered couch amid

Ben's stoned housemates and tries not to look uncomfortable. The lone other woman in the room, a girlfriend who comes and goes from the social group (Charlyne Yi), marvels at Alison's pregnancy, translating it into the comic register of the grotesque: "Aren't you scared? The way it's going to come out of you. It's going to hurt a lot, I bet. Hmmm, in your vagina. That's so sick!" This hazy, stream-of-consciousness dialogue immediately associates pregnancy with physical courage and ends with a remark that holds a double meaning, "so sick" being either grotesque or impressive. And the film does treat Alison's pregnancy as both grotesque and impressive, ideas that are explored in several ways in the succeeding scenes.

The fact that Alison has just been promoted to be an on-air personality for the E! network makes explicit how women's bodies are disciplined by intense expectations about appearance and comportment. Early in the film, two network executives, childishly named Jack and Jill (Alan Tudyk and Kristen Wiig), ask the already slender Alison to lose weight for her new on-air position. Given their request that she "tighten everything up," it is not surprising that Alison chooses to hide her pregnancy from her bosses until it is absurdly obvious, out of fear that she may lose her promotion. Indeed, there are several scenes of Alison working with her costumer (Tami Sagher) and her line producer (Bill Hader) to hide the symptoms of her pregnancy that have accidentally shown up on camera, including vomiting, fatness, and hormonal outbursts. These edges must be smoothed out and covered up for Alison's pregnant body to be acceptable for public consumption. When Jack and Jill finally confront her about the obvious pregnancy, Jack pitches to Alison a new segment where she will interview pregnant celebrities, quickly commodifying her bodily changes. Jill sits to the side during this exchange and delivers the taboo subtext to Jack's open enthusiasm:

> JACK: You're pregnant, they're pregnant. You can talk about being pregnant.
> JILL: It just grosses me out. When I know that people are pregnant. Because I think about the birth. Everything's so wet.
> JACK: And you can talk about everything that goes into it—none of the gross stuff, but hopes, dreams, whatever. It's going to be great.

Jack's acknowledgment that the public does not wish to know about the "gross stuff" marks contemporary motherphilia as a fetish, the trivializing overvaluation of the fetish object's surface features to alleviate anxiety about the fetish object's suppressed features. As a gross-out comedy, *Knocked Up* gives voice to those suppressed features through its persistent interest in bringing comments like Jill's into the light of day.

Introduction • 23

I take it to be one of the running jokes in the film that others respond to Alison as if her pregnancy makes her grotesque, while Heigl looks healthy, beautiful, and slender in the arms and face throughout the film. In one of the most absurd scenes, Ben becomes squeamish in the middle of sex, worried that his penis will poke the baby. At his request, Alison switches to a position on top of him, but she quickly becomes self-conscious about her body, particularly the movement of her breasts and what she imagines is his perfect view of her double chin (which does not exist). Perhaps most absurdly, a pregnant Alison and her sister Debbie (Leslie Mann) are denied entry to the same nightclub they had been waved into the night Alison met Ben because, the bouncer explains, "You old, she pregnant." Tania Modleski argues that in this moment, "both women are forced to consider the ways in which, beautiful as they are, they are quickly turning into female grotesques, the classic instances of which are the old woman and the pregnant woman."[31] Indeed, the bouncer later melds them into one, saying, "Can't have a bunch of old, pregnant bitches running around" inside the club. For most of the film, the idea of Alison's grotesqueness is framed as a joke—something outside herself, projected and imposed by other people.

The film draws together its threads of infantile masculinity and grotesque female embodiment in the birth scene, when Ben is able to channel his affinity for the "sick" into the genuinely necessary task of partnering with Alison through the process of childbirth. Having faced his grotesque baby double, Ben has reformed his lifestyle and read a few books about pregnancy and childcare to prepare for fatherhood. When Alison goes into labor, he shows himself prepared to support her through the physical challenges of labor:

> BEN: Have you had your bloody show?
> ALISON: What? What is that?
> BEN: It's a bloody mucusy discharge, but it only comes out right before the baby's going to come, so if that hasn't happened, we have time.

Here, Ben's comfort with the clinical facts of pregnancy emerges from his association with the grotesque. Bloody shows are his forte.

The labor scene is defined by the film's famous crowning scene, its signature moment of representational courage. Importantly, the baby's head crowning (emerging into the opening of the vagina) is shown three times, a test of the audience's endurance. First, when the doctor announces that the baby is crowning, Ben looks over the drape and reacts with shock and disgust. This prompts Alison to ask for a mirror so she can see for herself. "You don't want to see that," Ben says, but Alison insists and also looks at the baby crowning.

24 • It's All in the Delivery

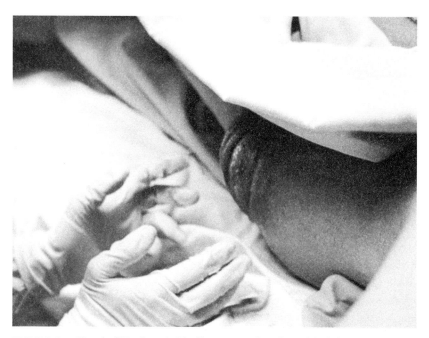

FIGURE 0.6. Knocked Up *(2007)*. *The film contains three shots of the baby's head crowning.*

Finally, one of Ben's friends, Jay (Jay Baruchel), alarmed by Alison's screams, barges into the room and catches sight of it before beating a quick retreat. This triple shot of the crowning is important, because jokes come in threes and because the moment is a triangulating bond among the three key characters, each with their own relationship to the grotesque: Ben, who needs to face the moment; Alison, who shows herself to be an equal participant in the world of gross-out by insisting on looking; and Jay, representing Ben's adolescent pals, who is chased away by the spectacle. Jay returns to the waiting room holding his midsection as if to contain his nausea, murmuring, "I shouldn't have gone in there, don't go in there, promise me you won't go in there," as though he had seen an uncanny horror.

Because childbearing is gross—it in fact requires far greater physical courage than any of the dumb stunts enjoyed by the male housemates—Ben's choice to confront the moment of rupture between the baby's body and the mother's is not a failure of masculine independence in favor of confining feminine domesticity. By making childbirth a test of courage, the film elevates it above the foolish stunting enjoyed by the permanent adolescents. Indeed, it is by far the "grossest" thing in the movie and is used as a climax to both the film's comic and sentimental plots. The fact that the crowning shots inevitably produce sounds of "ughhhh" from audiences suggests that it succeeds in shocking them with taboo embodiment, and yet a close look at the image surprises because it is so clean—no hair, no blood, no other mess on the table. The vagina and the baby's head are prosthetic, sanitized, and fake (figure 0.6). It seems that even this portrait of male courage extends only so far and no further in confronting the astonishing messiness of human reproduction.

In a deleted scene included on the extended DVD release of *Knocked Up*, Ben and his friend Jonah (Jonah Hill) watch an explicit birthing video and experience physical revulsion. The extended-cut DVD (labeled "unrated and unprotected") blurs out the actual birthing vagina of the woman in the video, as if this sight is too obscene even for Apatow fans seeking further thrills on the DVD extras.[32] Ben and Jonah watch the video as if they are watching a horror film, frequently raising their hands to their faces in gestures of self-protection while they say rude things about the video. Early reports from the production of *Knocked Up* indicate that actress Anne Hathaway, originally cast as Alison, left the project because she objected to the director's plan to use footage of an actual live birth in the hospital scene. Those plans were later scuttled, Apatow claims, because the state of California would have required a work permit for the birthing child, an impossible condition of employment.[33] The ways that pregnant doubleness is a challenge to the law's understanding of individual rights, particularly at the moment of childbirth, explicitly informs the film's inability to do its work of making the grotesque visible, bringing it out from behind the curtain.

The irony of all this fuss is that birthing videos are in fact common. The PBS Nova special *The Miracle of Life* showed a human birth on prime-time television in 1983 and has been used in high school curricula for generations.[34] *Knocked Up* is not even the first feature comedy to include a crowning scene, as Spike Lee had incorporated real birth footage in *Mo' Better Blues* (1990) and *She Hate Me* (2004). Of the latter, Lee claimed that he just went to Brooklyn Hospital and asked laboring women if his team could film the birth for a fee. That scene also produces shocked gasps in theaters; Lee mused, "It's interesting with audiences because they can deal better with bullets to the head than a child being born. That's a commentary."[35]

Further, there's a sort of meta-analysis of nudity on-screen in *Knocked Up* in the form of the website Ben and his friends are developing, Flesh of the Stars dot com. Their daily work is to review popular films to record the precise time codes at which the viewer can view female nudity. Alison at one point helps Ben with this work, pausing *Carrie* (1976) at the credit sequence and calling out, "Boobs and bush!" In this way, the film makes explicit the extraordinary hypocrisy of representational norms around the female body: directors, ratings agencies, studios, and audiences are extremely comfortable with fetishized sexual nudity, while reproductive display is still a taboo spectacle that *Knocked Up* cannot quite find a way to confront, even when it is the whole point of the movie.

Although *Knocked Up* grossed $219 million worldwide in 2007, the cycle of pregnancy rom-coms that appeared in its wake did little to grow the terms of pregnant representation.[36] For instance, the 2012 comedy *What to Expect When You're Expecting* is named after the famous pregnancy guidebook that has for years introduced pregnant women to the clinical facts of pregnancy. And yet screenwriter Heather Hatch, in an interview, described the process of adapting a medical guide into a romantic comedy: "No one wanted to see a movie about mucus plugs or, you know, leaking boobs, so it was really wide open what you wanted to do."[37] Instead, the screenwriters reverted to a mainstream comedy of hormones, weight gain, and some mild puking rather than a deep dive into the "mucus plugs or, you know, leaking boobs" that represent pregnancy's most candid form. Most of the history chronicled in this volume has followed this same logic, assuming that no one wants to see a comedy about gross lady stuff. This book exists to interrogate that assumption and to analyze the stories that have filled the vacuum that this idea has created in our cultural stories of the gestating body.

CHAPTER OUTLINE

The first two chapters of this book are roughly chronological, examining the early history of pregnancy's erasure and the euphemisms that came to stand in for the unrepresentable condition. Chapter 1, "Confinements: Enter the Stork," covers the first half of the twentieth century, during which both the word "pregnant" and the visible baby bump were largely absent from studio-produced films in the United States. By investigating how studio-era films worked within and around the rules of the production code, I argue that there is in fact a rich history of subversion that has pushed back against the era's regimes of seriousness and control. Chapter 2, "Hysterical Fatherhood: Male Pregnancy On-Screen," extends that history from the 1950s through the early twenty-first century to look at how the studio era's taboos against direct representations of pregnant female bodies created the conditions for comic fatherhood to fill the representational void, further marginalizing the pregnant woman's own subjectivity both in the studio era and long after.

The next three chapters each move back and forth between past and present to retrace various aspects of this history in more specific thematic terms. Chapter 3, "Bad Pregnancies: Social Problems and Bad Seeds," explores unwed and teen pregnancy and how popular comedy has often pushed back against the social problem framing of stigmatized childbearing practices. Chapter 4,

Introduction • 27

"Baby Bust: Infertility and Its Discontents," discusses infertility, miscarriage, and adoption in popular comedies. Taken together, chapters 4 and 5 trace how the stigmas of excessive or early fertility (Too early! Too much!) and the stigma of late fertility or childlessness (Too late! Too little!) are deeply connected.[38] The narrow ideal of childbearing bounded by these stigmas serves a eugenic function to justify racist and classist regimes of social control that rely on shallow moral judgments about childbearing and often meet in problematic practices and legal norms around adoption. Chapter 5, "Shmashmortion: Terminating Abortion Stigma through Comedy," examines how the tools of comedy can help disrupt abortion stigma and why doing so is essential to the cause of reproductive justice.

Finally, the conclusion, "It's All in the Delivery," focuses on what I find to be the most positive new development in popular representations of pregnant embodiment: the recent cycle of specials featuring stand-up comics in advanced stages of pregnancy. By confronting audiences with the visual spectacle of the very pregnant body paired with remarkably frank descriptions of the speakers' physically gross experiences of pregnancy, comics like Ali Wong, Amy Schumer, and Jena Friedman have produced shows that run counter to the century plus of obfuscation. This short and very transgressive history of pregnant stand-up offers reason for optimism that new voices, bodies, ideas, and jokes are accelerating the pace of representational change and working to obliterate a huge range of bad ideas about childbearing through comedy.

CONFINEMENTS
ENTER THE STORK

ALTHOUGH THIS BOOK IS PRIMARILY concerned with popular media produced in the United States, any history of comic childbearing on-screen must begin with cinema's own mother, who lived in France. Alice Guy-Blaché's *La Fée aux Choux* (*The Cabbage Fairy*), produced in 1896, is believed to have been one of the first fiction films ever produced. A scant minute long, the film consists of a single long shot of an elegant woman, the fairy, in a garden of giant cabbages (figure 1.1). She pulls first one and then another wiggling baby out from behind the prop cabbages and sets them on the ground in the front of the frame. She reaches for a third, this time clearly a doll; deciding it is not yet ripe, the fairy returns it to its cabbage to keep growing. This primal scene of feminine authorship is a comedy, bearing the one-two-three structure of a joke's setup, setup, and payoff. Jane Gaines has pointed out the rich symbolic importance of the first female filmmaker's signature film being a fantasy of painless, female-centered reproduction.[1]

In the course of making several hundred short films (including a few remakes of *La Fée aux Choux*), Guy-Blaché returned to the theme of childbearing several times.[2] In *Madame a des Envies* (*Madame's Fancies*) (1907), the titular Madame strolls down the streets in a state of advanced pregnancy (the baby bump is clearly a pillow arranged beneath the actress's dress), followed by her husband pushing a baby carriage. Experiencing uncontrollable pregnancy cravings, Madame steals and consumes first a child's lollipop, then a drinker's absinthe, a beggar's herring, and a salesman's pipe. Her long-suffering husband

FIGURE 1.1. La Fee aux Choux (The Cabbage Fairy). *Alice Guy-Blaché's 1896 fantasy centers painless reproduction.*

follows in her wake, pacifying the victims of her thefts. Finally, the husband confronts his wife about her behavior, and as they argue, she falls down into a cabbage patch. Her husband reaches down and picks up a baby out of a cabbage next to her. When Madame stands up, her baby bump is gone. She pats down her dress and takes the baby with delight. Her consternated husband flails about.

Guy-Blaché's fanciful excursions into the topics of pregnancy and childbirth were likely unique to their era, both in the candor of the disappearing baby bump (it seemed to disappear from the screen for decades to come) and in their unapologetic focus on women's experiences and fantasies. Guy-Blaché takes all pain, social stigma, and anxiety out of the process of producing babies and instead places women in control of a benevolent world where cravings are always satisfied, babies are always available, and childbirth is as easy as popping out to the garden.

These joyful dreamscapes answer a world where, for much of human history, bearing children was one of the most dangerous things that a woman could do.[3] Social rituals and medical norms of the late eighteenth century reflected this danger, cloaking childbearing in stigma, anxiety, and a cult of maternal sacrifice. These practices were stratified by class, with working-class women finding little respite from work and family obligations during pregnancy, and leisured women finding perhaps too much respite, being obligated to observe a period of several weeks' or months' "confinement" at home in late pregnancy. There are some ways in which confinement created a female-controlled space of community and care that predated the sterile hospital birth model of masculine control of reproduction. Historian Judith Walzer Leavitt notes that "parturient women, who felt vulnerable at the time of their confinements, armed themselves with the strength of other women who had passed through the event successfully."[4]

But the practice also reinforced a social logic that could be understood to treat advanced pregnancy as a private or shameful condition. Susan B. Anthony reported that her mother was profoundly embarrassed by pregnancy: "Before the birth of every child she was overwhelmed with embarrassment and humiliation, secluded herself from the outside world and would not speak of the expected little one."[5] Historians Richard Wertz and Dorothy Wertz describe the practice of confinement as an ideal extension of separate spheres gender ideology, as "leisured women of the nineteenth century embroidered the niceties of female conduct by withdrawing from social life."[6] Just as the fetus was enclosed in the woman, the woman was enclosed in the home; this tidy arrangement posited women of means as serene, dependent, regulated, and immobile vehicles of family reproduction.

When a dressmaker named Lena Bryant experimented with the mass production of maternity wear in 1900, the idea was novel because it implied that middle-class pregnant women would leave their homes in late stages of pregnancy.[7] At first "even the bravest often left their carriages a block away and shrouded their faces with veils before entering the little store on a side street."[8] A Lane Bryant ad from 1910 gives scant space to the design of the actual clothes and instead focuses on convincing women that going out in public during the visible stages of pregnancy was a healthful and socially appropriate choice at all:

> Will you be the "shut-in" mother? Hiding in darkness and gloom? Thinking only of things that depress?
>
> Or will you be the carefree one? Out in the brightness and sunshine? Out where gloomy thoughts are banished? Out where friends and happiness make every day a day of joy?
>
> You can put yourself in whichever picture you choose. And Oh, how much the choosing means to you! To choose right means a lifetime of health and happiness. To choose wrong may mean a lifetime of regret.[9]

These advertisements marked a shift in the culture of confinement among middle-class and wealthy women, which gradually dissolved over the first half of the twentieth century. Maternal and infant mortality fell, women's public roles increased, urban communities continued to draw social life out of the home, and the process of birthing emerged from the authority of midwives in the home to now be overseen by doctors in hospitals and clinics. Each of these evolutions created social, economic, and civic reasons for middle-class pregnant women to appear in public. And as with so many social shifts, as soon as pregnant women were recognized as a potential market for mass-produced goods and services, the profit motive helped accelerate and commodify the cultural change.

The concept of confinement and pregnancy's gradual release from the domestic sphere and emergence into a public space marked by middle-class consumption provide a guiding metaphor for this first chapter, which traces a process by which film and later television representations of pregnancy similarly transitioned from a set of firm representational taboos to a set of visual and verbal codes that were framed by new middle-class conventions of display and consumption as family activities. Along that arc from euphemism to proud display, the family comedies discussed in this chapter give a prismatic view of confinement, sometimes capitulating to its logic with coy euphemism and sometimes puncturing the absurdity of a taboo that was always a bit silly—and commonly doing both at the same time.

Pregnancy is, after all, the means by which every human on the planet was ever created. Though Western women of any era may have reason to wish to hide it, particularly because its visibility stood as evidence of sexual intercourse, the belly bump of late pregnancy is distinctive. Studio-era films developed a range of strategies to deal with this challenge of visual storytelling, from flat denial (as in the image of *Blondie* in the introduction) to half measures of obfuscation (housecoats, aprons, raincoats, a fluff of bedcovers) to simple absence from the screen, where pregnancy exists in a mysterious and private feminine world not visible in public.

In King Vidor's 1928 *The Crowd*, for instance, a young wife (Eleanor Boardman) beckons nervously for her husband (James Murray) to come closer to her so she can tell him a secret, even though they are alone in the apartment (figure 1.2). An intertitle provides half of her line, "I . . . I didn't get a chance to tell you—," but the rest of the sentence is not written out. Instead, the film cuts to a shot of the wife shyly mouthing, "I'm pregnant." A reaction shot of the young husband's smile clarifies the situation for anyone whose lipreading skills aren't up to the job. The next scene then jumps forward in time to the end of the pregnancy: the husband is at work, nervously waiting for news of his wife, who is in the hospital giving birth. Finally, he gets the call and rushes to the hospital to see his newborn son, the women's work of childbearing completed in his, and the camera's, absence. Pregnancy is thus framed three times as a secret, first by the wife's reluctance to speak, second by the intertitle's refusal to translate, and third by the narrative's immediate jump to the other side of the unrepresentable event.

FIGURE 1.2. The Crowd *(1928)*. *Coded pregnancy announcements were common in silent cinema. Here the wife (Eleanor Boardman) motions for her husband (James Murray) to come closer so she can tell him a secret, though they are alone in the room.*

The advent of sound did little to expand the conversation for several decades. *After the Thin Man* (1936), for instance, uses the common convention of knitting to craft a nonverbal pregnancy announcement that could have been lifted straight from the silents. Nora Charles (Myrna Loy) sits in a train car serenely knitting. Her husband Nick (William Powell) idly muses, "What's that, hmmm? . . . Looks like a baby's sock." A few beats pass, and Nick does a comic double take as realization dawns. Nora, amused, scolds, "And you call yourself a detective." The joke relies on the audience's certain knowledge that a woman knitting booties is pregnant, a cultural convention necessitated only by the taboo against saying so directly. The iconography of knitting is rich, because it posits the mother as a domestic agent, preparing for motherhood while her body is knitting together a new life. When glamorous actress Leslie Collier (Gloria Swanson) struggles to learn to knit in *Father Takes a Wife* (1941), her cynical aunt Julie inquires, "Wouldn't it be easier just to buy them?" "No," Leslie insists. "A little mother's always supposed to be knitting little things, and doggone it, I'm gonna do it." Knitting is the mark of natural motherhood to this character, and she must master it to inhabit the role.

These clichés were so familiar and so corny that for decades, clever comedies sought ways to make a joke of the euphemisms themselves, taking for granted

Confinements • 33

that audiences were in on the joke. In *Shall We Dance?* (1937), the unmarried Ginger Rogers character is assumed pregnant because she is observed knitting a tiny garment. It later turns out that she was repairing a dog sweater, her virtue intact. Early sitcoms, with their emphasis on domestic life during the postwar baby boom, made an art of the misread pregnancy euphemism. Both *I Love Lucy* and *The Honeymooners* use the false-alarm pregnancy joke. *The Honeymooners* got more mileage out of it, as Ralph (Jackie Gleason) frequently thought his wife Alice (Audrey Meadows) was pregnant, including when he saw her performing such innocuous activities as eating pickles (*The Jackie Gleason Show*, "Pickles," S1E7, November 8, 1952) or leaving a doctor's office (*The Jackie Gleason Show*, "Expectant Father," S4E6, November 3, 1956). The show made the familiar gag the entire plot of the 1976 reunion special, *The Honeymooners Second Honeymoon*, when Ralph finds an item Alice is knitting and jumps to conclusions, though he is a bit baffled that the small garment seems to have three armholes. (It turns out to be a bowling-ball cover.) Though these codes far outlasted the direct prohibition against naming pregnancy, the long tail of their use turns on American ambivalence about speaking pregnancy directly.

PRE-CODE AND POST-CODE

The various iterations of the Hollywood production code did not explicitly ban the representation of pregnant bodies or the word "pregnant," but then they didn't need to: those things were not much in circulation even in the pre-code era (1929–1934), during which the major studies toyed with racier subject matter. Pre-code melodramas used unwed pregnancy as a plot device quite liberally, comedies more sparingly, though there are some remarkable examples in *Reducing* (1931), *Many a Slip* (1931), *It's a Wise Child* (1931), *Blessed Event* (1932), *Doctor Bull* (1933), *She Done Him Wrong* (1933), and others.[10] Regardless of genre, the titillation focused almost entirely on the simple question of sexual guilt; there was no narrative requirement to bother with the visibly gestating body.

In *She Done Him Wrong*, for instance, a desperate young woman named Sally (Rochelle Hudson) passes out in a saloon after a failed suicide attempt. Though she wears a dress with a cinched waist and the word is never spoken, fainting often stood in for pregnancy in studio-era films. A worldly singer, played by Mae West, takes the young woman in and absolves her of shame, chiding, "It takes two to get one in trouble." The line is both more explicit than post-code films would be and still very much in the vein of euphemism, "in trouble" standing in for a past history, present condition, and future event

34 • It's All in the Delivery

that all go unspoken and unseen. Because this is a pre-code comedy, Mae West comes along and saves Sally from a life of degradation through some mysterious magic that might include an abortion. If it were a melodrama, degradation or death would likely be the order of the day. If it were post-code, Sally would have been dropped from the script.

The rapid-fire early talkie *Blessed Event* (1932) is particularly bold in its pre-code focus on pregnancy as scandal, but a credulous viewer could easily wonder what all the fuss is about. Lee Tracy plays a tabloid writer, Alvin Roberts, who fills his column with news of extramarital society pregnancies, thanks to a paid tipster in the New York Maternity Hospital. Though various agents of journalistic respectability spend the film chiding Roberts for his improper and overly feminine gossip items, he builds the paper's readership and quickly grows wealthy. Roberts's continual victories over his detractors echo Hollywood's pre-code strategy of exploiting the soft boundaries of permissible content. Though no visible pregnancies appear (a pregnant chorus singer who has been betrayed by Roberts's column wears a coat in later scenes but is definitely slim throughout), the state of pregnancy is continually under discussion.

> MOXLEY: Didn't I tell you to lay off that stuff about women having kids?
> ROBERTS: Yeah, but I invented a new way of saying it!
> MOXLEY: What new way?
> ROBERTS: "Anticipates a blessed event."

Roberts's euphemism is less a matter of invention (the term long predates the movie) than a willingness to exploit the term's hypocrisy by disingenuously applying the label "blessed" to stigmatized unwed or adulterous pregnancies. Later Roberts reads aloud a critical editorial in the rival paper: "If your wife is to have the sacred experience of motherhood, Mr. Roberts predicts the day and the hour for the public's amusement. Presently, it is not impossible he will be giving the full circumstances of the conception!" This direct line backward from (sacred) birth to (debased) conception anchors the film's interest in pregnancy as proof of sexual guilt. Much of the film's verbal comedy emerges from Roberts's critics being unwilling to name the problem with his column ("all that stuff about women having kids") because the more candid terms for illegitimate pregnancy are all too vulgar to speak, ceding the rhetorical terrain to the tabloid and its shameless faux reverence. Even this pre-code comedy that focuses its whole plot on the scandal of naming pregnancies barely scratches the surface of either the verbal or the visual qualities of its subject.

The production code reformers who took the reins in 1934 found it necessary to walk back the previous administration's boundary-pushing references to sexuality, conception, illegal activity, or bodily functions, but the idea that the baby bump itself was visually unrepresentable had held firm through the pre-code years; I can find no American equivalent to Alice Guy-Blaché's candid representations of baby bumps until much later in the twentieth century. The "sex" section of the production code lists a number of specific prohibitions, which include adultery, scenes of passion, seduction or rape, sexual perversion, white slavery, miscegenation, sex hygiene (birth control or venereal disease), "scenes of actual child birth," and children's sex organs, but nothing about the bodily changes of pregnancy. Olga J. Martin's 1937 code companion, *Hollywood's Movie Commandments*, elaborated on the rules, and here again, the focus is very much verbal rather than visual.

> Pregnancy, or expected "blessed events," should never be discussed as such in screen stories. Most censor boards not only frown upon, but almost always delete any such references. Any direct or crude reference to pregnancy is considered out of place exactly as it would be in any normal society where children are present. It is entirely acceptable, of course, to refer to the baby that is expected, but any reference to conception, childbearing, and childbirth is considered improper for public discussion.[11]

The code handbook explicitly separates the concept of the pregnant woman from "the baby that is expected." This prescription reinforces the idea that as separate entities, woman and baby are hygienic and morally sound, but joined together in a single body, they are obscene and sexually guilty.

Under the newly reformed code administration, sheer absence remained the most common strategy of safely representing a pregnancy. Audiences knew that a female character who disappeared for several months or through a change of seasons was quite likely to return with a baby. *Nobody's Baby* (1937) uses a headline to mark the passage of narrative time, "YVONNE STILL MISSING: No Word from Famous Dancer since Her Disappearance Some Months Ago." A dramatic wipe reveals a nursery full of newborns at a maternity hospital, answering the mystery of Yvonne's absence. *Private Number* (1936) follows a summer elopement with a shot of snow falling outside the family estate. The next scene features two servants confirming that the secretly married maid is expecting a baby. *Casanova Brown* (1944) begins in autumn, with its titular hero (Gary Cooper) returning home from a train trip and begging his confused fiancée (Anita Louise) never to let him out of her sight again. The film jumps immediately forward to spring, the eve of Brown's wedding. The exact timing of all this becomes important when Brown learns that

36 • It's All in the Delivery

the woman (Teresa Wright) with whom he had briefly eloped during that ill-fated autumn trip has just given birth at a Chicago maternity hospital. Pregnancy in all these cases is simple absence, a gap of time measured in months or seasons, separating conception from birth.

In cases where gestation was not entirely skipped over, it was easy to mistake a pregnancy announcement or pregnancy symptoms for some kind of debilitating illness. In *Brother Rat* (1938), for instance, military cadet Bing (Eddie Albert) thinks his wife Kate (Jane Bryan) is delivering bad news when she draws him into another room for a serious conversation. The nondiegetic music grows somber as well, exactly as if she is about to reveal an illness or crisis.

> KATE: Bing, I've quit my job.
> BING: You quit your job? Well, I thought you liked it in Roanoke.
> KATE: I can't go back there anymore. Oh, I didn't mean to tell you until it was all over . . . (sits and sobs)
> BING: What do you mean? Darling! Here, no, don't cry about it. Kate, what's happened?
> KATE: Bing, I don't know how to tell you.
> BING: Tell me what?
> KATE: I'm going to have a baby.

The two have secretly married—against the rules for cadets in Bing's military academy—but still the tone of the conversation is excessive for this situation. Kate's phrasing, "I can't go back there anymore" and "until it was all over," codes the pregnancy as a condition of shame and illness, despite the couple's marital respectability and her evident good health. While dramatic overstatement is hardly rare in narrative cinema, the particular parameters of this exaggeration code pregnancy as a catastrophic physical condition.

The representation of pregnancy as illness has deep roots and weighty implications. Jennifer Ellis West claims that medical practice treats pregnancy as "inherently pathological."[12] Leavitt asserts that the twilight sleep movement, which began in the 1920s and played a part in bringing birthing under the full medical control of male physicians, "helped change the definition of birthing from a natural home event, as it was in the nineteenth century, to an illness requiring hospitalization and physician attendance."[13] This connection of pregnancy with disease justified a number of regimes of control, within families, within medical infrastructures, and within states. In popular media, this connection renders pregnancy a problem to be solved by the film's comic narrative, eclipsing its roots in the greater complexities of sexuality, generative doubleness, or exciting reproductive power.

Confinements • 37

FIGURE 1.3. Boy Meets Girl *(1938)*. *Another bumpless mother-to-be (Marie Wilson) faints on the day she will go into labor.*

The most common method of catastrophizing pregnancy in the 1930s and 1940s was the use of fainting as a marker of early pregnancy. The Hollywood backstage comedy *Boy Meets Girl* (1938) shows pregnant waitress Susie (Marie Wilson) fainting in a producer's office, nearly spilling a tray of food. A callous actor comments, "That commissary shouldn't hire people with epilepsy," mistaking pregnancy for disability. A pair of screenwriters (James Cagney and Pat O'Brien), learning that she is pregnant, make plans to cast her unborn baby in a new movie. Later that diegetic day, she faints again, this time in labor, though she shows no sign of a baby bump beneath her waitressing apron (figure 1.3). This picture presents a bizarre conflation of fainting as both pregnancy announcement and sudden-onset-labor pain, bookending the woman's shockingly brief pregnancy arc with an all-purpose signifier of feminine distress and illness.

Other code-era examples often use a close rhetorical association with doctors and hospitals to render pregnancy a physical affliction. In *Four Wives* (1939), Ann (Priscilla Lane) learns that she is pregnant when she faints as she steps off the elevator at a doctor's office. Though she is only there looking for her sister, the spectacle of Ann fainting into a doctor's arms and being carried into the examination room suggests a terrible illness (figure 1.4). In *Three*

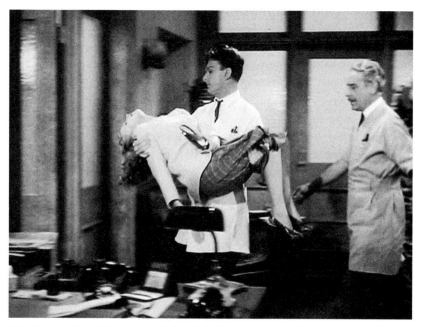

FIGURE 1.4. Four Wives *(1939)*. *Though she does not yet know she is pregnant, Ann (Priscilla Lane) experiences her first fainting spell at a doctor's office, creating this spectacle of medical emergency.*

Cheers for the Irish (1940), a grandfather-to-be (Thomas Mitchell) knows nothing of his daughter's pregnancy until he learns that she (Priscilla Lane again) has been taken to the hospital. "Hospital?" he frets. "She's been run over, ain't she?" In *People Will Talk* (1951), aspiring nurse Deborah (Jeanne Crain) faints during a dissection lecture, experiencing her first pregnancy symptom while surrounded by anatomical charts and figures in white coats.

In *Swing It Soldier* (1941), a pair of identical twin sisters (both played by Frances Langford) switch places in order to prevent the married sister from losing her job as a radio singer. Pregnant sister (Evelyn) disappears into confinement while her twin body double (Pat) continues her own normal activities, including dancing, drinking, and horseback riding, under Evelyn's identity. A confused radio executive (Jerry, played by Ken Murray), tasked by Evelyn's GI husband to keep an eye on his wife, is comically aghast to see a woman he believes to be pregnant living so recklessly and annoys her by offering her milk and asking her to sit down every time he sees her on her feet. The idea that pregnant women require regular monitoring, played for comedy in the film, reinforces the notion that pregnancy is a condition of extreme physical fragility.

Perhaps the most vivid example of pregnancy as dangerous illness appears

Confinements • 39

in the 1944 feature *Music for Millions*. Six-year-old Mike (Margaret O'Brien) is desperately worried about the health of her married sister Barbara (June Allyson). Barbara's friends won't let her carry heavy objects, she has to stop and catch her breath at the top of stairs, and she even passes out and falls in her apartment one night. She calls her friends "a crowd of crepe-hangers" (mourners) when they surround her bed in evident concern, noting, "You'd think I had some tropic disease or something." Mike chases the doctor down several flights of boardinghouse stairs to demand answers as to why her sister is so fragile, confessing, "I'm worried." Though Barbara wishes to keep her pregnancy a secret from the child, the doctor finally tells Mike, "Your sister is going to have a baby," to stave off Mike's very real fear that her sister is dying. Mike is relieved but continues to be confused and concerned as the pregnancy continues. "I've got to look out for you," she tells her sister later. "You don't want to be sick in bed when the baby comes, do you?" This curious dissociation of the woman's symptoms from the baby's arrival, though childish, neatly captures the ways that movies' feigned innocence about reproductive biology left a representational void into which the familiar and representable concept of illness tended to expand.

BIRTH CONTROL AND EUGENICS

It is perhaps a paradox that at the same time American popular cinema was struggling to articulate the process by which babies are born, it experienced even more difficulty in conveying how babies do *not* get born. Birth control occupied shadowy legal territory in these years. The Comstock Act of 1873 made it illegal to distribute "obscene" materials through the US mail, including educational materials about birth control. Activist Margaret Sanger opened her first clinic in Brooklyn in 1916, in defiance of these laws, and a wave of controversial "social problem films" dealing with birth control and abortion appeared in American theaters over the next few years, including *Where Are My Children?* (1916), *The Hand That Rocks the Cradle* (1917), and *Birth Control* (1917), as well as the later *Motherhood: Life's Greatest Miracle* (1925). Activists worked for decades to overturn the Comstock laws, and in 1936, the delightfully named Supreme Court decision *United States v. One Package of Japanese Pessaries* lifted all federal limitations on birth control for medical purposes (though it provided no protection for commercial distribution), a shift in official policy that punctuated a more complicated and ambivalent shift in public attitudes.[14]

Any celebration of these increases in bodily autonomy unfortunately must be balanced against the ways contraception was simultaneously being used as a tool of anti-democratic eugenics. During the years when Nazism was on the rise in Europe, America was experiencing its own eugenics movement, which informed the liberalization of family planning social policies as well as their ugly inverse: forced or coerced sterilization of poor, disabled, or non-white populations considered to be unfit citizens of the state. Rickie Solinger argues that "in a time of uniquely heightened economic, social, and political anxiety in the United States, many Americans saw reproductive control as an important remedy for everything that ailed that country."[15] "Reproductive control," while healthy and happy in the hands of the individual, becomes ominous as a tool of state and social repression. Both sides of this coin are visible in pre-code and code-era cinema, which includes evidence not only of growing social acceptance of birth control as a tool of family planning but also an incipient national anxiety about the "wrong" people reproducing.

In the years between World Wars I and II, eugenics was a common enough topic of social concern that a comedy play on the subject, *The Very Idea*, was produced on Broadway in 1917 and then adapted into films in 1920 and 1929.[16] In each version, the author of a eugenics textbook, *A Race of Thoroughbreds*, convinces his sister and her husband that although they are struggling to conceive a child, they should not select an infant from the local orphan home because they cannot be certain of the parents' fitness. His advice sticks with them: "There wasn't one among them all that we felt safe in taking," laments the would-be mother in the 1929 edition after she returns from the orphanage empty-handed. Spotting a chance to test his theories, the eugenics expert concocts a plan to pay the family chauffeur and maid—an engaged couple whom he considers excellent physical specimens—to produce a baby within a year. The surrogates accept the offer, but then at the end of the contract period, they refund the money, having bonded with their baby. All ends happily (in the manner of so many fertility fictions) when it turns out that the employers have conceived on their own during their relaxing travels.

The film is intended as satire, but its central eugenics argument is never really refuted. It is a running joke in the film that the would-be father is something of a dimwit, casting doubt on the whole idea of genetic superiority, which is found instead in the servant class. But this mild social criticism is eclipsed by the fact that the eugenics-loving uncle ends the film without ever receiving any comeuppance; instead, he is celebrated for making the generous decision to pay his chauffeur the promised money despite the broken bargain, a final gesture of benevolence bestowed on the whole human experiment he has sponsored. Meanwhile, a toddling orphan who is brought out as a punch line late in the film (to save the couple from social embarrassment after their maid refuses to surrender her child) displays such rude manners that he is returned to the asylum immediately and without regret. If the play and film

Confinements · 41

do lightly skewer the concept of eugenics, they treat it as a harmless eccentricity of the overeducated and idle rather than a dangerous mechanism to naturalize social inequality and effect genocide. The film, like other pre-code pregnancy comedies, seems far more interested in congratulating itself on the implicitly sexual nature of its breeding arrangement than in probing its political implications. When a character reads aloud from *A Race of Thoroughbreds* early in the film, there is some mild fussing over propriety until one of the men notes his approval: "I like a bit of spice." By thus reducing the notion of eugenics to a joke about sex, *The Very Idea* artfully skirts around the darker underside of its protagonist's problematic hobby.

Other early talkies put that pre-code social license to use for less dystopian ends. Sexual humor often created space for saucy references to birth control choice as an emerging social norm:

- In *Sunny Side Up* (1929), a reformer approaches a mother sitting on a stoop with her nine children. "Magazine, madam?" she asks, holding up a periodical titled *Birth Control Review*. The mother looks around at her many children and responds in an Irish brogue, "Sure, 'tis a fine time to be telling me! Go on with ya."
- The revue musical *King of Jazz* (1930) features a comedy skit with a young groom (Slim Summerville) asking his fiancée's father for his blessing on their marriage. The father (Otis Harlan) cautions him to consider whether he is ready for the financial commitments of marriage, noting, "After all, there may be children." "Well," Summerville deadpans, "we've been pretty lucky so far."
- In *International House* (1933), the W. C. Fields character and his companion find a litter of kittens on the front seat of a car. "I wonder what their parents are?" the lady muses. Fields responds, "Careless, my little dove cake, careless."

These unabashed references confirm a growing national culture of birth control, which had already slipped the bonds of the Comstock laws and circulated among the public. Many other films more subtly reference childbearing as a choice but do not specify how one goes about preventing the birth of children within marriage. A credible public could perhaps imagine that Bette Davis was referring to abstinence when, in *Ex-Lady* (1933), her character announces, "When I'm forty, I'll think of babies. Meantime, there are twenty years when I want to be the baby and play with my toys, and have a good time playing with them," but the prospect seems unlikely. It was not uncommon in this era for cinematic couples to reference the timing of children, though they do not make clear how exactly they intend to accomplish these delays. In *Employees' Entrance* (1933), a young husband tells his wife, "It won't be long now, darling . . . we'll have enough money to have a baby, if we want one."

LOOK OUT FOR MR. STORK

Though even roundabout references to birth control and reproductive choice largely disappeared from live-action films of the code era, those discourses survived through the euphemism of the stork. The stork was rather perfect as a replacement for the figure of the pregnant woman, precisely because it produced a complete separation between the woman's body and the expected baby. And in this space of the safely hygienic, the stork also made room for some discourses of childbearing that were heavily repressed in live-action features.

A familiar scene from *Dumbo* (1941), for instance, shows an elegant squad of delivery storks under a bright moon flying in formation like synchronized swimmers. They drop their bundles to the circus animals below, and every mother animal is delighted with her new offspring. Like the cabbage patch, the stork method of reproduction is uniquely painless and convenient. It is strange, then, that the lyrics to the accompanying song, "So look out for Mr. Stork / And let me tell you, friend / Don't try to get away / He'll find you in the end," sound almost menacing, as if the stork is an FBI agent on the trail of a supercriminal. Playful as they are, the lyrics acknowledge an alternate reality, where childbearing may not be joyful or individuals may fairly long to "get away" from the burdens and expenses of pregnancy and parenthood. Stork stories of the 1930s–1950s, particularly in animated form, frequently made room for ideas that were suppressed in code-approved comic representations of pregnancy, including the desire for contraception and anxieties about adoption.

The acknowledgment that not all reproduction is wanted referenced a social attitude that was spreading during the difficult years of the Depression, when even middle-class families felt the burdens of widespread economic hardship. Both *Mickey's Nightmare* (1932) and the later *Beau Ties* (1945) are animated shorts featuring male characters dreaming about marriage, happy fantasies that turn into nightmares when the stork goes berserk, delivering dozens of mischievous children who bring chaos and destruction to their homes. Another animated short, *Puzzled Pals* (1933), dramatizes a stork's dilemma when faced with a town where no one is willing to accept delivery of a baby. First the stork flies over the town and finds that his official destination

Confinements • 43

is blocked, with the chimney covered, all windows boarded up, and a Detour sign posted on the roof (figure 1.5). The stork then flies around town, looking for an alternate destination, but finds that every resident has taken precautions to prevent a new delivery: all the chimneys are covered over, and signs on the houses announce increasingly ludicrous reasons for quarantine, including measles, scarlet fever, leprosy, and seven-year itch. The stork soon finds an uncovered roof and is about to drop the baby down the chimney when five children run out of the house and begin shooting at it with toy guns and arrows. They are quickly joined by fourteen infant siblings and two parents. The father uses a hunting rifle and the mother a tommy gun to defend their home from the unwanted delivery. The cartoon is not subtle and boldly jokes about a rational desire for birth control in overstretched American families and neighborhoods.

All's Fair at the Fair (1938), on the other hand, includes a birth control joke so sly you can barely catch it. A couple of country bumpkins, Elmer and Miranda, stroll around the world's fair exclaiming "Wonderful!" as they gawk at all the fantastical modern innovations. A knitting machine? "Wonderful." A machine that makes furniture from logs? "Wonderful." Eventually, they approach a machine that produces prefab houses. As the houses roll off the production line, a stork approaches and drops a baby in each chimney. "Ain't that wonderful?" muses Miranda. "Nope," replies Elmer, at which his wife covers her mouth and giggles. The idea that not all couples want children was still a little bit naughty and particularly funny coming from this wholesome and naive pair. They may be baffled by the wonders of modern technology, but they understand storks perfectly well.

Storks were useful surrogates for the concept of birth control in the studio era because they drove a small wedge into the idea of reproduction's inevitability and divine predestination. Animated stork shorts of the 1930s–1950s show the process of delivery as something that does not always run smoothly— rather than being messengers from some daunting higher power, cartoon storks are often all too fallible and introduce chaos, obstacles, transgression, and choices into the story of reproduction.

While live-action films of the same period largely erase non-white reproductive practices, stork narratives also make room for a playfully diverse perspective on reproduction. A 1933 Warner Bros. cartoon, *Shuffle Off to Buffalo*, shows storks arriving in a sort of baby factory in heaven, where elves diaper and feed preborn babies and then dispatch them to earth. The popular song referenced by the title provides a rhythm for the factory and refers to the tradition of honeymooning at Niagara Falls, in upstate New York. So although all the action is set in the chaste baby factory, the excitement of marital consummation happening down on earth is always exuberantly present.

44 • It's All in the Delivery

FIGURE 1.5. Puzzled Pals *(1933)*. *Cartoons found creative ways to represent birth control: here, a family has boarded up its house against the stork.*

With sexuality thus relegated to a supporting role, much of the film's visual humor is based on ethnic jokes: a Jewish baby is stamped on the bottom with a "Kosher for Passover" seal of approval; Father Time pulls two babies out of a freezer to send in reply to a request from "Mr. and Mrs. Nanook of the North" (figure 1.6). These brief and stereotypical appearances relegate nonwhite reproduction to a marginal and humorous position, while white babies predominate, rolling by on a conveyor belt to be diapered, fed, and prepared for delivery. Though it was certainly a labor-saving device for the animators to render the white babies identical, this technique also produced a text that supports the idea that white babies are standard and normal, while minoritized babies are marked out as unusual and "funny." Very much in the tradition of vaudeville ethnic play (singer Eddie Cantor makes a cameo appearance), *Shuffle Off to Buffalo* is a sly, messy, ambivalent celebration of sexuality and reproduction that could exist only in the world of animated fantasy.

As the economic troubles of the 1930s gave way to the baby boom of the late 1940s and 1950s, animated storks reversed course a bit and frequently came to represent national fertility in overdrive. *The Farm of Tomorrow* (1954) is a faux newsreel touting innovative animal crossbreeding. The narrator explains, "Here, we've crossed the old reliable stork with a big-horn elk to

FIGURE 1.6. Shuffle Off to Buffalo *(1933)*. *In this ethnic caricature of the birth narrative, the stork is set to deliver twins to "Mr. and Mrs. Nanook of the North."*

accommodate you impatient newlyweds, who are in a hurry for a big family." The image shows a stork with a giant rack of horns, babies hung from each branch like Christmas tree ornaments. *Baby Bottleneck* (1946) starts with a drunken stork at the Stork Club complaining about its hectic delivery schedule. Labor conditions at the bustling baby factory are so excessive and chaotic that Porky Pig is installed as the new production chief, with predictably disastrous results.

Drunken storks are everywhere in animated films of the 1950s, mirroring the reproductive recklessness of the baby boom. These untrustworthy reproductive agents frequently deliver babies to the wrong houses, resulting in cross-species adoption narratives that work through stories of unwitting parents doting on genetically unrelated babies. *A Mouse Divided* (1953) sees a drunken stork bringing a mouse baby to a family of cats. *Goo Goo Goliath* (1954) shows a stork too drunk to carry a giant baby all the way to its new home at the top of a beanstalk. Giving up, the stork instead takes the baby to a human-size couple, who raise it as their own. *Lambert the Sheepish Lion* (1951) sees a stork leave a lion cub for sheep parents to raise. In *Apes of Wrath* (1959), a drunken stork loses an ape baby, so the stork kidnaps Bugs Bunny and delivers him to the ape parents instead.

These twin concerns, birth control and adoption, showcase the flexibility of the stork narrative in surfacing the hidden features of American reproductive practice. A final example dramatizes both ideas. In *Stork Naked* (1955), when a drunken stork delivers an egg to Daffy Duck and his wife, Daffy tries unsuccessfully to fight him off. Stuck with the egg, Daffy is delighted to see that the hatchling is a baby stork, not a baby duck. He immediately wraps up the chick and flies it back where it came from, muttering triumphantly, "For once, that stork is gonna get a taste of his own medicine." A bit of the subversive birth control logic of 1930s storks combined with the wrong-delivery excesses of the 1950s result in a portrait of the stork's role as a sly avatar of reproductive ambivalence.

THE MIRACLE OF MORGAN'S CREEK

Given these many ways that representations of pregnancy were "confined" in studio-era film comedies, a marker of the sheer audacity of Preston Sturges's 1943 screwball comedy *The Miracle of Morgan's Creek* is its absence of protective metaphors, as well as the insistent good health of its screwball heroine. In *The Miracle of Morgan's Creek*, pregnancy is a form of chaotic abundance, closer to the tradition of the animated storks described in the previous section than that of pre-code feature comedy euphemism. Sturges was a gleeful provocateur and regular antagonist to the Production Code Administration (PCA), using double entendre to develop jokes that flew under the censors' radar and making letter-of-the-law adjustments in response to production code requests, often keeping the racy spirit of a line or scene entirely intact.[17] The resulting film is an outlier, to be sure, and one that shows the cracks and inconsistencies in the ideology of pregnancy as an unrepresentable condition.

The Miracle of Morgan's Creek follows the adventures of Trudy Kockenlocker (Betty Hutton), a vivacious dingbat with a soft spot for the many soldiers stationed in Morgan's Creek on their way to the war. Trudy's popularity with the soldiers is a source of great distress to her strict father (William Demarest), the town constable. To evade his authority, Trudy asks her milquetoast friend Norval (Eddie Bracken) to take her to the movies one night so she can sneak out of the theater to attend a party with soldiers. Norval obliges, sitting through a triple feature while Trudy takes his car and dances the night away. When Trudy arrives back at the movie theater in the morning, she is unsteady on her feet and unable to remember much about the night before, and it's unclear whether she's suffering from drunkenness or from the concussion she received when an overenthusiastic dance partner banged her head into a chandelier. Norval bravely drives his disoriented friend home and faces her father's wrath.

Trudy's lost evening launches a narrative about an unsanctioned pregnancy and its social consequences. Discovering that she is pregnant, Trudy enlists Norval and her clever younger sister Emmy (Diana Lynn) to help her reconstruct her foggy memories of the lost night and find her baby's father. Trudy's best guess is that she eloped with one of the soldiers from the party. She thinks his name sounds something like "Ratzkiwatzki," but she has no marriage certificate and does not know how to find her missing husband, now deployed. From this point, the intricacies of the trio's quest to render Trudy legitimately married before her child is born are quite tangled to summarize, but it is necessary to try.

In brief, Norval dresses as a soldier to take Trudy to another town to marry her under the false name Ratzkiwatzki so that she may then legally annul the marriage to Ratzkiwatzki and marry Norval as himself. Norval is very bad at deception and soon gets arrested for impersonating a soldier, abducting Trudy, and perjury. None of it makes a bit of legal sense, but then this is the movie's most obvious and radical point: it persuades the audience not to care about the ambiguous state of Trudy's marriage and instead to care about her well-being, rendering the lost marriage certificate trivial and oppressive, a problem to be solved rather than a stain to be endured or a real quest for truth. Trudy is and is not married—either scenario is plausible. She was and was not drunk on the night of the conception—either scenario is plausible. The film evades both the legal logic of marriage and the PCA's rules about pregnancy by inhabiting these ambiguous spaces where evidence fails to produce a clear verdict and where any verdict says more about the arbitrariness of civic institutions than about the moral character of the pregnant woman.[18]

Trudy's father facilitates Norval's escape from authorities, and Norval spends several months on the run, seeking the real Ratzkiwatzki without success. When Norval returns to Morgan's Creek, he is once again arrested. Meanwhile, Trudy's father has been fired and the family has been evicted from their home, and are holed up in a remote farm. These few scenes that show Trudy in an advanced state of pregnancy do hide her body, but they are also more frank than Sturges's genre peers ever dared to be, and even the act of hiding her body confirms that late-stage pregnancy has visible symptoms. It is December, and Emmy plays "Silent Night" on the piano as her father hammers a star on top of the Christmas tree. One of the farm's cows has somehow wandered into the kitchen, giving a final ironic touch to the Christmas manger theme. Sturges's direction is both tongue-in-cheek and infinitely sentimental here, pointing up the hypocrisy of a society that would send an expecting woman out into the cold on Christmas at the same time that they celebrate the birth of a savior under similar circumstances. Trudy sits in a wing-back chair, which obscures her body from the camera's gaze. When her father tries tenderly to comfort her, she looks over the edges of the chair, refusing to meet his gaze. Though

48 • It's All in the Delivery

her midsection is obscured, Trudy's face is poignant with shame. The film's insistence on keeping her in the scene points to the ways that generations of cinema had missed out on representing the emotional subjectivities of pregnancy because of the ban on representing the physical symptoms.

In the end, Trudy's semiwed status is not so much solved as simply disappeared when she gives birth to sextuplets (besting Canada's world-famous Dionne quintuplets, born in 1934). Sensing an opportunity to bring international attention to his state, the corrupt governor pardons Norval, assigns him a position in the state guard, and issues a valid marriage certificate for Norval and Trudy, backdated to preserve the illusion of legitimacy. The cynicism of this "miracle" is extraordinary. The viewer cannot miss the ways in which social institutions relentlessly punish Trudy, Norval, and her family precisely up to the point at which the state sees the opportunity for profit. If, with a wave of his pen, a bureaucrat can relieve a family of the legal, social, and economic burdens of illegitimacy, then the rules that uphold that system of legitimacy must be as artificial as they are cruel.

And while the film's cynical ending is its first line of attack against a corrupt social order, *The Miracle of Morgan's Creek* is equally interested in bringing down civic and family authority through its tone of slapstick mayhem. Constant shouting, pratfalls, and broken objects disrupt the smooth flow of authority, particularly during the first half of the film, before Trudy's confinement. In a recurring joke, Mr. Kockenlocker hollers "It's not paid for!" each time his clumsy and exuberant daughter gambols around, literally breaking the house piece by piece. The characters break dishes, railings, and the glass storm door, a lively assault on the idyllic family home. The meaning of this breakdown shifts, however, when Norval later returns to Morgan's Creek after his six-month trip to find Ratzkiwatzki: he finds the house abandoned, decrepit, and for sale, completing the arc of its disintegration. The mortgaged suburban home falls to pieces after all, nothing as solid as it seems.

The characters' constant tumbles also make a mockery of the idea of a "fallen woman" as a trope of unwed pregnancy narrative. Trudy takes her share of pratfalls in the first half of the film (figure 1.7), culminating in her collision with an inconveniently placed chandelier. The film thus undermines the conventions of the "fallen woman" film, as Trudy's sexual transgression is integrated into her general clumsiness. Though Trudy becomes a bit more sedate in pregnancy, the imagery of the fallen woman is revisited when she confides in despair to Norval that she is thinking of throwing herself into Morgan's Creek. When Norval mentions that the creek isn't very deep this time of year, the two get into a comic discussion of the mechanics of suicide that robs the idea of its melodrama. Norval reasons, "I'm a very good swimmer, and they say that whenever they get in a situation like that, they just naturally swim

FIGURE 1.7. The Miracle of Morgan's Creek *(1944)*. *The film plays with the convention of the "fallen woman." Trudy (Betty Hutton) takes many tumbles, but they are pratfalls rather than moral slips.*

right out." "I'm a very good swimmer too. I hadn't thought of that," Trudy replies. In this way, Sturges refuses the idea of a fallen woman as a tragic condition and instead renders unwed pregnancy as more of a pratfall, a condition produced by an excess of physical vigor, doing no permanent damage.

In the end, Trudy's disruptive sexuality creates the conditions for what comes to be framed as patriotic reproduction: six male children, a platoon. A montage of newspaper headlines linking the babies' birth to the success of the US war effort culminates in the collapse of America's enemies abroad, undone by Trudy's heroic fertility. "Nature Answers Total War!" one headline crows. Frenetic scenes of the governor granting Trudy and Norval marital legitimacy are intercut with scenes of disorder among the Axis leadership, culminating in one of Mussolini's emissaries falling down as he sprints to deliver the terrible news of American reproductive dominance. The sheer audacity of this ending, where Trudy's problematic pregnancy literally brings about victory in Europe, is matched by its frenetic and ridiculous energy. The film piles excess upon excess, fortifying its defense of sexually exuberant semimarital fecundity behind such an avalanche of wish fulfillment that all basis in civic order is simply dislodged and carried along for the ride. Blurring the lines between satire and farce, *The Miracle of Morgan's Creek* applies the tools of comedy to prevailing hypocrisies around reproduction with exceptional force.

BREAKTHROUGHS

Although *The Miracle of Morgan's Creek* was an outlier in many ways, its themes do point to a pivot in representational strategies around the moment of World War II. Pregnancies between soldiers and the wives they left behind become common sentimental plot points in World War II home-front pictures, including *Tender Comrade* (1943), *The Human Comedy* (1943), and *Music for Millions* (1944). These sentimental comedy dramas, with their emphasis on generational continuity and the birth of a new American family out of the destruction of World War II, anticipated the fetish for nuclear families that would define the postwar baby boom beginning in 1946.

Although pregnancy rates had been dropping in the United States from 1909 to 1940, tracking the popularization of birth control throughout the country as well as the economic anxieties of the Depression, the baby boom of 1946–1964 swung the pendulum back in the other direction, positioning the nuclear family as the cornerstone of postwar home-front virtue. The emphasis on rebuilding a new America centered around the single-family home enabled pregnancy to take up more space in the visual rhetoric of family formation. This same ideal also expanded the previous decades' representation of doctors exercising sanitary authority over pregnancies of all kinds. *My Blue Heaven* (1950) opens with Kitty (Betty Grable) sitting on a couch, an expression of bliss on her face as she buttons up her blouse over an exposed slip. A male voice off-screen asks, "Does your husband know anything about this?" A quick cut reveals that the speaker is Kitty's obstetrician, and by "this" he means her newly diagnosed pregnancy, but the opening joke teases the idea of Betty Grable's sexuality for the audience while also acknowledging the doctor's centrality to the 1950s model of American pregnancy. The medical practitioner takes the place of the father in the pregnancy's narrative origin story.

The decline of the production code after 1948 and cinema's competition with television also enabled a bit more frankness in studio features as the 1950s dawned. *People Will Talk* (1951) features a scene between the (secretly unmarried) Deborah Higgins (Jeanne Crain) and the slightly eccentric Doctor Praetorius (Cary Grant), who has run some tests to determine the cause of her fainting spell. The doctor tells Deborah she is perfectly well, at which she is flooded with relief. Then he asks her to make a follow-up appointment with either himself or an obstetrician of her choice. Concerned, Deborah asks, "Didn't you say I had nothing to worry about? That everything was all right?"

The doctor replies, "It couldn't be any better, Mrs. Higgins. You're pregnant." His candor startles her, but the doctor insists on treating the subject with frankness. They go on to discuss the possibility of medical error and the exact species of frog used in the pregnancy test. It is not insignificant that both the word "pregnant" and the refusal of any discourse that treats pregnancy like an illness converge in this conversation. The doctor's insistence that pregnancy is "all right" is the film's justification for discussing it openly.

The public reception of *People Will Talk* showed only mild objection to the use of the word "pregnant" or its frank discussion. The trade publication *Harrison's Reports* noted that the film was "adult in theme, but there are no objectionable situations."[19] *Modern Screen* expressed outrage not at the pregnancy plot, but at the film's depiction of a medical school classroom: "I don't think any medical school trots a corpse with a madeup face and long black hair into a class room (if they do, I'm against it)."[20] The *Los Angeles Times* called the film "occasionally daring and, by conventional movie standards, even shocking— although by standards of the adult theater there is nothing to raise more than an eyebrow over."[21]

Speaking of adult theater, the relatively rapid progression of visual codes in these years happened more quickly in prestige drama and melodrama than in comedy. Drawing heavily from theater and international arthouse conventions, these pictures were more likely to take advantage of the flexibility associated with the decline of the production code and the rise of independent producing options to push the boundaries of visual representation. Ida Lupino's 1949 social problem film, *Unwed Mother* (also released as *Not Wanted*), features a whole line of young women with padded bumps washing dishes in a home for unwed mothers. Reviews did not tend to note the visible pregnancies as an innovation, though the *New York Times* did speculate that the film's delivery scene "may possibly be offensive to some audiences."[22] The scene, while not graphic, is indeed remarkable: a tonal jazz soundtrack plays over an extended sequence of woozy point-of-view shots that slip in and out of focus as the laboring woman watches the masked medical team select instruments and lean over the foot of her bed, ominously backlit by surgical lights. In a different realist tradition, *A Streetcar Named Desire* (1951) makes visible and verbal reference to the uncomfortable final weeks of pregnancy Stella Kowalski (Kim Hunter) endures in the heat of a New Orleans summer, though it does not use the word "pregnant." In the tradition of 1950s social realism, and influenced by European art films of the postwar period, these movies are also significant for dramatizing the traumas of working-class pregnancy in quite a different way than the suburban fantasy of many family comedies or sitcoms.

Family comedies of the early 1950s, though chronological peers of these urban dramas, tended to dress pregnant characters in maternity smocks but

FIGURE 1.8. Cheaper by the Dozen *(1950)*. *Lillian Gilbreth (Myrna Loy) packs to go to the hospital to deliver this same day. It was common for comedies of the early 1950s to use the volume of fabric in maternity smocks to stand in for the bodily changes of pregnancy, without apparent padding underneath.*

without obvious padding underneath, such as those worn by Myrna Loy in *Cheaper by the Dozen* (1950), Betty Grable in *My Blue Heaven* (1950), Meg Randall in *Ma and Pa Kettle Back on the Farm* (1951), and Elizabeth Taylor in *Father's Little Dividend* (1951). In *Cheaper by the Dozen*, Myrna Loy's character, Lillian Gilbreth, remains slender beneath her smock even as she is packing for her visit to the hospital to deliver this very day (figure 1.8). Maternity fashions of the 1950s abetted the ambiguity of the transition from unpadded to padded bumps by covering the waist in loose folds of excess fabric. The straight-down line from bust to hip split the difference between obfuscation and acknowledgment while still creating a far more realistic impression of bulk than earlier depictions, such as in *Blondie's Blessed Event*.

I LOVE LUCY

Situation comedies began as radio shows, where the physical changes associated with pregnancy posed no problem. Characters could welcome babies without showing any physical changes, and actresses could carry pregnancies to term without disturbing the delicate sensibilities of the American public. When television entered the scene after World War II, the domestic conventions of the sitcom encountered some inevitable obstacles. If an actress in a film became pregnant, usually she would just be replaced or the shooting schedule adjusted.[23] But in a sitcom, the new combination of a visible lead actress and a serial narrative created a situation where the shooting schedule and lead performer were not quite so easily shifted around.

Lucille Ball was actually pregnant and hid her second-trimester figure in a series of bulky costumes when she filmed the 1951 pilot episode of *I Love Lucy*, but she had given birth before the studio shot the actual first season that aired later that year.[24] When Ball informed the network about her second pregnancy in 1952, producer Jess Oppenheimer and Desi Arnaz fought hard to avoid canceling the series, challenging standard studio practice by seeking to simply make Ball's character pregnant as well. It's hard for modern audiences to imagine how a married couple having a baby in a sitcom could be other than wholesome, even in a world where the married couple in question had twin beds in their TV bedroom. But the negotiations between the show's producer, the CBS head office, and the show's sponsor, the cigarette company Philip Morris, betrayed deep discomfort with the plan to incorporate Ball's pregnancy into the show's narrative.

First the studio asked that Ball's figure be hidden behind furniture, unacknowledged. Arnaz refused—and it is significant that Ball's importance as a physical comedian justified the refusal and helped break the taboo. Then the studio agreed to the pregnancy plot but wanted it confined to two episodes to minimize the impact. Arnaz refused. Eventually, Oppenheimer came up with the idea to have a priest, a minister, and a rabbi review each script and be present at the filming of each episode to ensure that the material met all possible standards of Judeo-Christian decency. The studio conceded.[25] In the end, the clerical trio heartily approved the seven episodes dealing with Lucy's pregnancy. When asked if they found anything objectionable after a dress rehearsal, they are said to have asked, "What's wrong with having a baby?"[26] Famously, the episode announcing Lucy's pregnancy is titled "Lucy Is Enceinte" (S2E10, December 8, 1952), coyly substituting the French word for "pregnant," though no French is used in the episode itself. After all that fuss, the very next episode of the season was titled "Pregnant Women Are Unpredictable" (S2E11, December 15, 1952) because—as has often been the case with censorship practices—there was no great consistency in studio and sponsor rule-making or enforcement.

In many ways, Lucy's pregnancy brought further into focus the issues of private versus public that were the show's hallmark. Lucy's world is still centered in her apartment, and her physical comedy becomes a bit gentler, but perhaps the most radical aspect of her pregnancy is how much she still claims ownership of the space outside her home. In "Lucy Is Enceinte," Lucy tries to tell Ricky the news of her pregnancy when he comes home for lunch but is repeatedly interrupted. She follows him to work, but when Ricky asks the whole band to quiet down so his wife can tell him something, she is too embarrassed to continue. Finally, she dresses up and visits his nightclub during prime time, slipping a note to the floor manager as she enters. Ricky reads the note onstage, explaining that a member of the audience is expecting a "blessed event" and wants him to sing his song "We're Having a Baby, My Baby and Me" as a way of making the announcement to her husband. Ricky begins singing as he strolls from table to table, asking each woman if she is the mother-to-be. When he gets to Lucy, he smiles and jokingly asks, "Is it you?," to which she nods. The realization overwhelms Ricky, and he can barely contain tears as he embraces his wife and sings to her. By placing this tender moment in the public space of the nightclub, this pivotal episode carefully navigates how the pregnancy fits into the Arnaz-Ricardo dynamic of two professional entertainers enacting a scripted, comic, topsy-turvy version of their own marriage for the viewing public.

Breaking the logic of confinement both diegetically and extradiegetically, Lucy's pregnancy did not put even a temporary end to her character's playful forays into the public world. In "Lucy's Show-Biz Swan Song" (S2E12, December 22, 1952), Lucy tries to crash Ricky's nightclub show, auditioning for his "Gay '90s Revue" in a ludicrous hoop skirt that covers her expanded middle. She is humiliated when the pantaloons she wears beneath the skirt fall down around her ankles, forcing her to shuffle awkwardly offstage, shackled by her own drawers, ably demonstrating that pregnancy and physical comedy need not be mutually exclusive.

Unlike any peer, *I Love Lucy* had great fun with its star's baby bump as a costume element. When downstairs neighbor Fred throws Ricky a men's baby shower at a stag club, Lucy and Ethel dress as male reporters to crash the party and monitor the men's behavior ("Ricky Has Labor Pains," S2E14, January 5, 1953). In drag, Lucy's baby bump becomes an audacious beer belly tucked beneath an old-fashioned waistcoat (figure 1.9). In a different kind of drag, Lucy, Desi, Ethel, and Fred all dress up as Santa Clauses for a Christmas episode ("Lucy's Show-Biz Swan Song"). While the others use pillows to pad their stomachs, Lucy's belly fills the costume perfectly. With these episodes, *I Love Lucy* presented a vision of pregnancy very much at odds with the legacy of treating the condition as an unmentionable feminine secret. Lucy's pregnancy was, rather, a physical condition that did not radically transform the couple's

Confinements · 55

FIGURE 1.9. I Love Lucy ("Ricky Has Labor Pains," S2E14, January 5, 1953). Lucy's pregnant figure was incorporated into the costumes for several of her ludicrous schemes, as when Lucy (Lucille Ball) and Ethel (Vivian Vance) pose as reporters covering Ricky's stag party.

companionate public-private marriage. Instead, it provided the opportunity for a new kind of social play. Not since Alice Guy-Blaché had the pregnant body itself been shown as being in any way fun.

Though there certainly wasn't any large-scale controversy around Ball's public pregnancy, the *Chicago Tribune* did publish excerpts from reader letters expressing a range of views. One reader objected on aesthetic grounds: "Lucy looked like a barrel on two sticks. A woman's place is in the home at that stage." Another objected on moral grounds: "What can you possibly like about Lucille Ball and her sex exhibitions?"[27] Despite these outliers, there is no question that the experiment of Lucy Ricardo's sitcom pregnancy was a transformational success, which further made history when forty-four million households (68 percent of the total viewing audience for the night) tuned in on January 19, 1953, to see the episode in which Lucy gave birth to little Ricky ("Lucy Goes to the Hospital," S2E16) on the same day that the real Ball gave birth to Desi Jr., a broadcasting event made possible through the magic of prerecorded taping and a scheduled cesarean section.

Curiously, while studio executives and sponsors were wringing their hands about the necessity of delicate handling, the fan press went in the opposite direction, publishing extraordinarily detailed accounts of Ball's real-life pregnancy, the publicity event of the decade. A *Modern Screen* profile, for instance, not only uses the word "pregnant" without apparent concern ("Besides everyone knew I was pregnant—with Desi it's impossible to keep a thing like that quiet") but also describes many details of her experience that would never have made it on the show, including how Ball knew she couldn't hide her condition after about the fifth month, that she chose her own due date to deliver by cesarean section, and a very detailed description of the delivery: "At 7:00 a.m. Lucille was wheeled into the delivery room. Dr. Harris gave her a spinal. During the course of the delivery, Lucille asked a nurse, 'Is it a boy?'"[28] An adoring fan base, then, would have seesawed from television's heavily regulated delicate treatment of the subject of pregnancy to the nitty-gritty details that are the currency of tabloid culture. By showing that the public would not just tolerate but enthusiastically consume a very unconfined pregnancy, Lucy's adventures in childbearing helped reveal a public appetite for greater and more candid discourse regarding marital reproduction in both television and film.

CONCLUSION

After the breakthrough of Lucille Ball's televised pregnancy, and fueled by the national baby boom, the early 1950s saw rapid progress in the frank depiction of pregnancy and, in a strange way, carried on as if visible bumps had been the norm all along. The 1952 romantic comedy *You for Me* uses the word "pregnant" and a padded bump to signify a supporting character's pregnancy without any diegetic fuss. In 1956, *The Opposite Sex* doesn't use the word "pregnant," but the character of Edith (Joan Blondell) leans back from the table and pats her padded belly by way of announcing her pregnancy to a gossip columnist. The character shows remarkable comfort with her own body and indeed makes a joke of her frequent pregnancies, which have taken on the quality of a routine.[29] The gossip columnist does not regard the situation as news.

The 1956 domestic comedy *Full of Life* provides an apt conclusion to this chapter in media history because it focuses on the emotional and physical comedy of late-term pregnancy unusually directly and marks a decisive (if ambivalent) end to the taboo of confinement. The movie begins with Emily (Judy Holliday), heavily pregnant and dressed in a nightgown, unable to sleep and making herself a snack. A pretitle scene opens with a narrow shot of the character's feet and the hem of her nightgown as she walks into the kitchen. Medium shots frame her against the counter, making a sandwich of lunch meat, butter, mustard, and raw onion. Finally, the camera pulls back to show

FIGURE 1.10. Full of Life *(1956)*. Judy Holliday is abundantly padded.

her full pregnant figure as the title, *Full of Life*, appears on the screen, showcasing the pregnant body as the film's featured spectacle (figure 1.10).

The discomfort and heft of Emily's pregnant body are a key diegetic topic of the film's story and dialogue. "It takes so long to have a baby," she tells her husband in a moment of late-term weariness. "Just centuries and centuries." The character experiences backaches, food cravings, cleaning binges, and sleep disturbances, and she tolerates her husband's unchivalrous sexual frustration with the change in her figure. Holliday's performance of pregnancy invites identification from the viewer in a way that is empathetic, good-humored, and quite novel. In one scene, she just stands in front of a mirror in her nightgown, examining herself and going through a range of emotions as she ponders the vast changes in her body and life. Judy Holliday's sensitive performance communicates an impression of precisely how strange, exhausting, and exhilarating she finds the experience of carrying this pregnancy.

Though most critics praised the film for its warmth, Bosley Crowther of the *New York Times* reviewed *Full of Life* with a nearly audible yawn, calling it "a very broad and obvious discourse on modern maternity," plagued by "a set of obvious jokes."[30] In just a few short years, marital pregnancy had evidently traveled the short distance from taboo to cliché without ever being acknowledged as a common and remarkable human experience.

If the gradual decline of the pregnancy taboo in feature films and television turned out to be a bit anticlimactic, it also proved frustratingly incomplete. Although the baby boom helped usher in a generation in which pregnancy became representable in a literal sense, the deep ambivalence that defined American attitudes toward pregnant embodiment continued to skew representational practices for generations. The next chapter builds on this history of confinement to show that while American popular media were and still are very uncomfortable confronting the physiology and doubleness of the pregnant female body, those same media have long given far more room—literal and figurative—to the figure of the expectant father.

Chapter 2
HYSTERICAL FATHERHOOD
MALE PREGNANCY ON-SCREEN

> PEG: Here. Here's something I've been knitting.
> CHESTER: A mitten! Just what I need.
> PEG: It's a bootie.
> CHESTER: It *is* pretty.
> PEG: Not a *beauty*, a *bootie*. Well, I guess I better tell ya. We're going to have an addition to our home.
> CHESTER: Aw, don't be silly, Peg. We can't even pay the rent for this joint; why should the landlord build us a dining room?
> PEG: There's a little stranger coming to our house.
> CHESTER: Oh, so that's what you mean. Well, I don't want that sawed-off runt of an uncle moving in here with us.
> PEG: Aw, it's not an uncle, it's a little (whispers in his ear).
>
> *The Life of Riley* ("Riley's Firstborn," S1E16, January 17, 1950)

ONE OF THE MANY CODES for pregnancy outlined in chapter 1 was a woman whispering news of her pregnancy into a man's ear, as in the silent comedy *The Crowd* (see figure 1.2) or this exchange from the early sitcom *The Life of Riley*. Although one might expect this convention to die out once the word "pregnant" entered mainstream film and television in the 1950s, promotional

FIGURE 2.1. *Clockwise, from top left:* The Miracle of Morgan's Creek *(1943)*, Casey Bats Again *(1954)*, Fools Rush In *(1997)*, Nine Months *(1995)*. *A woman whispering into a man's ear is used to signify pregnancy.*

images ranging from 1941 to 1997—over fifty years—suggest the ubiquity and longevity of this trope (figure 2.1). The gestational news in each case creates a kind of visual joke written across the man's face, his obvious surprise and alarm a confirmation that the woman is in charge of reproduction, composed and feminine, often smiling, while the man is taken off guard, baffled or insensible at his first exposure to his partner's whisper. The idea that pregnancy is a woman's secret knowledge, bestowed on her partner, far outlived the cultural necessity of secrecy. Clearly there is something going on here besides euphemism.

Fancifully, I think of this whisper as a Freudian joke of reverse insemination:

the man puts his sperm in the woman, the child is conceived, and then she puts her whisper in his ear, essentially inseminating him back with the news of his expectant fatherhood. Thus the circle is closed and cishet male pregnancy is born. Understood in these terms, this euphemistic whisper is an apt figure to capture the thesis of this chapter: that the inherited taboo around the representation of how women conceive and bear children created the conditions for the emergence of representational tropes that centered men. But even after that taboo began to decline, deep-seated cultural anxiety about women's reproductive power as secretive, uncanny, or undermining male control drove the perpetuation of these norms and ensured that the experience of pregnancy in film and television comedy would ultimately be focalized through the male character and often played out through his body instead of hers over the course of decades.[1]

Although one might expect this asymmetrical attention to fatherhood to decline as pregnancy grew more representable through the mid-twentieth century, this chapter argues that the tendency to centralize fathers in reproductive narratives both long predates the production code and has persisted in one form or another through the present day, perversely coding pregnancy as a male experience and a male burden. Indeed, watching comedies from the 1930s through much of the 1990s—far later than mainstream cinema and television ceased to censor the baby bump—one would think that pregnancy was a condition that primarily affected men. The titles of many American pregnancy comedies centralize a male perspective: *Stork Bites Man* (1947), *So You're Going to Be a Father* (1947), *Father's Little Dividend* (1951), *Paternity* (1981), *Father of the Bride Part II* (1995), *My Baby's Daddy* (2004). Sitcom episodes, too: "Ricky Has Labor Pains" in 1953 (*I Love Lucy*, S2E14), "The Expectant Father" in 1963 (*The Joey Bishop Show*, S2E31), "Fred Sanford Has a Baby" in 1976 (*Sanford and Son*, S5E16).

The old canard that women aren't funny similarly helped ensure that male performers would function as the bankable star in generations of comedies.[2] Pregnancy as an occasion for panic was particularly a justification for male physical comedy: the frenetic motion, the rubber face, the pratfalls and physical comedy gags strung together into a Rube Goldberg machine of hilarity. Fathers in comic films and sitcoms often specialize in faux haplessness, characters who perform their lack of domestic control even as the entire household unambiguously centers around their antics. Their female costars have frequently been framed as more sensible "straight men" or even as decorative supporting characters. In this way, comic films about pregnancy were doubly stacked against women, layering an asymmetrical genre convention on top of a taboo. But even as women's pregnant bodies on-screen emerged from behind closed doors, heavy bedclothes, bulky smocks, and polite euphemisms, the

Hysterical Fatherhood • 63

FIGURE 2.2. Vanity Fair *and* Spy *magazines (1991). Groundbreaking representations of pregnancy provoke co-optation and parody, as in these paired images of actress Demi Moore and her husband, actor Bruce Willis.*

conventions of male pregnancy did not disappear, but rather expanded to hysterical proportions.

When Demi Moore appeared, for instance, naked and pregnant, on the cover of *Vanity Fair* in 1991, the photo provided a shot across the bow of decades of obfuscation. And still, pressure from newsstand dealers pushed *Vanity Fair* to ship copies of the issue in white paper sleeves so that retailers could choose whether to display the full cover image at the point of sale.[3] This push-pull is typical of moments of cultural change, which nearly always lead to backlash, commodification, and fetishistic reappraisal of the taboo as it declines, all of which are visible in this case. With pregnancy, that backlash also took the form of masculine co-optation, as in the immediate publication of a *Spy* magazine parody image of Moore's husband, Bruce Willis, photoshopped in a similar pose cradling a naked, pregnant belly (figure 2.2). In these years of transition, the idea of pregnancy as essentially a male problem reemerged as a counterweight to this growing cultural candor about childbearing, a way to contain, reframe, and undermine the spectacle of women's reproductive power.

The ways that comic pregnancy is performed through the male body recall the medical diagnosis of couvade syndrome, in which the male partners of pregnant women may experience sympathetic symptoms, including nausea, back pain, and weight gain. Although, as William Marsiglio notes, research on couvade as a medical or even a psychological condition "remains sketchy," the concept of men experiencing pregnancy symptoms or even reenacting labor rituals has been remarkably durable across eras and cultures.[4] The term "couvade," from the French *couver*, meaning "to hatch," was used to describe rituals common in early modern Europe, when a laboring woman's husband would take to bed and mimic the pains of labor in his own body. When the child was born, it would be given to the father as if he had birthed it himself. In the psychoanalytic era, theorists and therapists have frequently described biologically male patients dealing with fantasies or anxieties of pregnancy and have interpreted those symptoms as evidence of a deep-seated envy of biologically female reproductive power.[5]

The whole notion of couvade syndrome activates some pretty primal concepts of psychosocial identity, which is to say that psychoanalysis may provide a lens to understand how this fantasy of male reproductive centrality may help satisfy some of the open wounds of gender identity and biological essentialism that Freudian theory has identified. Karen Horney's psychoanalytic theory of "womb envy" suggests a starting point. In 1926, Horney postulated, as a counter to Freud's famous suggestion that women's psychosexual development is built around "penis envy," that a parallel process defines masculine maturation, as cisgender boys come to learn that they do not possess the physical organs to bear and nurse children:

> But from the biological point of view woman has in motherhood, or in the capacity for motherhood, a quite indisputable and by no means negligible physiological superiority. This is most clearly reflected in the unconscious of the male psyche in the boy's intense envy of motherhood. . . . When one begins, as I did, to analyze men only after a fairly long experience of analyzing women, one receives a most surprising impression of this envy of pregnancy, childbirth, and motherhood, as well as of the breasts and of the act of suckling.[6]

This notion of womb envy has some explanatory power for understanding why cultural narratives of creation have often substituted a male figure for a female one in the pro/creative act, as when Eve is born from Adam's rib, when Athena emerges from the head of Zeus, or when Pygmalion crafts his ideal partner from clay.[7] The erasure of the mother figure in these stories restores the father to centrality, eliminating the nine-month phase in which female physiology hides the developing child from masculine knowledge or control. The possibility of deception—that a father's knowledge of his biological paternity is never certain (or became more certain only recently with the development

Hysterical Fatherhood • 65

of DNA tests)—further underscores this drive to reassert authority, as well as the stigmatization of female biology as inherently gross, dark, or threatening. Female bodies and the physical privacy of the reproductive event happening inside those bodies represent a direct challenge to the very possibility of total patriarchal social control.

Womb envy as a concept helps illustrate how misogyny, at a deep level, can be traced to masculine anxiety about what Horney calls women's "by no means negligible physiological superiority," a claim that undermines the most cherished myths of male supremacy. Once activated, these anxieties must be answered with social organizations, cultural norms, and unconscious psychological structures that distort female biology and reframe it as abject and grotesque, in need of masculine control. These ideas are evident throughout this book but apply most strongly to this chapter, which literalizes womb envy in films and shows that use pregnancy to structure comedy narratives that focus on cisgender male bodies and subjectivities, thereby excluding, appropriating, or minimizing women's experiences of childbearing.

I use the term "male pregnancy" playfully in this chapter to refer to three different forms of hysterical masculine appropriation: (1) a visual and narrative focus on the father that treats him as the principal actor in a text; (2) literal stories of pregnant cisgender men, framed as dreams, witchcraft, satirical science fiction, or farce; and (3) a recent cycle of what I call "sperm comedies," which apply a gross-out comedy aesthetic to stories of male reproductive mishaps. Looking at these male pregnancy jokes and stories as a group makes visible the extent to which playful masculine appropriations of pregnancy can be understood as attempts to deal with pregnancy as a challenge to patriarchal dominance. The representational strategies associated with male pregnancy, then, are specifically positioned to recenter masculine subjectivity, developing a hysterical masculine comic trope, a father-to-be who expresses this anxiety through frenzied action and excessive emotional displays that decenter the pregnant woman from the comic frame.

APPROPRIATIONS

For much of the twentieth century, during and after the period in which the production code banned "scenes of actual childbirth," this is what childbirth looked like: A nervous father paces around the hospital waiting room or outside the door of the bedroom where his wife labors—unseen—under the care of a doctor or midwife. Sometimes the doctor asks for towels or boiling water. Sometimes the father smokes. Sometimes other fathers are pacing there with him. The tension is finally broken by the cry of a healthy baby from behind a door or a visit from a smiling nurse, followed by great relief and cigars. Sometimes the father faints.

This trope was so familiar to audiences by midcentury that films and sitcoms routinely riffed on these conventions to freshen the material. In *The Great Lie* (1941), the father is absent, so adoptive mother Bette Davis paces outside the delivery room in riding breeches. In *Seven Brides for Seven Brothers* (1954), the six uncles-to-be make a visual joke of pacing in choreographed patterns around the cabin while their sister-in-law labors upstairs. In the animated *One Hundred and One Dalmatians* (1961), both expectant father dog Pongo and human owner Roger pace the floor while mother dog Perdita gives birth in the next room. The sitcom father in *The Joey Bishop Show* ("The Baby Cometh," S2E34, May 11, 1963) organizes the pacing fathers in military order so they don't run into each other. A book of popular vaudeville skits offers several comic sketches for the waiting father, including this one:

ED: . . . How can she know the pain I'm experiencing? Some people are heartless! (*Do business of having paper under fingernails, biting them, and spitting them out. The nurse enters.*)
NURSE: Mr. Lowry, Mr. Lowry, news, news! It's a beautiful baby girl.
ED (*joyful*): Oh, a girl! Thank heaven! Good fortune has smiled on me! What luck!
NURSE: Mr. Lowry, you seem elated. Men usually prefer a boy.
ED: What, I should bring a boy into this world to suffer as I just did? God forbid![8]

The punch line, which mocks the father's self-pity, also reveals a secondary truth. If women's pain was unrepresentable, grotesque, or taboo, sanitized but hysterical male suffering would gladly expand to hyperbolic proportions to take up all the space created by this vacuum.

As scenes of labor and childbirth entered the visual realm in film and television, this transference of labor pain and panic from the mother to the father continued, often spurring the father to frenetic motion. The Keystone Kops–style rush to the hospital, the core joke of so many pregnancy movies from *The Crowd* (1928) to *Bridget Jones's Baby* (2016), is ludicrous when considered alongside the facts of actual labor, which in the case of first childbirths normally lasts twelve to eighteen hours. It is comprehensible only when it is understood that the man is not rushing the woman to the hospital because the baby will arrive any second. He is rushing her to the hospital because he understands her body to be in the grip of an alien and grotesque process and is desperate to entrust her care to a sterile medical establishment, thereby relieving himself of anxiety about it. This persistent convention reframes the female experience, and even the female body, as a prop for male heroism, panic, and distress.

In sitcoms and comedy movies, fathers-to-be have often channeled this anxiety of female otherness and the uncanny process of birthing into meticulous planning and packing, which imposes a superficial orderliness on the uncontrollable timing of unmedicated childbirth. This planning is promptly undone by the father's frenzied panic with the onset of labor, disrupting that veneer of order. This schtick was played out across dozens of film and television scripts beginning in the 1940s, with the father leaping from bed and throwing on clothes over his pajamas or revealing that he had gone to bed in his clothes in the first place. He grabs suitcases and dashes to the door, causing some kind of havoc along the way, all the while ignoring his wife's pleas for calm and order. This joke was revisited like any other favorite old vaudeville routine in *Father's Little Dividend* (1951), *The Dick Van Dyke Show* ("Where Did I Come From?," S1E15, January 3, 1962), *The Life of Riley* ("Riley's Firstborn," S1E16, January 17, 1950), and many others. In a frequent variation, the father pulls the car out of the driveway, forgetting his wife altogether before doubling back for her, as in *Father of the Bride Part II* (1995), *The Flintstones* ("The Blessed Event," S3E23, February 22, 1963), and *The Cosby Show* ("The Birth," S5E6, November 10, 1988). The neglect of women in childbirth literalizes the idea that this whole enterprise is really an exercise for and about the father; the birthing woman is an afterthought.

In some cases, the father (or other attending male) simply replaces the mother as the suffering patient. In one episode of *The Odd Couple*, for instance, a young supporting character goes into labor unexpectedly and is escorted into an off-screen bedroom to await the ambulance ("Natural Childbirth," S2E1, September 17, 1971). Meanwhile, Felix (Tony Randall) performs male hysteria in the on-screen living room, stammering into the phone and doubling over with stomach pains of his own. When the ambulance arrives, the medics assume Felix is the patient and place him on the gurney, fully replacing the medical condition of labor with the hysterical condition of male suffering.

In an example that draws this visual language of male suffering into the late twentieth century, the birth scene from *Fools Rush In* (1997) shows Isabel (Salma Hayek) experiencing an emergency unmedicated delivery by the side of the road in a rainstorm, attended by her estranged husband, Alex (Matthew Perry). Though Isabel is the one experiencing pain, the framing of the shots in this sequence centralizes Alex's face and his reactions, while Isabel's face and body are almost off-screen (figure 2.3). The film thus tries to redirect the discomfort generated by viewers' experience of her pain by using Perry's mugging as literal comic relief. This strategy of misdirection implies that labor is really a male problem: the woman does the bodily work of childbirth at the edge

FIGURE 2.3. Fools Rush In *(1997)*. *The laboring woman (Salma Hayek) is nearly out of frame, so the expression of distress of the father (Matthew Perry) replaces hers.*

of the screen, what we might call "out of her head" with pain, and the man occupies the position of head in the same frame, channeling the labor through his experience rather than hers.

Though the comic father's masochistic appropriation of labor pain in comic media has long roots, it grew particularly acute in the late twentieth century. Beginning in the 1970s, childbirth in America underwent several important developments: changes in anesthetic technology and protocols meant more women were awake and alert during hospital births; hospitals and community centers started to offer birthing classes and parenting classes, encouraging couples to learn about and take a greater role in birthing choices; and in the context of these changes, men began to be welcome in the birthing suite while their children were born rather than being exiled to the waiting room.[9] All these changes were processed and satirized in popular media through the lens of the baffled father rather than the laboring mother.

In a 1973 episode of *The Carol Burnett Show* (S7E8, November 3), one sketch dramatizes a couple feuding as the woman goes into labor, the husband (Paul Sand) blurting out his grievances: "You get all the attention, you get all the presents, and you get all the pain!" His wife (Carol Burnett) reassures him: "Darling, a pregnancy is a sharing experience between a husband and his

Hysterical Fatherhood • 69

wife. I'm going to share everything with you, even the pain." She goes on to describe in detail the pain of a contraction, and he rapidly begins experiencing sympathy pains with her, doubling over and panting from the force of it. The sketch ends with Burnett's character picking up the phone and calling for an ambulance to collect the debilitated couple, announcing triumphantly, "My husband and I are having a baby!" This fantasy that modern companionate marriage can be taken to an extreme that allows couples to "share everything," even labor pains, is framed as a dubious feminist triumph, satirizing the couvade conundrums of this generation.

More iconically, Bill Cosby's 1983 stand-up routine describing his wife's natural childbirth quickly became a cultural touchstone, both daring and wholesome in its insights into the intimate and formerly taboo process. It is impossible to write about comedian Bill Cosby in the present tense without acknowledging the fact that over sixty women have now credibly accused the actor of sexual assault, most of those incidents compounded by forced sedation. At the time of this writing, Cosby has served jail time for a conviction related to a 2004 incident, but the conviction was overturned on the basis of a due process violation. Several civil suits have been settled against the actor for cases that were not processed criminally. The net effect of these revelations has been a very necessary public conversation about professional predation and women's safety, and the courage of Cosby's accusers helped lay the groundwork for the #MeToo movement in the United States.

I include Cosby's work here as a matter of historical interest, as his stand-up and sitcom career significantly shaped the public discourse around male pregnancy and sensitive fatherhood in the 1980s and 1990s. It is right and proper that Cosby's work should undergo reevaluation, for reasons both textual and extratextual. As in many related cases, the history of Cosby's career teaches us to mourn for the work that generations of creative women were never able to create, their own careers discouraged, cut short, or eclipsed by the industry's protection of predatory men in positions of power. Brittney Cooper and Bambi Haggins have both written on what the loss of Bill Cosby as a specifically Black comic icon has meant to them, and both note that Cosby's legacy as the leading proponent of "respectability politics"—in which racial equality was conditioned on the successful performance of middle-class values—was always problematic and had grown increasingly toxic even before the comedian's public disgrace.[10] That emphasis on respectability politics in Cosby's persona and work is particularly relevant here, because Cosby's role as a father narrating the absurdities of natural childbirth was essential to his emerging persona as an emblem of bourgeois respectability in the last two decades of the twentieth century, placing patriarchal understandings of family life at the center of his professional identity.

Cosby's story of childbirth in *Himself* lays claim to middle-class respectability by defining himself both within and against trendy middle-class California parenthood. Wearing an urbane suit, comedian Cosby notes that he and his wife were star students at the natural childbirth classes they had taken to prepare for the birth of their first child, mastering the art of breathing together as he helpfully added "push" at rhythmic intervals. After the usual jokes about the onset of his wife's labor and the mad rush to the hospital, Cosby proceeds to narrate the process by which his wife's pain quickly exceeded their plans for a drug-free birth. Let me note that it's a bit challenging to narrate the sound effects and gestures that punctuate Cosby's delivery in this famous routine. The comedy of the bit is built on the vivid contrasts between Cosby's patient, anecdotal patter and the urgency of the laboring situation.

> Now, the first real pain hit my wife ("boom") and my wife said, (shocked inhale of breath), and I said, "push?" . . . Carol Burnett described what labor pains feel like. She said, "Take your bottom lip and pull it over your head." . . .
>
> The second pain hit, ("whoooo"), and my wife said, "Whaaaaaaaaaaaa," and stood up in the stirrups, grabbed my bottom lip, and said, "I WANT MORPHINE." I said, "But dear . . ." and she said, "You shut up. You did this to me!" . . .
>
> And on the next contraction, she told everybody in the delivery room that my parents were never married.

The representation of the woman's pain as uncanny, producing an exorcist-style levitation from the bed and unnatural strength, reframes her body as alien or animal, while his reactions to her remain calm and understated. This famous stand-up routine was very funny and in some ways attentive to the birthing woman, whose anger is framed as an utterly justified reaction to real pain. He even cites a female comic, Burnett, to describe the experience, giving her credit for the observation and the joke. At the same time, his wife's voice is comically reframed through Cosby's own body, his sound effects, and his calm commentary. Sensitive fatherhood takes center stage here, a new version of the father handing out cigars in the waiting room, but one that equally implies that the mother's body is a challenge to be managed rather than a comic subject with her own experience of the event.

Cosby's famous stand-up set the stage for his character on *The Cosby Show* (1984–1992), Dr. Heathcliff Huxtable, both a father of five (like Cosby himself) and an ob-gyn (unlike Cosby himself). Each episode focuses primarily on the domestic comedy of the prosperous Huxtable family, whose small-scale problems rarely include explicit encounters with individual or institutional racism. Because racist critiques of Black family life, as codified in the Moynihan Report, tend to isolate single mothers and absent fathers as an origin point for generational dysfunction or criminality, the emphasis on fatherhood in Cosby's comic persona carries particular weight.[11] His sitcom work explored the idea that benevolent, prosperous fatherhood could insulate a Black family against a racist world. Dr. Huxtable's role as an obstetrician located this particular version of paternalism specifically in the realm of reproduction.

Though the heart of *The Cosby Show* is its famous family living room, most episodes also feature a brief B plot involving a diverse cast of pregnant patients and their partners visiting Dr. Huxtable's medical practice in the basement of his family brownstone. Taken together, these two worlds (the home and the doctor's office) give Cosby a kind of ultrapaternal authority as someone who not only raises his own children but also oversees the process of bringing others' children safely into an idealized, multiracial urban community. The show generally frames these B plots through Dr. Huxtable's paternal gaze and with an emphasis on the trials and tribulations of the expectant fathers who enter his circle: the ex-military father who has to be dissuaded from the idea that he was "the boss" of his pregnant wife ("Father's Day," S1E13, December 20, 1984), the father who faints at even the mention of labor ("Rudy's Sick," S1E12, December 13, 1984), the expectant grandfather who supports his daughter in the delivery room because her husband is deployed in Iceland ("Calling Dr. Huxtable," S3E17, February 12, 1987). These stories of sensitive fathers (or fathers who must learn to be sensitive) reframe the ob-gyn office as a place that is only occasionally about pregnant women themselves.

Consistent with this pattern, during his eldest daughter's diegetic pregnancy, much of the comedy focuses on her hapless, overly sensitive husband Elvin (Geoffrey Owens), while Sondra (Sabrina Le Beauf) herself is at ease. In the double episode depicting Sondra's labor ("The Birth," S5E6, November 10, 1988), Elvin enacts all the most extreme stereotypes of paternal panic, from driving to the hospital without his wife in the car to labor room hyperventilation to sympathetic contractions. Sondra, meanwhile, is serene and passive, stationary in her birthing bed, while her husband chews the scenery. The model of sensitive paternity as an evolution of middle-class masculinity transitions the father from the waiting room into the birthing room, but without displacing him as the primary agent of labor hysteria.

After the babies' birth, the new twins' grandparents crowd into the room and inquire after Sondra's well-being, sharing stories of past births in the family. For several very interesting seconds, the women ask Sondra about her pain and go on to reconstruct a brief history of middle-class pain management practices in their hospital birth experiences, with Elvin's mother (Marcella Lowery) declaring, "I kissed my anesthesiologist," and Sondra's grandmother (Clarice

72 • It's All in the Delivery

Taylor) chiming in, "Hey, with Heathcliff, I was out cold the whole time!" These reminiscences are interrupted when Elvin butts in jokingly, "Nobody's asking me how I'm doing!" "That's because you don't count," scolds Cliff. The overstatement is telling. The gendered norms of comedy require male joking to provide "comic relief" that literally interrupts the women's conversation about their own bodily experiences as if that conversation (mild though it is) is annoying, dull, or obscene. The return to male pregnancy restores the balance of power in the delivery room to match the show's celebration of sensitive Black patriarchy, where the father's sensitivity anchors his claim to centrality in family life. No one in the diegesis seems to notice how the women's stories must be sidelined in the process.

Cosby's work helped make male pregnancy fashionable, but it was not alone in updating hysterical fatherhood for the Reagan era and beyond. In the 1980s and 1990s, nearly all the social changes in pregnancy and childbirth were represented through a comic male lens, usually long before being considered from the pregnant person's perspective.

- Surrogacy: In 1981, Burt Reynolds starred in *Paternity*, a comedy about a confirmed bachelor who hires a surrogate (Beverly D'Angelo) to have his baby.
- Sensitive birth partnering: *Micki & Maude* (1984) stars Dudley Moore as a man with so much love to give that he cannot end a relationship with either Micki (Ann Reinking) or Maude (Amy Irving) and becomes a bigamist instead, providing sensitive support to both their pregnancies.
- Infertility and biological clocks: *Funny About Love* (1990) stars Gene Wilder as part of a couple struggling with fertility, who begins to feel his biological clock even more acutely than his wife does. Indeed, the fertility crisis ends their marriage, and the Gene Wilder character continues to work through his ticking biological clock in relationships with other women.

Father of the Bride Part II (1995) manages masculine hysteria at the spectacle of female fertility by taking refuge in the comforting embrace of commodity consumption. The film sees Steve Martin painfully coping with the pregnancies of both his daughter and his wife, a crisis that at first throws him into a midlife panic of bad behavior. But as in the first *Father of the Bride* (1991), he undergoes a loving conversion in the third act and happily takes on the role of willing servant to evolving feminine domestic rituals. He transforms his life for the two women, running out for takeout, remodeling the house, and paying for an elaborate double baby shower. The film treats pregnancy as a consumerist enterprise, one in which men can and must participate by providing a great deal of very attractive stuff, filtered through the taste-making function of the vaguely European, vaguely gay lifestyle assistant played by Martin Short. In sum, as in the earlier *Father of the Bride*, Martin's character (unironically named George *Banks*) has to stop buying the wrong things and start buying the right ones in service to his perfect prosperous white family. In this way, *Father of the Bride Part II* wrapped the threatening aspects of pregnancy in the updated traditional logic of breadwinning.

I close this section on masculine appropriations with a text that exemplifies this tendency for hysterical couvade to take the form of slapstick excess, the weirdly frenetic *Nine Months* (1995). The film stars Hugh Grant as Samuel, an upwardly mobile professional horrified by his girlfriend's unexpected pregnancy. Despite, or likely because of, his day job as a child psychologist, Samuel begins the film hating children. When some children trample his carefully planned romantic picnic and their parents do nothing to stop them, Samuel mutters to his girlfriend Rebecca (Julianne Moore), "You see? Breeders." The pejorative renders parenting as an animal enterprise, beneath the aspirations of the urban professionals.

Samuel's best friend Sean (Jeff Goldblum) espouses a philosophy of independent masculinity that relies on childlessness as a sign of virility and liberty. At the beginning of the film, Sean has just ended a relationship with a woman who wanted a baby, saying, "She was hungry for seed." He goes on to describe his phobia of female reproductive control: "I'm not ready to be biologically extraneous. She would have devoured me from the head down, you know, chewed up my manhood, swallowed my youth, gobbled me up like some praying mantis."

The casting of Jeff Goldblum in this part is an intertextual joke, as his comments recall his iconic role in David Cronenberg's *The Fly* (1986) as a scientist who accidentally fuses his own body with that of an insect. In that film, the titular fly terrorizes his pregnant girlfriend, but here Goldblum's character paints himself as a victim of grotesque predatory female reproductive sexuality. Samuel is so intensely influenced by this suggestion that he has a comic nightmare of waking up in his bed next to a giant green mantis, who rolls over and tries to embrace him before he wakes in a cold sweat and shrinks from Rebecca, as if her true nature has been revealed to him in the vision.

The mantis is a key clue that *Nine Months* is best understood not as a comedy, but as a comic horror film. It speaks to masculine anxieties about the reproductive female body: its uncanny doubleness, its unruly growth, and the way it locks the reproductive event into the closed space of the womb, where it exists outside of masculine control or influence. Indeed, it is the way that Rebecca appears to *control* the unexpected pregnancy that most deeply triggers

Samuel's anxiety. When she speculates aloud that she must be pregnant, Samuel immediately crashes the expensive sports car he is driving, physically panicked by the idea, the token of his masculine identity already in shambles. While they wait for a tow truck, Samuel berates Rebecca for the pregnancy and speculates that she might have sabotaged her birth control on purpose, muttering sarcastically, "I suppose I just thought that birth control had a little teeny element of actual, umm, control about it." Later, at her first doctor's appointment, they learn the baby's due date, and Samuel leaps up from his seat to accuse Rebecca of infidelity, thinking the child must have been conceived while he was away on business. His shoddy math is quickly corrected, but Samuel's disavowal of paternity is both a last-ditch effort to escape responsibility for the pregnancy and an expression of his desperate anxiety that Rebecca's superior knowledge and control place her in a sinister position to deceive him.

It's worth noting that this business of accusing a guiltless partner of infidelity, while it seems outrageous as a plot point in a family comedy, is also used in *Father of the Bride Part II*. Steve Martin's character leaps up from his seat and shouts "You whore!" at his wife (Diane Keaton), before she reminds him of an afternoon some weeks earlier when they had celebrated the freedoms of their new empty-nest lifestyle with a quickie on the kitchen floor. These hysterical disavowals of a partner's pregnancy underline the very literal logic of control that unsettles male pregnancy.

To balance and validate all this masculine neurosis, the female partners of the male heroes of pregnancy comedies are often infantilized or fetishized, the sympathetic center around which the frenzied father orbits. In *Nine Months*, praying mantis Rebecca is a teacher of children's ballet, a low-paying, high-class career that is pleasantly unthreatening, promises physical fitness, and puts her in cute pink tights for part of the movie. Referencing horror scholar Barbara Creed, Sarah Arnold argues that "the [maternal] horror film copes with the abject pregnant body by invoking the concept of the child, by personifying it."[12] Cuteness simplifies the uncanny doubleness of the pregnant woman by reducing her to a single figure, the child itself. The childlike design of much 1990s maternity fashion supported this logic (see figure 2.4), cloaking the fashionably pregnant behind floral prints, pinafores, big buttons, and other girlish details that conflated the pregnant woman with the future child, reducing the threatening doubleness of her body.

Despite Rebecca's unthreatening femininity, Samuel's paternal neurosis builds through the first two acts of the film, reaching a crisis when he misses a long-scheduled ultrasound appointment. Rebecca leaves her neglectful partner, and a dejected Samuel later watches the ultrasound video alone in his apartment. Faced with the spectacle of the fetus, his eyes fill with tears, and

FIGURE 2.4. Nine Months *(1995). Two pregnant characters (Julianne Moore and Joan Cusack) are dressed and framed as little girls, reducing the threatening doubleness of pregnancy into a single figure, the child itself.*

he begins his transformation into a good father. This character arc is typical of comedies of reluctant paternity, where the sonogram often serves as the occasion for fathers to recommit to their partners' pregnancies after a period of confusion or ambivalence. Chapter 5 explores more deeply the paradigm shift associated with ultrasound technology, which for the first time allowed doctors, parents, and legislatures to perceive the fetus in a photograph or video that literally looks through the mother's body, dissolving her out of the frame.

Here, new ultrasound technology allows Samuel to bond directly with the fetus while Rebecca isn't even in the room. The editing puts Samuel into a shot/reverse shot relationship to the fetus, the camera slowly pulling in on each of them as Samuel's eyes fill with tears. For Samuel, the ultrasound video settles the anxiety of Rebecca's doubleness and relieves the mystery of her physical mastery of the pregnancy. Also, he learns it's a boy, reinforcing the child's confirmation of his masculinity.[13] A transformed Samuel expresses his new paternal engagement by trading in his sports car for a family van and then lying in wait for Rebecca at a local park so he can show how much he loves children. The film then proceeds through their reconciliation, marriage, and the inevitable mad rush to the hospital.

The labor itself is a scene of unmitigated masculine hysteria. Forced to share a delivery room with another couple (Tom Arnold and Joan Cusack), and attended by an incompetent and inexperienced ob-gyn (Robin Williams), Samuel battles to protect his wife from the chaos while inadvertently amplifying it. Williams, Arnold, and Grant enact some manic slapstick that includes a fistfight between the two fathers and concludes with Grant and Williams both fainting at the foot of Rebecca's delivery bed, overcome by the sight of the baby's emergence. Later, the trio of male comic actors stand outside the nursery sharing a group hug, and the doctor rejoices, "We did it!" The women are completely off-screen.

It is, as it sounds, appalling. Clearly, as with Cliff Huxtable's "You don't count," the joke is on the men who take over the scene of labor as a test of their own fortitude and sensitivity. Audiences of the 1990s knew this was the "wrong" attitude and could perceive the irony of "We did it!" as a self-aware critique of paternal self-absorption. At the same time, the narrative logic of the film, its fetish for anxious fatherhood, its camera's fascination with the manic physical comedy of three particularly gaudy male comic actors—Grant, Williams, and Arnold—all militate against the critique. These performers are also working under the direction of Chris Columbus, whose most recognized work to that date—*Home Alone* (1990) and *Mrs. Doubtfire* (1993)—had equally focused on cartoonish male excess disrupting the domestic sphere. Romantic lead Julianne Moore and comic character actress Joan Cusack are sympathetic but largely irrelevant. Though the viewer feels for their predicament, the film offers no alternative glimpse of how pregnancy might be understood as something other than a specifically male problem to be solved through vigorous, if purposeless, action. It would fall to a later cycle of films even to begin the process of decentering this norm.

GETTING LITERAL

A second set of films and television texts, small but persistent, explores questions of male pregnancy in a more literal way, by using dream sequences, science fiction scenarios, or pure farce to tell fictional stories of actual pregnant men. Unlike the above examples, in which masculine self-pity marginalizes or even demonizes female experiences of pregnancy, comedies that literalize male pregnancy tend to open up greater ideological space for carnivalesque explorations of gender role reversal and can create opportunities for empathy and creative ideological critique by making visible the absurdity of many of the representational clichés around pregnancy.

They also frequently replicate a long history of satire that uses the thought exercise of male pregnancy to dramatize the importance of reproductive choice as a fundamental human right. Most famously, Gloria Steinem argued that "if men could get pregnant, abortion would be a sacrament."[14] The formula has proliferated well beyond Steinem, spawning dozens of memes and political slogans, as when a 2012 *Saturday Night Live* "Weekend Update" segment featured a female commentator opining, "If men could get pregnant, abortion clinics would be like Starbucks: there would be two on every block and four in every airport. And the morning-after pill would come in different flavors like sea salt and cool ranch."[15]

Artist Barbara Kruger used this joke in a 1991 project for which she installed posters of pregnant men on bus shelters around New York City. Though the men in the photos bear no physical markers of pregnancy (one was a vintage photo of a young George H. W. Bush), the text of each poster is written as a first-person description of a pregnant man's dilemma of first-trimester choice. One poster read, "Help! I've got a great job. My wife just got a promotion. We're beginning to make a dent in the mortgage but it's tough in this economy. I just found out I'm pregnant. What should I do?" The use of male figures to anchor first-person pregnancy vignettes is both a joke and a provocation. The posters alienate the gendered norms of pregnancy to make visible how deeply these dilemmas about bodily autonomy, vulnerability, and choice are framed as female problems. Similarly, comedies that literalize the idea of male pregnancy present implicit challenges to the premise of male physical entitlement, the idea that cisgender men never need worry about the loss of their rights under a legal system that treats masculine subjects as individuals and women as potentially always two subjects in one body, subject to paternalistic social and legal oversight.

An early example, the 1940 comedy of the sexes *Turnabout*, uses male pregnancy as an opportunity to give its female lead the last laugh. In this farce, a magic Indian statue that they call Mr. Ram casts a spell on a feuding married couple to trade bodies for one day. The arrogant executive Tim (John Hubbard) and his materialistic wife Sally (Carole Landis) quickly learn to appreciate each other more, and in the end, they get down on their knees before the idol and beg to be returned to normal. The idol grants them their wish but admits a mistake: he switched back every aspect of their bodies except that Tim is now carrying their child instead of Sally.[16] The film ends with Sally laughing at the alarmed Tim as he faints. The couple's reconciliation, then, does not end with Sally's capitulation to being a better wife, but rather with her ultimate triumph in evading the physical labor of pregnancy, which is transposed to her husband. It is a compellingly ambivalent, transgressive, unrecuperated ending, which implicitly acknowledges that gestation is difficult and that Sally may have reason to celebrate her liberation from it.

A couvade episode of *Bewitched*, "A Very Special Delivery" (S2E2, September 23, 1965), uses male pregnancy to push back against a medicalized regime of masculine control. In the beginning of the episode, father-to-be Darrin insists on doing all the housework, despite Samantha's assurances that she feels fine. Later, Darrin's boss Mr. Tate scolds him for spoiling his wife:

78 • It's All in the Delivery

TATE: I've read up on this motherhood routine. As a matter of fact, a well-known doctor has written a book on the subject, *The Joy of Labor for Labor's Sake*. The more active the mother, the more she does for herself, the happier she'll be and the healthier the child.

DARRIN: Really?

TATE: Well, it makes sense if you stop to think about it. You know, in the pioneer days, women used to plow the fields, have their babies during the lunch break, and go right on plowing again.

The marks of unearned patriarchal authority are all here in Mr. Tate's bad advice: the reference to a nameless "well-known doctor," the faddish book title, the use of inaccurate history as justification for women's subjugation. Bowing to his boss's questionable wisdom, Darrin comes home and refuses to help Samantha lift a heavy pot in the kitchen. Samantha's mother Endora (Agnes Moorehead) is outraged by his attitude, but Darrin defends his domestic authority, saying, "She's my wife, and I know what's best for her . . . I know every ache and pain that she has, and it hurts me more than it hurts her." Annoyed, Endora mutters, "It doesn't yet, but it will." The next morning, Darrin wakes up with a backache, nausea, strange cravings, and weight gain. He goes to work and quickly gets into an emotional argument with his boss. At an important lunch meeting, Darrin disrupts the group several times to lay claim to the other men's pickles from the catered lunch. By the time Samantha discovers her mother's spell and reverses it, a mortified Darrin has developed a healthier attitude toward his wife's experience. Endora's mischievous use of actual pregnancy as a punishment for politicized masculine appropriation of pregnancy presents an early and spirited feminist critique of precisely the displacements detailed in this chapter.

Rabbit Test (1978) was a less coherent social statement. The film is most interesting for how it was framed as a parental experience for director Joan Rivers. Advertisements and posters for the film featured images of Rivers herself (already a recognizable stand-up comic and sometimes talk-show host) wearing a plain black T-shirt labeled, in white letters, "DIRECTOR PERSON." She is pointing straight at the protruding belly of star Billy Crystal, her other hand pressed to her face in mock astonishment (figure 2.5). This visual joke places Rivers in the masculine role of both director (boss) and father/creator, as if she has impregnated the hapless Crystal—and indeed, her authorship of the film is the generative force behind his pregnancy.

Unlike the sharp advertising campaign, the film is visual and narrative chaos, a series of sight gags and one-liners that seem interested in satirizing gender roles, media sensationalism, and religious hypocrisy but veer so crazily

FIGURE 2.5. Rabbit Test *(1978)*. Joan Rivers put herself on the movie poster as "DIRECTOR PERSON," emphasizing the film's gender-flipping qualities.

around these topics that any potential satire devolves into simple farce. Lionel Carpenter (Crystal) is a mild-mannered, sexually inexperienced teacher who lives with his mother (Doris Roberts). His first sexual experience—with an aggressive sexpot who lays him down on a pinball machine in the back of a bar—leaves him pregnant for reasons that are never explained. A series of capers ensues as the president sends the army to pursue Lionel and his new girlfriend, a gypsy immigrant named Segoynia (Joan Prather). *Rabbit Test* seems to want to take the side of outsiders and the innocent against powerful and corrupt institutions, but again, its rat-a-tat-tat gags often wander off in all directions or turn back against the socially marginalized. In particular, the protagonist's trip to Africa is plainly offensive, marked by a blackface performance, a barefoot king, and a pair of diapered royal attendants holding basketballs as ceremonial objects. Late in the film, an army of activists concerned about global overpopulation pursue Lionel to try to force him to have an abortion.

The film ends abruptly with the fugitive couple hiding out in a cabin at Christmastime. Lionel goes into labor and announces beatifically, "I think it's time," at which point the camera pulls back to show wise men in robes approaching the cabin as snow falls peacefully outside. The final punch line is a voice of God emanating from the clouds: "Oh my God! It's a girl!" This final reversal, the farcical nativity scene producing a female messiah, again suggests that the film hopes to assert its gender play as satire. Unfortunately, by this time the coherence of the joke is largely lost.

In 1989, during *The Cosby Show*'s sixth season, one episode ("The Day the Spores Landed," S6E8, November 9, 1989) takes the show's long-standing fascination with male pregnancy to its logical extreme: a dream sequence impregnates all four of the show's main male characters through a science fiction MacGuffin about spores. The episode's first act sees Cosby performing a lengthy physical comedy routine around the difficulties of sitting down on (and getting up from) a low couch while in the third trimester of pregnancy. Notably, daughter Sondra, pregnant with twins, had simply avoided the same couch when she entered the house during the previous season's "The Birth" episode, explaining to her husband, "If I sit down there, I'm never going to get up," a joke that evoked gentle laughter from the studio audience. Pregnant Cliff, on the other hand, chooses the low couch on purpose, then milks the moment through multiple dips and restarts, trying every possible geometric positioning of the human body before settling into a nearly horizontal orientation. The audience's laughter confirms the renewed hilarity of each new silent decision, as Cosby depicts the complicated paradox of late-pregnant embodiment's delicacy and clumsiness. The bit—performed so differently by Sondra and by Cliff—implicitly suggests that physical comedy is so much the province of masculinity that the full comic potential of the pregnant body is realized only when the condition is portrayed by a male performer.

The rest of the episode explores the contradictions between masculine identity and pregnant embodiment, as Cliff, son Theo (Malcolm-Jamal Warner), sensitive son-in-law Elvin, and military officer son-in-law Martin (Joseph C. Phillips) commiserate about their discomfort and humiliation and endure insensitive comments from their wives. The episode dwells, with a fascination bordering on obsession, on the subject of pain. Elvin worries aloud that labor will be painful. Martin scolds the others, declaring that men can handle pain better than women and that they should all tolerate labor with a stoicism befitting their gender identity. "No matter how bad the pain gets," he asserts, "we won't let on." They shake on this ludicrous premise, announcing, "All for one, and one for all," the four Musketeers of foolhardy machismo.

This fixation on the pain of childbirth serves as a pressure point where male gender identity breaks down: How can male illusions of bodily superiority survive the challenge of facing extreme and feminizing pain? And predictably, all four men break this oath immediately upon the onset of labor, moaning and whining, gripping their bellies and arching their backs, and generally having a grand time in imitation of labor pains. Boastful Martin is the first to crack, screaming "I can't take it!" as the others scold "Shut up!" to snap him out of his cartoon hysteria. Elvin eventually slaps him, as panicking women are often slapped in disaster movies. At the hospital, the Huxtable family encounters a neighbor, Jeffrey (Wallace Shawn), who has just given birth. He frightens the laboring men with his story: "The horror! I don't understand how Mother Nature could allow such terrible suffering to happen to a human being! . . . Excruciating, searing, grueling, unbearable, piercing pain. And when I think of where that baby came out of . . . aaah!" This final remark, unusually graphic for *The Cosby Show* (though Jeffrey never actually specifies where the baby came out), points to the episode's perverse fascination with pregnancy as an assault on the male body. The performative appropriation of labor pain is particularly galling in light of the earlier episode ("The Birth") in which Elvin and Cliff had cut short a brief conversation among the women of the family describing their lived experiences of pain management.

The tension of this impossible paradox of masculine gender identity and the physical violence of labor is finally relieved when the men give birth to inanimate objects, each a token of its "mother's" masculine social identity. A female doctor (Elayne Boosler) draws the objects out from under a stirrup drape covering the lower half of each birthing bed: Martin births a toy sailboat, Theo a sports car, Cliff a comically large sandwich and orange soda. Curiously, the dream dissolves before Elvin's "child" is revealed. The episode ends with Cliff waking up from the nightmare and embracing his sleeping wife Clair, telling her, "I think women are the most wonderful people on the face of this earth." She ignores him and keeps sleeping, which seems about right. The common empty praise for women's ability to endure the discomforts of pregnancy and the pain of labor is revealed as a particularly neurotic form of womb envy. Cliff is able to sleep peacefully after he assures himself that it is right and proper that women dwell in the realm of sentimental melodrama, while men bring forth instead a comic exuberance that is incompatible with the real pain and labor of human reproduction.

The theme of male pregnancy produces more coherent satire in the 1994 Arnold Schwarzenegger film *Junior*, casting the alpha male actor as a pregnant man. Unlike the Cosby version of male pregnancy as macho appropriation, *Junior* uses the iconic Aryan masculinity of its star paradoxically to find room for a far more gender-fluid, playfully queer understanding of the doubleness of the pregnant body. The film begins with Schwarzenegger as Dr. Alex Hesse (note the androgynous name), a cold and ambitious fertility scientist, disappointed that the FDA has rejected human trials of Expectane, a fertility drug that prevents miscarriages by suppressing the pregnant person's immune system so that it does not reject the implanted embryo. Forced to give up his lab space to Dr. Diana Reddin (Emma Thompson), a pioneer in egg-freezing technology, Alex is ready to return to Austria when his partner, an ob-gyn named Dr. Larry Arbogast (Danny DeVito), persuades him to stay and test the drug on himself to bypass the FDA process.

Arbogast steals a frozen egg from a tube labeled "Junior" in Diana's lab, not knowing that it is one of her own, and fertilizes it with Alex's sperm before implanting it in the wall of his abdomen. Alex plans to carry the embryo for twelve weeks and then discontinue the Expectane, at which point his body would reabsorb the embryo. Instead, Alex grows attached both to the embryo and to the emotional and physical changes he is experiencing in pregnancy and decides to carry the pregnancy to term. Alex's budding romance with Diana, aided by his estrogen-enhanced personality, hits a snag when she learns that he is carrying her stolen egg; she becomes enraged at this violation. Eventually, they reconcile before their child, a girl, is born by cesarean section. Diana names her Junior.

Producer Beverly Camhe described the writing team's intention to destabilize gender as a practice of idealism: "We had both been in Jungian therapy and were searching for a way to reconcile the antagonism between the yin and the yang, a favorite Jungian question and a good theme for a movie. Then it struck us: If men could have babies, the wall would come crashing down."[17] Director Ivan Reitman, presumably less informed by Jung, was attracted to the premise's comic ambivalence, admitting, "There's the feeling that it will make men queasy. I mean it made me uncomfortable just to think about this."[18] This discomfort is part of the comedy, and yet it is striking how little Alex's body is rendered abject or grotesque through either the narrative or the mise-en-scène. The film is playful rather than stigmatizing as it reverses and combines gender norms in its attempts to reunify human subjectivity across the schism of biological difference.

If appropriative comedies of male pregnancy posit fatherhood as a process of panic, spasmodic motion, and threatened disavowal, *Junior* breaks that mold by giving its hero inner peace, physical rest, and a total lack of ambivalence about his own doubleness. It is as if the film satisfies the concept of womb envy, opening up a space for male reproduction untainted by anxiety. Schwarzenegger's performance is quite earnest, dignifying Alex's transformation. "If you could feel for just one minute the feeling of absolute joy and connection that carrying a baby brings," he tells Arbogast, without irony, "you would understand." He keenly seeks out the community of pregnant women, first as a man, finding common ground with Arbogast's pregnant ex-wife Sharon; later in Arbogast's waiting room, where he bonds with the other patients; and finally, in a curiously touching form of drag as he spends his final months of gestation hiding out in a spa for expectant women. These images show the hero joyfully immersed in these pastel feminine worlds, physically surrounded by a mise-en-scène of nourishment, communion, and mutual care.

Julia Cooper points out how the iconicity of Schwarzenegger as prototypical alpha male lends impact to his physical transformation: "If it is bodybuilding steroids that are responsible for sculpting Schwarzenegger into *Terminator*, in *Junior*, it is estrogen that renders his body soft, feeling, and queer."[19] The iconicity of Schwarzenegger's dominant masculinity allows the film to make the project of male pregnancy into a field of play. The actor is visibly having a blast with this character, as is Emma Thompson, gender-bending less dramatically as an unglamorous scientist, striding about in a ponytail and pleated pants, falling down a lot, and getting cheese stuck to her face and toilet paper stuck to her shoe. She is also the sexual instigator in the relationship, demanding that they sleep together before the birth, quipping, "Well, call me old-fashioned, but I'll be damned if I'm going to have a baby with a man I've never slept with." While Thompson's performance, like Schwarzenegger's, is grounded in the star's reliably heteronormative gender presentation and star persona, her game adoption of masculine tropes rounds out the film's interest in breaking the binary code of the romantic comedy.

The dialogue applies this same misgendering logic to reproductive discourse, producing soft-boiled but heartfelt political satire. Arbogast, for instance, scolds Diana for her late-breaking involvement in the pregnancy, using the language of paternal custody cases: "Just because your egg's in some guy doesn't make you the mother." In a more striking reversal, Alex rebuffs the film's villain (a corrupt research director trying to shut down the experiment and assume custody of the fetus) by announcing, in the same flat tone familiar from Schwarzenegger's action movie one-liners, "My body, my choice." I don't want to oversell what is at its core a pretty heteronormative spectacle: it is naturally not ideal that it takes a hypermasculine spokesperson to make the point that bodily autonomy is a human right. At the same time, *Junior*'s queer disruption of the by this time prevalent narrative of pregnancy as a spectacle of male panic in the face of a female creative event feels like relief from the dominant representational norms of the decade. Like many gender-bending comedies, these literal comedies of male pregnancy, at their best, condemn sexist social, legal, and economic conditions by imposing those conditions on a male subject not socially conditioned to tolerate them. In doing so, they denaturalize and challenge familiar regimes of control.

SPERM COMEDIES

The 1972 sex comedy *Everything You Always Wanted to Know about Sex* (*But Were Afraid to Ask)* features a vignette in which creator Woody Allen plays an anthropomorphized sperm, preparing for deployment (ejaculation) (figure 2.6). The other sperm are enthusiastic about fulfilling the mission for which they have been training: "to fertilize an ovum or die trying!" The sperm played by Allen expresses doubts, however, and begins to fret, "I don't want to go out there." He has heard stories that "there's this pill these women take, or sometimes the guys will slam their heads up against a wall of hard rubber." "Or what if it's a homosexual encounter?" "What if he's masturbating—I'm liable to wind up on the ceiling!" "It's dark out there!" As the sperm line up in the white tunnel representing the urethra, a lone Black actor among white ones begins to bounce off his colleagues, muttering, "What am I doing here?" Eventually, the whole squad exits through the tunnel's opening, bound for an unknown fate in the darkness beyond. These sperm jokes recall some of the issues of masculine fragility that have been explored already in this chapter, including uncertainty of paternity, the dread of female control, and self-abjection.

I start this section with the figure of the sperm as an anxious little white man because it unlocks a key understanding of male reproductive biology as intolerably fragile. Anthropologist Emily Martin has pointed out the ways scientific descriptions of sperm and ovum often reflect cultural attitudes toward male and female roles, even sometimes in defiance of the actual mechanisms that animate these cells. Quoting a variety of scientific textbooks, Martin documents the received logic of active, questing sperm and passive (or even demurely resistant), immobile egg:

> It is remarkable how "femininely" the egg behaves and how "masculinely" the sperm. The egg is seen as large and passive. It does not move or journey, but passively "is transported," "is swept," or even "drifts" along the fallopian tube. In utter contrast, sperm are small, "streamlined," and invariably active. They "deliver" their genes to the egg, "activate the developmental program of the egg," and have a "velocity" that is often remarked upon. Their tails are "strong" and efficiently powered. Together with the forces of ejaculation, they can "propel the semen into the deepest recesses of the vagina." For this they need "energy," "fuel," so that with a "whiplashlike motion and strong lurches" they can "burrow through the egg coat" and "penetrate it."[20]

Hysterical Fatherhood 85

FIGURE 2.6. Everything You Always Wanted to Know about Sex* (*But Were Afraid to Ask) *(1972). Woody Allen plays a sperm worried about its future.*

Martin goes on to debunk these gendered ways of describing fertilization, explaining that the sperm's propulsion is actually quite weak, and the protective coating of the ovum, long presented as a barrier for sperm to "penetrate," is something more like flypaper, a "sperm catcher" that initiates a complex biomechanical process by which the egg absorbs the genetic material of the sperm.[21] The process of fertilization is not, then, a race followed by a triumphant penetration, but rather a complex process of selection and joining completed by both sperm and egg.

These physical particulars are less important to my analysis than the general idea that in both popular and scientific literature, sperm have been figured as miniaturized agents of heteromasculine virility—striving, traveling, penetrating, engendering new life. But just as this concept of virility fails as a description of actual sperm, it equally fails when put into conversation with lived realities of reproductive agency. And so the shadow concept of the hapless and neurotic sperm emerges as a counterweight to impossible myths of masculine virility, reflecting the anxieties of failure and the experiences of uncertainty and abjection that are suppressed by the notion of the hypermasculine sperm.

Thus the hysteria that animated 1990s-style comedies of slapstick fatherhood has, in recent years, been increasingly channeled into what I am calling "sperm comedies." These new meditations on reproductive fatherhood treat prospective fathers not just as simple sperm donors but almost literally as sperm themselves, confused, hypermobile, anxious, and out of control. The imagery in these films centers around actually keeping men blind to the results of their reproductive efforts, often physically separating them from the women they impregnate and eliminating the pregnant woman from the frame, replicating the male-focused logic of early twentieth-century comedy, but with the new element of gross-out jokes and physical indignities centering on testicles, ejaculation, and semen. These films center on male frustration with women's perceived control of the reproductive process and vent the resulting anxiety and disempowerment by reducing masculine identity to a figure of hapless proliferation.

An early example of the trend, Spike Lee's *She Hate Me* (2004), tells the story of a young African American executive who is fired for blowing the whistle on his firm's corporate corruption. John Henry Armstrong (Anthony Mackie)—his apartment decorated with paintings of his namesake, the mythical hammer-wielding Black laborer—finds his bank accounts and credit frozen by his corrupt bosses. Lacking access to the official economy, he enters the underground economy by selling his sperm to lesbians recruited by his ex-girlfriend Fatima (Kerry Washington). Inexplicably, all his clients except Fatima's new girlfriend Alex (Dania Ramirez) choose to be inseminated through intercourse rather than through mediated methods. The midpoint of the film is a montage of sex scenes between the superdonor and a parade of lesbian clients of many different races, ethnicities, body types, and personalities, who demand a variety of different services and seem to experience tremendous pleasure during the act. The modern John Henry fuels his long nights with energy drinks and Viagra, debased and exhausted by the work of five inseminations per night. Interspersed with the montage of sex scenes are fanciful animations of John Henry's sperm, each one bearing an image of his face (figure 2.7), racing up fallopian tubes, muscling each other out of the way, and joining with each woman's egg. Every insemination is successful except the one he made in a cup, and Alex later shows up at his doorstep looking for intercourse. This tryst produces a viable pregnancy, reinforcing a host of problematic social myths about Black male virility, the fluidity of lesbian sexual identity, and the role of sexual pleasure in conception.

Though *She Hate Me* is clearly satire, its social critique is a bit murky. The corporate overlords prosecuting their vendetta against whistleblower John Henry discover his sperm donation business and have him arrested on unclear charges. The film ends with his testifying (seemingly about both his corporate and his reproductive "crimes") in front of a congressional committee, while hundreds of women rally to his defense, holding signs that say things like "Jack, I'm next!" and "My Eggs/Your Sperm." Eventually, our hero is acquitted, and the corporate evildoers are led away in handcuffs. All the sperm recipients have healthy babies, and a family photo shows John Henry at the center of his prodigious family, a diverse, utopian community of mothers plus

Hysterical Fatherhood • 87

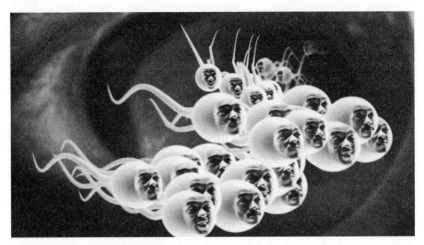

FIGURE 2.7. *Sperm as proxy for masculine agency in* She Hate Me *(2004). Each sperm is playfully stamped with the face of superdonor John Henry Armstrong (Anthony Mackie) as they muscle each other aside and race toward the waiting egg.*

one father, all delighted with their children. In the final scene, John Henry, Fatima, and Alex form a three-way romantic partnership, ready to raise their two children. The film emphasizes a contrast between the deadly sterility of corporate corruption and the joyful abundance of urban diversity. In connecting the political problems of women's uncertain reproductive autonomy and the extraction of Black men's labor, Lee's messy satire skewers an economic system that thrives on the exploitation of both.

As a celebration of the power of Black reproductive excess to create utopian, anti-corporate social outcomes, *She Hate Me* is a genre outlier—I know of no peers in this area. But the emphasis on sperm itself as a key narrative feature anticipates the direction of millennial comedies of male pregnancy. As the early 2000s progressed, comedies centered around the interplay between masculine identity and literal sperm proliferated, though later iterations of the idea centralized crises of a specifically white, neurotic fatherhood. A brief roundup of plot summaries illustrates the trend.

The Brothers Solomon (2007) follows two socially awkward brothers (Will Forte and Will Arnett) as they seek a surrogate to be inseminated with their commingled sperm so that their comatose father will have a grandchild before his death. The white surrogate (Kristen Wiig) and her African American boyfriend (Chi McBride) bond with the two lovable goofballs, and when her child is born Black, the dim-witted brothers give no indication that they realize that the surrogacy arrangement has failed. The fivesome become a nontraditional family.

Due Date (2010) shows a father-to-be, Peter (Robert Downey, Jr.), frantically road-tripping across the country to reach his wife in time for the scheduled delivery of their baby. During the trip, Peter is thrown together with a neurotic companion, Ethan (Zach Galifianakis), who needles him about his paternity, insisting that his wife's ex-boyfriend (Jamie Foxx) must be the real father of the child, who will be born "a zebra." When they arrive at the hospital to witness the birth, Peter at first enters the wrong room and mistakes a Black newborn for proof of his wife's infidelity. Finally, he is reunited with his wife in time for their daughter's birth but passes out from injuries sustained during the catastrophic trip.

The Switch (2010) tells the story of a single woman, Kassie (Jennifer Aniston), who decides to have a child through artificial insemination. She hosts a party to celebrate this decision, leaving the vial of donor sperm in her apartment bathroom. Her best friend Wally (Jason Bateman), drunk and frustrated by unrequited love, picks up the specimen vial and accidentally spills the contents down the sink. Hastily, he masturbates into the vial and replaces it on the shelf. Seven years later, when Kassie's son starts exhibiting neurotic behavior that mirrors Wally's, the truth is revealed. Kassie forgives Wally, and the three become a family.

In *Delivery Man* (2013), David (Vince Vaughn) is a lovable working-class screwup who made hundreds of deposits at a New York sperm bank in the 1990s to fund a dream trip to Venice for his dying mother. Now, twenty years later, 134 of his 533 biological children are bringing suit to learn the identity of the donor code-named "Starbuck" in the fertility clinic records. As he weighs his complicated feelings about this situation, David's on-again, off-again girlfriend (Cobie Smulders) informs him she is pregnant with his child but wants to parent the child alone. The film uses these mirrored crises to meditate explicitly on paternal rights and reproductive choice: David feels helpless, being on the one hand conscripted into the role of father to the hundreds of children he engendered for money and on the other hand locked out of the role of father to the child he conceived in affection. In the end, he embraces and is embraced by both extended families.

The Babymakers (2012) (tagline: "She's fired up. He's firing blanks.") follows the misadventures of Tommy (Paul Schneider), who discovers that his sperm are too slow to successfully impregnate his wife Audrey (Olivia Munn). When his circle of friends learn of this problem, Tommy is subject to a barrage of intrusive advice, humiliating medical treatments, and emasculating social encounters. By bizarre coincidence, Tommy sold a batch of (presumably healthy) sperm to the local sperm bank several years before, and he is able to recover his lost virility quite literally by joining together with a ragtag bunch of friends to hire a reformed criminal, the Indian gangster Ron Jon (Jay

Chandrasekhar), to help them rob the sperm bank. The bumbling criminals succeed, but not before a lengthy slapstick scene involving a slippery floor covered in spilled semen, followed by a scene of full-frontal male nudity designed to distract the police officers on their tail.

A deceptive epilogue shows Ron Jon in the delivery room, welcoming a brown-skinned baby being born to a white mother. Has Audrey been inseminated with the wrong sperm? A reverse shot reveals that the mother is not Audrey, but a female acquaintance whose naked photos had been circulated as masturbatory inspiration for much of the film. Tommy and Audrey are then shown celebrating their own triplets' first birthday. Not only has the white father's sperm survived this misadventure, but it has also engendered an abundance of healthy children, confirming his uncompromised masculinity.

These five films together suggest a remarkable figuration of contemporary masculine reproductive anxiety that reduces the white male figure to something like actual human sperm: anxious, hyperactive, and blind (in the case of the Solomon brothers, almost literally blind); they are defined by manic motion, seeking purchase in a highly uncertain world controlled by women, fertilizing or failing to fertilize without discretion. These heroes are cut off from control over and often even knowledge of their progeny. The repeated jokes about white men being deceived by women carrying the children of non-white fathers (three jokes in five films, and honorable mention to the lone Black sperm in Woody Allen's sketch) make visible the intolerable fragility of racial and sexual codes of dominance in the face of a reproductive biology that locks men out of easy knowledge or control of the final resting place of their innumerable sperm. Ultimately, the through line of male pregnancy narratives is precisely this hysterical fragility.

CONCLUSION

Perhaps the happiest legacy of these male-centered pregnancy comedies is that they have provided abundant targets for mockery. Indeed, many contemporary pregnancy comedies take obvious pleasure in puncturing the cherished myths of male pregnancy detailed in this chapter. A 2010 episode of *The Office* ("The Delivery: Part 1," S6E17, March 4, 2010), for instance, revises the trope of masculine labor panic as Pam (Jenna Fischer) and Jim (John Krasinski) have decided to try to hold out until midnight before they check into the hospital, thereby ensuring an extra night is covered by their health insurance after the child's birth. This jab at the anti-humanism of America's bureaucratized healthcare system builds its tension not by instigating manic motion, but by withholding it. Instead of a spectacle of rush, the labor episode is an absurdist exercise in stasis as Pam's contractions get closer together and the office organizes a lame talent show to try to distract her from the pains. Pam is stoic as the contractions increase in frequency and intensity, while Jim becomes nervous as their agreed-upon threshold of seven-minute intervals passes and she still refuses to budge.

Pam's refusal to leave the office functions as her way of taking control back from a medical system and masculinist work environment that relentlessly discipline her body within an economic system ruled by the clock. Pam's refusal recenters her as the central figure in her own labor, defying generations of comic precedent that treat her body as an object to be delivered to a medical authority in great haste.

The ways fatherhood has dominated the visual rhetoric of pregnancy and childbirth in popular media has high stakes for conversations around reproductive rights and justice. Although the pregnant father can be used to make an argument for abortion rights and reproductive choice, as in *Junior*, the representation of pregnancy as a domain of male obsession also reinforces patriarchal ideas about how the mother's body should be owned or controlled by male partners or institutions. The chapters to come look at a generation of comic films and television shows that have done the work of moving forward from these lingering taboos and hysterical appropriations, slowly and incompletely. Later cycles of pregnancy comedies have their own problems and blind spots, but it is to be celebrated that they generally at least acknowledge that the pregnant person should perform a leading role in narratives of gestation and birth, rather than serving as a prop for paternal hysteria. Baby steps, let's say.

Chapter 3
BAD PREGNANCIES
SOCIAL PROBLEMS AND BAD SEEDS

MIKE JUDGE'S 2006 SATIRE *IDIOCRACY* opens with a short lesson in eugenics. Over an image of the earth floating in space, a voice of God narrator (Earl Mann) begins to explain:

> As the twenty-first century began, human evolution was at a turning point. Natural selection, the process by which the strongest, the fastest, the smartest reproduced in greater numbers than the rest—a process which had once favored the noblest traits of man—now began to favor different traits. Most science fiction of the day predicted a future that was more civilized and more intelligent. But as time went on, things seemed to be heading in the opposite direction: a dumbing down. How did this happen? Evolution does not necessarily reward intelligence. With no natural predators to thin the herd, it began to simply reward those who reproduced the most and left the intelligent to become an endangered species.

This little valentine to the pseudoscience of eugenics is illustrated with a case study. The next shot shows a young, white, professional couple, Trevor and Carol (Patrick Fischler and Darlene Hunt), sitting on a couch to be

FIGURE 3.1. Idiocracy *(2006)*. *High-achieving Trevor and Carol overthink their approach to childbearing and never have any children.*

interviewed. Trevor explains, "Having kids is such an important decision." Carol adds, "We're just waiting for the right time." As they are speaking, their IQs are written across the screen: 138 and 141, respectively (figure 3.1). The film suggests that these people would give birth to "good" children.

The scene abruptly cuts to the inside of a noisy, messy trailer home, where a woman announces, "Aw, shit, I'm pregnant again!" Her partner, a man named Clevon (Ryan Ransdell) (IQ 84), puts down his beer and replies, "Shit. I've got too many damn kids!" As if to prove his point, wild and unkempt children tear through the scene. These are "bad" children.

From here the montage skips ahead in five-year intervals, as Trevor and Carol continue to delay childbearing and then pursue fertility treatment when they are finally ready to conceive. Clevon, meanwhile, continues to father children thoughtlessly, with two pregnant lovers now living side by side in a duplex, throwing pans and insults at each other, children running wild around them. Soon Clevon Jr. (IQ 74) reaches his teens and begins impregnating high school cheerleaders, producing four children of his own.

Eventually, Trevor dies of a heart attack while trying to produce a sperm sample for fertility treatment, but Carol soldiers on: "I have some eggs frozen, so as soon as the right guy comes along . . . ," she trails off, crossing her fingers for the camera. And so Carol and Trevor's family line dies off, while Clevon's family continues breeding out of control, the family tree filling the screen over an image of a parked pickup truck suggestively rocking (figure 3.2) Thus the satirical "idiocracy" is born, a society no longer able to maintain its infrastructure, civic institutions, or economy because its population is just too dumb.

94 • It's All in the Delivery

FIGURE 3.2. Idiocracy (2006). Low-achieving Clevon fathers too many children and grandchildren, contributing to the downfall of human civilization.

I am all for giving comedy quite a lot of wiggle room to play with stereotypes and satirize cultural foibles. But a long history of genre theory shows that comedy achieves its ethical potential when the creators are "punching up" rather than "punching down" (that is, stigmatizing the already stigmatized). Using this same logic, Adam Johnson argues that "the film's legions of defenders call it satire . . . [but] Satire isn't a get-out-of-jail-free card for all vulgar and illiberal ideas; it has to be pointed and targeting the powerful, not targeting vague notions of idiocy illustrated by Appalachia accents and trailer parks without consideration for what caused the idiocy in the first place."[1] In fact, blaming the rise of "idiocy" on the reproductive practices of the poor rather than factors such as the defunding of healthcare, public education, public services, and arts programs is both intellectually lazy and morally shortsighted.

This chapter examines comedies about "bad" pregnancies—usually nonmarital, usually under conditions of economic precarity—a frequent topic of sensationalized and sometimes explicitly racist public concern in the late twentieth and early twenty-first centuries. These social problem framings of pregnancies stigmatize parents from marginalized groups, ascribing parasitic intentions and criminal indifference to their reproductive choices rather than suggesting ways to support families and prospective parents. Reproductive rights are human rights, and the freedom to make choices to bear or not to bear children is fundamental to human dignity. The idea that the childbearing practices of poor or non-white mothers are a "social problem" has historically been used to justify abuses such as forced sterilization, child removal, and coercive adoption. This chapter begins with the premise that no chosen pregnancy is bad.

And while *Idiocracy* makes its bad seed a white male—almost certainly an intentional choice to evade the association of eugenics with racism—it still echoes all the baggage of racial and ethnic difference that has informed scolding reproductive politics of the post-Reagan era. Clevon's name evokes rural Appalachia, but it is also a name more common among Black families than white ones, pointing to the character's function as a representative of "failed whiteness," a form of white precarity in which racial privilege has failed to give evidence of its promised economic and social superiority.[2] He is listed in the credits simply as Trashy Guy. John Hartigan argues that middle-class white identity can maintain its hegemony as an unmarked category of "normal" identity only by casting off or Othering the category of "white trash" in which "the decorum of the white racial order has been breached and compromised or, perhaps more important, where the imagined boundary between whiteness and blackness is undermined. White trash is used to name those bodies that exceed the class and racial etiquettes required of whites if they are to preserve the powers and privileges that accrue to them as members of the dominant racial order in this country."[3] Clevon's failed whiteness serves as a denial that this parable of genetic doom is a story of race, but meanwhile all the details of this opening vignette provide a kind of dog whistle reference to precisely the types of racialized eugenics then circulating in the millennial era.

For instance, the prominent role of IQ scores, written across the screen as a verdict on human value and reproductive worthiness, taps into a long history of "hereditarian" pseudoscience that was designed to reify and preserve power relations around class, race, gender, and nation.[4] IQ claims to be able to quantify inherent human potential, ignoring social and economic factors that amplify or suppress that potential as well as the ways human value might be expressed in terms other than what is conventionally known as intelligence.

Idiocracy was released in the decade that followed Richard Herrnstein and Charles Murray's incendiary 1994 bestseller, *The Bell Curve: Intelligence and Class Structure in American Life*, which makes the argument that America's successful system of meritocracy is inevitably leading to the concentration of high and low intellectual achievement at the top and bottom of the American class system, outcomes that then reproduce themselves through the genetic heritage of each generation.[5] Indeed, the preface of *The Bell Curve* asks the reader to picture a scenario uncannily similar to the *Idiocracy* opening:

> A great nation, founded on principles of individual liberty and self-government that constitute the crowning achievement of

96 ⬧ It's All in the Delivery

statecraft, approaches the end of the twentieth century. Equality of rights—another central principle—has been implemented more deeply and more successfully than in any other society in history. Yet even as the principle of equal rights triumphs, strange things begin to happen to two small segments of the population.[6]

The book goes on to describe the highest "cognitive class" of the population thriving, while the lowest is plagued by drugs, crime, and the breakdown of the traditional family, effecting an ever-widening gulf between the smart and the dumb. Notoriously, *The Bell Curve* further correlates IQ and race, giving the veneer of statistical inevitability to racial economic inequality by blaming it on genetic inequality of potential. Though these ideas have been roundly debunked, they persist in the cultural imagination in ways this chapter also explores.[7]

All this to say that when eugenic discourses proliferate in popular media, the agents who get blamed for littering the planet with failed offspring are not usually white fathers but non-white mothers. Consider, for instance, how the media circulated phobic discourses such as Ronald Reagan's "welfare queen," having children to increase the size of her assistance check; right-wing media's "anchor babies" being born to stake an immigrant parent's claim to citizenship or benefits; or physically damaged "crack babies" born to drug-addicted women. The emphasis on crack, a street drug associated with Black users rather than the more white-coded cocaine, alcohol, or opioids, points to the inherently racial logic of this label. There was no attendant panic about "Valium babies."

Dorothy Roberts traces the history of public hysteria over the supposed public health crisis of "crack babies" in the late 1980s, noting that the image of the irresponsible Black woman poisoning her children easily built its tone of moral panic on a preexisting "iconography of depraved Black maternity," particularly regarding out-of-wedlock births and public assistance.[8] The news media extrapolated wild price tags for the care of these children. Following on Reagan's anti-welfare ideology, one newsletter projected that the crack baby epidemic would "cost this nation $100 billion in remedial medical and developmental costs over the next decade."[9] Other coverage emphasized that prenatal crack exposure could lead to an underdeveloped capacity for empathy, making this category of babies particularly dangerous, a generation of violent future criminals. Later research has shown that, while substance abuse is dangerous for anyone, issues like poverty, prenatal care, and maternal stress were far more predictive of infant well-being than substance abuse alone, and policymakers might have better invested their attention in social services or

Bad Pregnancies • 97

economic justice rather than efforts to test and criminalize birthing mothers, which had the effect of further driving impoverished women out of the health-care system and separating mothers from their infants.[10]

I lead with these ugly portraits of American classism, sensationalism, and white supremacy to set up the ways comedy films and shows of the millennial era have both used and revised these conventions and the binary of good versus bad pregnancies that animates them. This chapter and the next examine two forms of reproduction that have been framed as social problems in both popular discourse and fiction media: unwed, unplanned, or teenage pregnancy (too soon!) and infertility and medically assisted childbearing (too late!). As in the *Idiocracy* example, these two forms of pregnancy are often treated as being in tension with each other, as if women who rush childbearing and women who delay childbearing are caught in a personal tug-of-war that feeds off racism, class grievances, public judgments about who deserves babies, and a market logic of specialized services. Within this discourse, *both* "good" and "bad" pregnancies occur under conditions of surveillance designed around a eugenic logic of protecting babies from the bodies and choices of bad mothers, a system that polices the boundaries of "good" and "bad" in ways that treat all pregnant bodies with possessive suspicion.

UNWED PREGNANCY AND THE SEXUAL REVOLUTION

Nonmarital pregnancy was not invented in the second half of the twentieth century. Chapter 1 of this volume catalogs a large number of pre-code and code-era films that incorporate unwed or ambiguously wed pregnancy plots. As was typical of these decades, the comedies generally ended in marriages or the revelation of secret marriages to "fix" the problem of the pregnancy. Melo-dramas more often employed fallen woman tropes to impose years of suffering as if in punishment for the heroine's unregulated sexuality.

A number of midcentury social changes forced revisions to this formula, shifting nonmarital pregnancy into a more visible social problem register. *Sexual Behavior in the Human Male* (1948) and, even more controversially, *Sexual Behavior in the Human Female* (1953), known as the Kinsey Reports, drew attention to patterns of teen and young adult sexual activity outside of marriage that had long been hidden from public view.[11] Although it is true that greater proportions of young women reported having nonmarital sex in the 1960s than in previous generations, largely enabled by advances in the effectiveness and availability of contraception, it is also true that teenagers and young women of the 1970s and 1980s who experienced unplanned or ill-timed pregnancies were far less likely to marry to "solve" the problem. Rising divorce rates, relaxing sexual mores, and greater awareness of the negative impacts of early or unsuitable marriage led both teenagers and sometimes their parents to conclude that young women should not be forced to compound a difficult situation with an unwise legal coupling.[12] The evolving social "problem" of unwed parenting in these decades, then, reflected several factors, including the salutary decline of hasty teen marriage as a solution for unwed pregnancy. This decline, however, meant that teenage premarital sexual activity became increasingly visible in the gestating bodies of unwed girls, a shift that produced moral panic.

Starting in the 1960s, film comedies began to make nonmarital pregnancy more visible as well. Most commonly, studio comedies tease at the idea of unwed pregnancy as a salacious plot device but hastily retreat to traditional marital values, often in the form of a last-minute wedding, in the mold of *The Miracle of Morgan's Creek*. Crucially, the pregnant belly becomes a visual joke in these movies, punctuating the character's predicament in a more visually defiant way than previous texts had been able to do. *Auntie Mame* (1958) plays the apparently unwed pregnancy of hapless secretary Agnes Gooch (Peggy Cass) for laughs until a climactic telegram reveals that she is actually married. *Irma la Douce* (1963) and *Generation* (1969) both make visual jokes of their heavily pregnant brides taking marriage vows just before the onset of labor. The Doris Day–Rock Hudson comedy *Lover Come Back* (1961) ends with the central couple taking their vows as Day is being wheeled into the delivery room, after the Hudson character discovers that their one-night, hastily annulled marriage had resulted in a pregnancy.

When Sandra Dee took a role in the 1967 unwed pregnancy comedy *Doctor, You've Got to Be Kidding!*, the press billed it as an attempt to change her good-girl image. The film was advertised as if it were a sex farce, with the tagline "It's the funniest who done it!" embedded in a cartoon showing four different potential fathers, each of whom is falling backward as if in shock over Dee's predicament and his own role in creating it (figure 3.3). But in fact, the film is not an investigation of sexual promiscuity, and the viewer is always quite certain that Dee's character, Heather, conceived her child during an on-again, off-again engagement to her demanding boss (George Hamilton), not the wild season of sexual experimentation suggested by the poster. Heather's three other nutty suitors are all well-meaning friends who offer to marry her to provide for her child, while the child's real father does not learn of the pregnancy until Heather goes into labor. Dee's costuming as the single mother-to-be is a study in cute maternity fashion that further domesticates her supposedly scandalous diegetic pregnancy. The film's climax sees Heather

Bad Pregnancies · 99

FIGURE 3.3. Doctor, You've Got to Be Kidding! *(1967). Advertising for studio-produced 1960s pregnancy comedies often promised a lot more sex farce than they delivered.*

being chased into the delivery room by three enthusiastic potential fathers and a very confused priest, but the baby's father shows up on cue as well. *Doctor, You've Got to Be Kidding!* is not a "who done it" at all.

Similarly, the 1969 comedy *How to Commit Marriage* uses unwed pregnancy as a sexual punch line, one easily resolved through the application of middle-class marital values. The film begins with a middle-aged couple (Bob Hope and Jane Wyman) deciding to divorce just before their daughter, Nancy (JoAnna Cameron), announces her engagement to a young man she's met at college. Crushed by the dissolution of her parents' marriage, young Nancy abruptly cancels her own wedding. She and her boyfriend join a hippie band and consummate their relationship on the road. When Nancy's parents attend a concert many months later, they are shocked when Nancy turns sideways onstage, revealing a baby bump beneath her gown. The moment is presented as a visual joke, the sudden reveal punctuated by Hope's and Wyman's outsize double takes and instant astonishment. "She's pregnant!" marvels Wyman. "Maybe it's gas," deadpans Hope.

Nancy's pregnancy is her parents' wildest comic fears come true: their chaste middle-class daughter has transformed into a pregnant hippie rock star. And yet the concerned parents soon bring the wayward youngsters back into the fold through the device of their own reconciliation. Although the young couple do not marry before the birth of their child, *How to Commit Marriage* still takes a cautious approach to its unwed pregnancy, locating it inside a committed, conventional pairing of young people who will be altar-bound once some silly plot complications are cleared up.

Slowly, studio films caught up with changing social mores, and unwed pregnancy came out from under the shadow of family romance, sometimes even standing as a symbol of defiance. In *Funny Girl* (1968), a fictionalized biopic of Broadway star Fanny Brice, Brice (Barbra Streisand) often jokes about her appearance, which she considers homely. She is horrified and embarrassed when producer Florenz Zeigfeld (Walter Pidgeon) insists that she appear as a glamorous bride in a musical number set to a sentimental song about beauty. When Zeigfeld refuses to hear his star's concerns, Brice exacts her revenge by slipping a pillow under her bridal costume just before the number begins and revealing her "pregnant" belly by turning sideways at the climax of the production number (figure 3.4), thus turning the lyrics of the song "His Love Makes Me Beautiful" into naughty comedy. The diegetic audience bursts into laughter, while Zeigfeld storms out of the theater in a rage. This is a rare case of a female comic star using a belly bump as a punch line not against herself, but as an act of defiance against the conventions of sentimental romance, against the objectifying gaze, and against a tyrannical boss. This defiance is enabled by emerging changes in sexual mores that had begun to shake the foundations of pregnant spectacle as the 1960s wore on.[13]

Sheer defiance also drives the unwed pregnancy plot in the feminist satire *Stand Up and Be Counted* (1972). The film begins with a dark screen and a baby's cry, then fades in to show a doctor leaning over an unnamed birthing mother to tell her, "It's a girl." The mother turns her face directly to the camera with an expression of strained neutrality and says, "Oh," in a disappointed voice. After this dispiriting commentary on the status of women, the film's main plot follows the experiences of a journalist (Jacqueline Bisset), ambivalent about the new women's movement, who returns to her hometown of Denver to cover the impact of feminism on middle America. A key subplot follows a particularly radical young leader, Karen (Lee Purcell), who seeks out a dim-witted sports coach (Alex Wilson) and pays him to help her conceive a child to raise on her own. The scheme succeeds, and the final scene of the film is a match to the opening, except that now it is Karen giving birth. When

Bad Pregnancies • 101

FIGURE 3.4. Funny Girl *(1968)*. *Barbra Streisand (as Fanny Brice) using a padded baby bump as a defiant punchline.*

the doctor says, "Karen, it's a girl," the new and still-unwed mother turns her face toward the camera with a beaming smile. Helen Reddy's "I Am Woman" fades in on the soundtrack, marking the moment as a feminist triumph of self-definition and generational optimism.

Less explicitly feminist titles, such as the Walter Matthau vehicle *Kotch* (1971), also explore the idea that unpartnered pregnancy can be something other than a tragedy, a reason for marriage, or a dirty joke. The story, a bit syrupy, follows garrulous grandfather Joseph Kotcher (Matthau) trying to find his place in the world after his adult son and daughter-in-law ask him to move out of their Los Angeles home. Rejecting the prospect of a retirement community, Kotch instead devotes himself to caring for Erica (Deborah Winters), a pregnant teen now living on her own in Palm Springs. In the story of two outsiders who come to rely on each other, there is little catastrophizing over Erica's pregnancy. It is a condition that produces obvious problems, mostly financial, but not one that is held up as a moral, intellectual, or social failing. During the film, Kotch falls into frequent reveries because Erica reminds him of his own late wife and the happy time in his life when he had a young family to care for. The connection between Kotch's memories of an idealized marital family and his current life within a patched-together found family confers a nostalgic beauty on Erica and her pregnancy.

These unapologetic comic portraits of unwed pregnancy quickly fell out of favor amid a new conservatism of the 1980s, as the news media became gripped by a so-called epidemic of teen motherhood as a new site of moral panic. The theme was most often explored in melodramas, where the moral stakes were clear, such as in the TV movies *I Want to Keep My Baby!* (1976), *Babies Having Babies* (1986), *When Innocence Is Lost* (1997), and *Fifteen and Pregnant* (1998). Kelly Oliver points out that the language of a teen pregnancy "epidemic" implicitly suggests that the condition is a contagious disease.[14] If popular media are one of the means by which this epidemic spreads, then it would make sense that such film and television representations would take steps to condemn the condition to inoculate teen audiences against any romantic notions of childbearing they may harbor. Certainly, later reality melodramas such as MTV's *16 and Pregnant* (2009–2014) and *Teen Mom* (2009–2021) take this approach, making clear how difficult it is for teen mothers to handle the physical rigors of pregnancy, the economic strain on their families, the constant negotiation with parents adjusting to a new relationship with their child, the inherent stresses of caring for newborn children, and the frequent troubles of custody-sharing relationships with their boyfriends, no more prepared for parenthood than the girls.

And although comedies have historically been more resistant to "social problem" framings than melodramas, teen comedies of the 1980s frequently did respond to the era's conservatism by treating their stories as cautionary tales. The John Hughes comedy drama *For Keeps* (1988) shows a high-achieving high school couple bending under the pressure of an unintended pregnancy and new baby. Teenagers Darcy (Molly Ringwald) and Stan (Randall Batinkoff) are happy together, hardworking, academically gifted, and nice to their parents—until one day Darcy discovers she is pregnant. The high school counselor parrots the logic of teen pregnancy as a contagious condition when she asks Darcy to shift her classes to night school so that other girls in the school don't see her succeeding and emulate her choices. The couple's lives quickly devolve into chaos as they fight with their families, move into a dingy and unsafe apartment, squabble over money, and later try to manage Darcy's postpartum depression. Significantly, Darcy and Stan do marry after they decide to keep their baby—a situation that would have been considered a resolution in an earlier generation of films, but here it does nothing to reduce their stress as the young pair try to hold on to their dreams of college while facing economic hardship and family squabbles. Though the film ends happily with the family reunited after a crisis, its warning was clear.

Comedies about Black teen pregnancy have been far rarer; few filmmakers have taken on the task of representing the subject through comedy without accidentally reinforcing stereotypes of Black teen pregnancy as ubiquitous or pathological. The gritty independent release *Just Another Girl on the I.R.T.* (1992) walks a fine line between representing the challenges of an ambitious Black sixteen-year-old managing an unplanned pregnancy and insisting that her future still contains promise and possibilities, in defiance of social messages that essentially condemned young mothers to a life of poverty and social abjection. A rare independent film of the 1990s written, directed, and coproduced by a Black woman, Leslie Harris, *Just Another Girl on the I.R.T.* won a Sundance Special Jury Prize and widespread distribution in the year of its release.[15] Chantel (Ariyan A. Johnson) is a Brooklyn high school junior with ambitions to graduate early, attend college, and become a doctor. She maintains good grades despite working part-time and taking care of her two young brothers while her parents work long hours. Chantel refuses easy categorization as either a model kid or a troubled one—she is both. Richard Brody says of the character, "Her intense and serious emotion and breezy comedy, freewheeling excitement and acerbic cruelty, self-awareness and self-delusion tumble upon one another with a hectic clash of tones that evokes the whirling spectrum of Chantel's emotional world."[16] Chantel's subjectivity is foregrounded through frequent direct address to the camera, as when she announces early in the film, "I don't let nobody mess with me, and I do what I want when I want."

The film takes pains to show exactly what authority figures she is rebelling against: the callous teachers and school administrators, her overwhelmed parents (whose lives she wishes to avoid), the entitled white shoppers at the store where she works. Chantel is seeking a way out, and when she meets Tyrone (Kevin Thigpen), who seems rich to her because he has a Jeep, he appears to fit the bill.[17] When Chantel becomes pregnant, Tyrone gives her $500 for an abortion, but she blows the money on a shopping spree with her best friend. She later decides in earnest that she is ready for an abortion, but the pregnancy is too far along for an elective procedure. Chantel's "bad" choices put immediate gratification ahead of her long-term goals, but the arc of the film emphasizes that her life has taught her to seize gratification where she can find it; still a kid, she also thinks she is cheating the system and will figure out a solution to the problem of her pregnancy later. Harris researched the film by visiting Planned Parenthood clinics and other sites where teens seek sex education and treatment. She explains, "I think in a lot of films you have teenagers who appear to be older than they actually are or act older."[18] When Chantel and her friends discuss sex, condoms, and the possibility that douching with soda after intercourse will prevent pregnancy, their theories of the body are juvenile and fantastical.

The film's ending is a shocking mix of dark and light tones. In a harrowing extended sequence, Chantel goes into early labor in her bedroom, has her baby without medical intervention, and instructs Tyrone to put the newborn in a garbage bag and throw it away. He takes the baby away in the bag but is unable to follow through with this plan; he brings the baby back to Chantel, and the two decide to raise their new daughter. A brief, happy epilogue shows Chantel and Tyrone at community college, baby girl in tow. Harris explains, "I don't want this character to speak for everybody. But at the same time, I think that she has a right to be who she is."[19] In the years when teen pregnancy, particularly among inner-city Black girls, was a political punching bag, *Just Another*

104 • It's All in the Delivery

Girl on the I.R.T. used rapid tonal shifts to convey the emotional chaos of Chantel's experience in a way that humanized and juvenilized her struggles and framed her as a unique, ferocious individual rather than "just another" statistic.

The scrappy, low-budget *Manny and Lo* (1996) similarly shows a lot of unsentimental compassion for its messy protagonist, an orphaned, pregnant white teenager (Lo, played by Aleksa Palladino), who springs her nine-year-old sister Manny (Scarlett Johansson) out of foster care and takes her on a penniless road trip marked by shoplifting, trespassing, and convenience-store food. Worn out by life on the road, the two kidnap Elaine (Mary Kay Place), a know-it-all clerk from an upscale baby boutique, and compel her to coach them through the final months of Lo's pregnancy while the three are holed up in an abandoned ski lodge. The girls don't find happiness until they submit to being mothered, allowing Elaine to manage their diet and manners and to address them by their given names, the more feminine Amanda for Manny and Laurel for Lo. Elaine delivers Lo's baby in a quiet culvert by the side of a road, and the characters drive away onto paths unknown, all of them awed by the enormity of what they just experienced. *Manny and Lo* reimagines teen pregnancy as a woodland fairy tale in which runaway children can be brought under control, transformed from outlaws to good girls by a bossy fairy godmother.

MURPHY BROWN

Given that the national conversation on unwed pregnancy was hyperfocused on teenagers in the early 1990s, the fracas over the unpartnered pregnancy of sitcom character Murphy Brown (Candice Bergen) in 1993 was always a bit odd. Vice President Dan Quayle was already on the conservative side of public opinion when he famously scolded a television show for its unsavory impact on the public: "Bearing babies irresponsibly is, simply, wrong. . . . It doesn't help matters when prime time TV has Murphy Brown—a character who supposedly epitomizes today's intelligent, highly paid, professional woman—mocking the importance of fathers, by bearing a child alone, and calling it just another 'lifestyle choice.'"[20] Bonnie Dow points out that the shallow media frenzy that ensued utterly neglected the larger context of Quayle's remarks, which sought to address the causes and lessons of the recent Los Angeles riots by commenting on the supposed pathology of Black families. Quayle argued that poverty results from "a poverty of values," and that "the anarchy and lack of structure in our inner cities are testament to how quickly civilization falls apart when the family foundation cracks." He goes on to claim, dubiously, that "marriage is probably the best anti-poverty program of all."[21]

So although the character of Murphy Brown was financially capable of raising her child alone, Quayle was criticizing her for setting a poor example that could influence women without independent means, returning to the "epidemic" logic of unpartnered pregnancy as a contagious condition. Significantly, the Bush-Quayle political campaign was heavily focused on "family values" as a reelection theme, a kind of catchall concept that valorized an idealized suburban family structure as the cornerstone of American prosperity and social order. As Jimmie L. Reeves and Richard Campbell argue, the political slogan of "family values" conveniently flipped cause and effect by "cynically converting the material advantages of the bourgeois nuclear family into a virtue," framing poverty "as a moral transgression" to be cured through firm paternalistic and legal structures of authority rather than through economic relief.[22]

The popular press immediately glossed over the racism of Quayle's accusations in favor of a dumb and lengthy celebrity media feud. The story of Quayle's remarks appeared on the front pages of national newspapers, including the *New York Times* and *USA Today*, and was the lead story on ABC's *World News Tonight*.[23] Coverage of the remarks was so extensive that it overshadowed the Bush administration's intended agenda for the week, as Quayle found himself confronted with questions about *Murphy Brown* at every stop of his Los Angeles tour, and President George H. W. Bush faced questions from the press while trying to discuss his trade talks with Canadian prime minister Brian Mulroney. "I don't know that much about the show," Bush erupted at a press conference. "I've told you, I don't want any more questions about it."[24]

While a trite GOP versus Hollywood framing dominated coverage of the issue, the rare commentator recognized the larger issues at work in the condemnation of Murphy Brown. National Urban League president John E. Jacob noted, "We know that when they say Murphy Brown from Hollywood they mean Lizzie Brown from southeast San Diego."[25] Unfortunately, this commentary was in a short article buried in the back pages of the *Los Angeles Times*. Meanwhile, a *New York Times* page-one story crowed, "Today the high councils of government were preoccupied with a truly vexing question: Is Murphy Brown really a tramp?"[26] There were far more promiscuous characters on prime-time television in 1992 (Blanche from *The Golden Girls* had been looking for action since 1985 but had attracted no attention from the White House), so this label "tramp" is an intentionally incendiary description that makes plain the fact that campaigns against unwed pregnancy have historically been unclear about whether they were promoting abstinence, birth control, early marriage, or all three.[27] Producer Diane English also took aim at this ambiguity when she battled back, "If the vice president thinks it's disgraceful for an unmarried woman to bear a child, and if he believes that a woman cannot adequately raise a child without a father, then he'd better make sure abortion remains safe and legal."[28]

It is an important feature of this feud that the vice president made his famous remarks on May 19, 1992, the day after the television season of Murphy's pregnancy (September 16, 1991–May 18, 1992) ended with the birth of her son. In fact, the season had played out as if anticipating and preemptively defending itself against precisely the kind of family values moralizing that the vice president would later provide. Several episodes had already dealt with fictionalized authority figures criticizing Murphy's pregnancy, framing these attacks as some of the many challenges Murphy faces in navigating her role in a high-pressure workplace and in the public eye dealing with an unpartnered pregnancy. When she tells her producer Miles (Grant Shaud) in one episode ("Uh Oh: Part 2," S4E1, September 16, 1991) that she thinks she's pregnant, his reply is to mutter:

> My God, how could you do this to me? . . . You are a major network news star—a role model. How many unmarried pregnant role models have you ever seen on prime time? . . . And what about the job? How will you get stories? What happens when your face gets like a casaba melon and we have to use the jaws of life to get you out of the anchor chair?

The network president reacts just as badly to the news: "Our first priority is getting you married as soon as possible." He then threatens to take her off the air when she refuses.

These workplace offenses are always the butt of the show's jokes, and Murphy always prevails, putting her bosses in their place through a quip or a prank, building a defense of her own bodily autonomy episode by episode over the course of the season. In the episode "I'm as Much of a Man as I Ever Was" (S4E3, September 23, 1991), for instance, Murphy needs a quote from President Bush to complete a news story and knows the only way to get a candid interview is to join the president and Secret Service detail for their morning jog. When her doctor advises against jogging, Murphy obtains a bicycle and accidentally mows down the president in her zeal to keep up with the joggers. After the Secret Service returns her to the network, Miles scolds an unrepentant Murphy.

> MILES: You haven't learned one thing from this, have you?
> MURPHY: Yes, I have, Miles. I've learned that for the next nine months, I'm just going to have to be a little more creative.

MILES (whimpering): Oh God, a more creative Murphy Brown. And now there'll be two of her.

In his anxiety, Miles stumbles upon the idea that Murphy has increased her trickster power in pregnancy, as now there are "two of her." This unruly and delightful framing of Murphy's pregnancy as a superpower of doubled agency serves as a counter to the catastrophizing practiced by the show's ludicrous authority figures. *Murphy Brown* always reveled in puncturing the pompous and patriarchal norms of government and journalism, and Murphy's pregnancy provided a strong new angle to push back against dehumanizing workplace norms that fail to contain the star's growing body and nonmarital sexuality.

Murphy's pregnancy also offered the show an opportunity to satirize the family values discourse that had overtaken political speech of the time, particularly during a fictionalized Senate investigation in "Send in the Clowns" (S4E18, February 24, 1992). As the episode begins, Murphy has just presented a news segment criticizing senators for squandering taxpayer money on foreign trips and parking tickets. Embarrassed, a Senate committee immediately calls her to testify, asking her to name the source who leaked this confidential information to her. Murphy invokes the First Amendment and refuses to name the source. One senator (of the all-white, all-male, scathingly caricatured panel) asks how she knows what confidential information is in the public's interest to disclose, and she replies that she uses her "personal judgment as a journalist." He fires back, "Would that be the same personal judgment that led you to become an unwed mother?" The remark is clearly out of line (ignoring her modifier "as a journalist"), and Murphy emerges from the hearing not just victorious but defiant. Throughout the episode, the senators are presented as buffoonish, self-interested, and pompous, trying to divert attention from their own failures and intimidate the press by invoking platitudes and hot-button issues. The episode was such a prescient dress rehearsal for the real quarrel with Vice President Quayle precisely because the family values discourse of the Reagan-Bush years, which used a reproductive ideal of middle-class heterosexual respectability to stigmatize political opponents, was such a constant figure on the nightly news that it was nearly inevitable someone would eventually take the bait. Quayle did.

In the wake of Quayle's remarks, the Murphy Brown season 5 premiere ("You Say Potatoe, I Say Potato: Parts 1 and 2," S5E1–2, September 21, 1992) milked the controversy for all it could, cleverly editing the vice president's remarks into the fictional diegesis of the show, as if Quayle had criticized Murphy Brown the political journalist rather than *Murphy Brown* the sitcom. An exhausted new mother, Murphy goes on air to defend herself and other single parents:

> These are difficult times for our country, and in searching for the cause of our social ills, we could choose to blame the media, or the Congress, or an administration that's been in power for twelve years, or we could blame it on me. . . . The Vice President says he felt it was important to open a dialogue about family values and on that point we agree. Unfortunately, it seems that for him, the only acceptable definition of family is a mother, a father, and children, and in a country where millions of children grow up in non-traditional families, that definition seems painfully unfair.

Murphy goes on to introduce a racially diverse group of "non-traditional" families to give visual evidence of how out of touch Quayle's narrow definition of family is in a leader and policymaker. Never one to stick to the high road, the fictional Murphy then has a truckload of potatoes dumped on the vice president's lawn (a reference to his famous 1992 gaffe at a New Jersey spelling bee in which he coached a child to add an "e" at the end of the word "potato"). Trying to end the feud graciously, the real Dan Quayle sent a card and a stuffed elephant to star Candice Bergen and gathered a group of single mothers to watch the season 5 premiere, claiming it was the first time he had seen the show.[29] Probably it was.

The *Washington Post* later noted, "Sixty-seven million viewers tuned in— about 31 million more than the votes the Bush/Quayle ticket got six weeks later when they lost reelection."[30] And yet while Dan Quayle may have proved an easy target for satire (the show had included a Dan Quayle joke in every episode's script even *before* this controversy erupted)[31] and soon left his role as vice president, it is important to note that this electoral loss in no way ended the family values rhetoric that implicitly blamed poor or nontraditional reproductive practices for crime and poverty. In his 1995 State of the Union address, Bush's successor, President Bill Clinton, called on community leaders across the nation "to help us stop our most serious social problem, the epidemic of teen pregnancies and births where there is no marriage."[32] The new president's pledge to "end welfare as we know it" operationalized the family values discourse that had underscored the previous administration's clumsy parting shots in the culture war over reproduction and family structure. The basic idea that bad pregnancies were a threat to American health and prosperity remained dominant.

Bad Pregnancies • 109

THE *"JUNO EFFECT"*

Despite the continued social problem discourse, and perhaps in defiance of policy decisions that intentionally made life harder for single parents, the first decade of the twenty-first century did evince a shift away from the cautionary-tale framing of teen pregnancy comedies. The pregnant-cheerleader-armed-robbery movie *Sugar and Spice*, released in 2001, foregrounded the radical idea that teen parents' only real deficit is money. The film's cheerleading squad launches a highly organized bank robbery to support pregnant squad leader Diane (Marley Shelton). The film shows the girls using their social intelligence, organizational skills, and cheerleading acrobatics to accomplish this goal, transforming undervalued feminine traits into unexpected criminal competencies.

Diane's can-do spirit and relentless optimism ground the film's campy tone, which uses the language, aesthetics, and rules of cheerleading to frame the girls' bank-robbing adventure as a team activity. On the day of the heist, the squad members dress in identical "Betty Doll" masks, and those who are not pregnant pad their own bellies to be indistinguishable from the pregnant Diane (figure 3.5). This comic teen-girl solidarity reframes Diane's pregnancy not as tragedy but as provocation for defiant collective action. Diane uses the proceeds from the robbery to provide for her new family. The film's epilogue shows her marrying dim-bulb boyfriend Jack (James Marsden) and raising their twins as he runs successfully for the Senate. Diane's family eventually starts the Diane Bartlett Scholarship Fund for Pregnant Cheerleaders, another of the film's reminders that teen pregnancy is often a financial problem, never a moral one. The film was successful enough in changing the subject away from the social problem discourse of teen pregnancy that critics were far more concerned about its association of teens and guns than about its general positivity toward Diane's pregnancy.[33]

A few years later, the wicked satire *Saved!* (2004) similarly pushed back against the social problem framing of teen pregnancy by focusing on naive born-again Christian Mary (Jena Malone), who is bedeviled not so much by her pregnancy itself, but by the hypocrisy of her cartoonishly pious peers, who use religion as a weapon to enforce the rigid hierarchy of their teen social networks. Mary, a "good girl," has sex with her boyfriend Dean (Chad Faust) to try to cure him of his homosexuality (it doesn't work). When Dean is then sent off to a gay-conversion camp, Mary is left alone to deal with her unexpected pregnancy. Though at first Mary suffers the sanctimonious cruelty of her classmates, she eventually assembles a new non-normative family: Mary's new boyfriend, her supportive single mother, her brother and his iconoclastic girlfriend, and even biological father Dean, who returns accompanied by the

FIGURE 3.5. Sugar and Spice *(2001)*. *The cheerleading squad members dress as identical pregnant "Betty Dolls" (and one shortish Richard Nixon) in a show of solidarity during the bank robbery.*

new boyfriend he met at camp. The film ends with a snapshot of this nontraditional family gathered around Mary's hospital bed, joyfully welcoming the new child. The satire, though broad, resists the mandate that all socially responsible representations of teen pregnancy should take pains to condemn it in order to discourage impressionable teens from replicating on-screen behavior. Instead, it locates the origins of Mary's pregnancy in her abstinence-only naivete about sexuality and reproduction, an ignorance nurtured by the same religious intolerance that animates the stigma against her pregnancy as it develops. Rather than brutalizing its teen mother, *Saved!* invests its comic energy in taking down the ways purity culture promotes ignorance, hypocrisy, and cruelty.

Another film that critiques purity culture, *Quinceañera* (2006), is the story of fourteen-year-old Magdalena (Emily Rios), who becomes pregnant after her boyfriend accidentally ejaculates on her leg. Magdalena's father, a preacher, throws her out of the house, but she is taken in by her kind great-uncle, Tío Tomas (Chalo González). Tomas has a practice of taking in all the family's strays, including Magdalena's cousin Carlos (Jesse Garcia), who has been thrown out of his family for being gay. This is one of the rare pregnancy comedies not to end with the euphoric birth of a child. Instead, Magdalena's happy ending is a reunion with her parents (after an ob-gyn appointment has confirmed her virginity) and the celebration of her own quinceañera, a traditional fifteenth birthday party and coming-of-age celebration. By freezing the ending in the midst of her coming-of-age party, the film leaves Magdalena poised between girlhood and womanhood and restores the adolescence that premature motherhood is expected to rob her of.

In a more rhetorically direct vein, *Juno* (2007), the story of a pregnant teen (Elliot Page) who decides to give her baby up for adoption, rehearses the argument condemning teen pregnancy and then forcefully refutes it. In the middle of the movie, an ultrasound technician, visibly uncomfortable with Juno's pregnancy, expresses relief when she learns that Juno intends to give the baby up for adoption, "Oh, well, thank goodness for that! . . . I just see a lot of teenage mothers come through here; it's obviously a poisonous environment to raise a baby in." Provoked, Juno replies, "How do you know that I'm so poisonous?," before her stepmother Bren (Allison Janney) launches into a more spirited defense, pointing out that there is no guarantee an adoptive couple will provide an ideal home: "Maybe they'll do a far shittier job of raising a kid than my dumb-ass stepdaughter ever would; have you considered that?" In addition to shaming the technician for her judgment toward Juno's pregnancy, this takedown lays bare the logic of class that underscores condemnations of teen pregnancy. Intentionally using coarse language, Bren refutes the technician's assumptions that Juno's pregnancy is proof of the family's dysfunction and that being born to a teenager would condemn the child to a lifetime of economic scarcity and social stigma.

Though Juno does not choose to raise the child herself, the film's refusal to condemn teen pregnancy as a social blight—expressed both in this scene and in the upbeat tone of Juno's verbal quirks, cute maternity wear, and unflappable attitude—raised the ire of several national groups. In the summer of 2008, the national press picked up a minor story out of the working-class, majority-white suburb of Gloucester, Massachusetts: seventeen students turned up pregnant at Gloucester High, whose school nurse reported that the girls seemed too happy about their pregnancies. There were rumors of a "pregnancy pact," through which the girls set out to conceive children at the same time so they could raise them together. *Time* magazine called this the *"Juno* Effect," attributing it to the recent spate of films that presented unwed motherhood as something other than a catastrophe, particularly *Juno* and *Knocked Up*.[34] District officials later called the whole narrative of a pregnancy pact into question, insisting that the high school principal had based his comments on an unconfirmed rumor. A couple of girls confirmed that they had made a pact to raise their children together after they found out they were pregnant, but no preconception pact was ever verified.

Still, the idea of the *"Juno* Effect" stuck in the public imagination. NPR picked up the term and amplified it by producing a story in which host Mike Pesca interviewed University of North Carolina professor Jane Brown, director of the Teen Media Project. Brown quotes research indicating that girls with "heavier sexual-media diets" are more likely to become sexually active by age sixteen—a fact with dubious relevance to this issue, as the original charge against *Juno* was that it presents an idealization of teen pregnancy rather than that it promotes teen sex.[35] Indeed, the film has very little sexual activity at all, the conception scene being presented in flashback, without nudity or passion. Further, the fictional Juno gives her child up for adoption, a significant element not copied by the Gloucester teens who made plans to raise their babies together.

The issue reached the peak of tabloid handwringing when a Lifetime Original movie, *The Pregnancy Pact* (2010), fictionalized what was probably a fictional news event in the first place. In reality, the rate of teen pregnancy has been dropping pretty steadily for thirty years and fell several percentage points in 2007–2008, during the time the "*Juno* Effect" was in the news.[36] There was no such effect. Ultimately, the condemnation of *Juno* for an overly sympathetic view of teen pregnancy reflected the longevity of moralizing political discourses, which resumed with new urgency even as pregnancy comedies pushed back against them.

ADOPTION

The *Idiocracy* vignette that opened this chapter pairs teen and unpartnered pregnancy with infertility and delayed conception, as if babies being born to and raised by "inappropriate" poor or too-young parents exist in tension or competition with babies born to and raised by "appropriate" economically secure and educated couples. The clash of too soon/too many and too late/ too few becomes particularly visible in adoption stories, as in the conclusion of *Juno*, when the teen mother gives her child to infertile professional woman Vanessa (played by Jennifer Garner, a celebrity with an "ideal mom" tabloid persona). Adoption is often treated as a tidy solution to the problem of too early/too late, simply to transfer the child from an inappropriate home to an optimized one. Importantly, this solution also skips over the need for abortion, serving a political function to justify ongoing reductions in reproductive rights. The availability of adoption as an apparent solution to the problem of unwanted or ill-timed pregnancy strongly animates contemporary political arguments that led to the fall of *Roe v. Wade*.

In 2023, as I am completing this book draft, the US Supreme Court has formally released its judicial decision overturning *Roe v. Wade* and enabling state legislatures to place restrictions on abortion. One aspect of the majority's reasoning in this decision was expressed by Justice Amy Coney Barrett during the hearings when she pointed out that all fifty states have "safe haven" laws allowing mothers to surrender children for adoption without conditions. Addressing the argument that forced pregnancy and parenthood deny women equal access to education and economic opportunity, Justice Barrett seemed to argue that changes in employment law, declining social stigma around pregnancy, and liberalized adoption practices had obviated the need for abortion as a means to protect equality. Noting that being required to carry a pregnancy to term is not the same as being forced to parent the child thus born, Justice Barrett asked the petitioner, "Why don't the safe haven laws take care of the problem?"[37] This question was echoed in the court's final opinion, which quotes a 2008 CDC report indicating that "nearly one million women were seeking to adopt children in 2002 (i.e., they were in demand for a child), whereas the domestic supply of infants relinquished at birth or within the first month of life and available to be adopted had become virtually nonexistent."[38] Taken together, this chapter and the next one both bump up against this seductive logic, which promises to fix all reproductive problems through the judicious reassignment of human babies.

The idea that adoption is a tidy solution to the twinned problems of over-fertility and impaired fertility first rose to prominence in the United States in the 1950s. Reproductive historian Rickie Solinger argues that one result of America's baby boom mania for suburban family life was a cultural revision in the ways unwed pregnancies in young white women were handled by families, churches, and state institutions.[39] The eugenic fretting about an illegitimate infant's presumed genetic defects (so central in *The Very Idea*, discussed in chapter 1) dominated social management of unwed pregnancy in the 1930s precisely because there was little "market" for adoptable babies during the Depression. Child abandonment was presumed to place children in perma-nent state care, so unwed mothers were encouraged to keep and raise their children in the hope that motherhood might serve as a penance to address the moral stain on the young woman and her child.

These ideas fell out of fashion during the baby boom as young, middle-class white couples increasingly sought to build their families by any means nec-essary, and orphan homes evolved into sanitized consumer spaces that could fulfill the hopes and dreams of economically secure young couples. As this mar-ket for adoptable white babies emerged, the ideology of unwed motherhood conveniently and rapidly shifted to match the needs of the marketplace. Now young, unwed white mothers, if they were not willing or able to marry their partners, were encouraged, coerced, or forced to give their babies up. Girls and women who resisted the mandate to relinquish their children were routinely diagnosed as neurotic or unfit (wishing to raise their own children as single mothers was used as evidence of unfitness) so the decision could be enacted without their consent.[40] The system appeared to produce perfect results: unwed mothers could restore their marriageability, unburdened by children, while the children could become moral and genetic blank slates, unstained by illegitimacy or maternal defect, ready to be welcomed into adoptive families and raised in more prosperous and socially sanctioned surroundings.[41] Later studies revealed that the coercive tactics used by maternity centers for unwed white mothers produced deep, long-term harm for women whose babies were forcibly removed under this system, and in some cases for the separated children as well.[42] Margaret Atwood's *The Handmaid's Tale* is built on an amplified version of this same idea, envisioning a reproductive dystopia where fertile women are enslaved and raped in order to provide offspring to an infertile ruling class.[43]

Solinger explains: "With . . . the decline in the belief in the genetically flawed illegitimate mother and child, white babies were born out of wedlock not only untainted but *unclassed* as well. Thus, the salient demographic fact about white unwed mothers was that they were white."[44] There being no parallel market for Black infants in the decades after World War II, unmarried Black girls and women most often kept their babies or gave them to family members to raise. This racial segregation of the experiences of unwed mothers both reflected and proliferated the long-term stereotyping of Black women as irresponsible single mothers, political attacks on public assistance assumed to support Black mothers, and the pseudoscientific logic of studies like the Moynihan Report (1965), which scapegoated Black family structures and specifically female-headed households for persistent economic inequalities that would be better explained by racist patterns of policing, segregation, housing, banking, and educational opportunity.[45] The postwar move to eliminate the social phenomenon of white unmarried women raising their own children furthered all these racist ideas by widening the gap between Black and white family norms.

This historic backdrop of racialized reproductive injustice provides important context for *Juno*, a film that examines both halves of the stigmatized childbearing binary among white mothers: the working-class teen pregnancy and the infertility of the older professional woman. *Juno* is a canny exploration of the market dynamics of this system and a revealing portrait of how whiteness structures adoptive families' infertility as well as their market power as professionals and consumers.

In contrast to the contemporary norm of open adoption, in which an adopted child retains regular and structured ties with their birth parent or parents, Juno requests that her child be adopted under a closed system, in which she expects no further contact with the birth parents after the relinquishment of the child, a system that has fallen out of favor in the realm of domestic adoptions in the United States (though international adoptions often remain closed and can be subject to similar economic coercion of birth mothers). *Juno* was criticized by adoption activists, who asserted that the film's glorification of the now-antiquated closed system of adoption is bad character psychology. Most prominently, an opinion piece in *USA Today* argued:

Bad Pregnancies   •   115

> *Juno* makes an unwanted pregnancy look like a great experience, akin to a year in the Peace Corps. The film's light finale, with Juno unchanged by what she has gone through, is harmful fiction of the worst kind. She is seducing girls and young women into believing that they could—and even should—give away their own child, as if they were giving away a favorite toy, just to be nice.[46]

I want to complicate this critique by examining how, although the film does not make visible the emotional fallout from closed-adoption culture, it does a far clearer job of expressing the complicated class dynamics that have made closed adoption seem like such an ideal solution to the social problem of white unwed pregnancy for many years. Those class dynamics are an important and underrecognized part of the conversation quoted above, which often refers to women's emotional lives as though they exist outside of class. Even within this opinion piece, the author, Jean Strauss, derides screenwriter Diablo Cody as "a former stripper who has never relinquished a child nor even given birth."[47] This reference to Cody's employment history is clearly meant to influence the reader to identify against her, again placing true motherhood in the realm of the middle class.

Juno is explicitly interested in class. The film makes much of the fondly cluttered mise-en-scène of Juno's home, as well as her parents' professions: Dad (J. K. Simmons) is a heating and air-conditioning specialist, and stepmom Bren is a nail technician. Mark and Vanessa Loring (Jason Bateman and Jennifer Garner), the adoptive parents Juno chooses for her baby, are a commercial composer and an attorney, well-paid professionals who live manicured lives inside their suburban home. The film delights in playful references to how their perfection is bound up in cultural codes of whiteness. The perfect housing development where they live is called Glacial Valley Estates. Richard Dyer has memorably explored the associations of whiteness with coldness and cold places: the northern European homeland of Aryan and Caucasian races. "Such places," says Dyer "had a number of virtues: the clarity and cleanliness of the air, the vigour demanded by the cold, the enterprise required by the harshness of the terrain and climate, the sublime, soul-elevating beauty of mountain vistas, even the greater nearness to God above and the presence of the whitest thing on earth, snow."[48] The inside of the Lorings' house, spare and quite white, continues to play with this imagery, as do the corny photos of Mark and Vanessa, frolicking in matching white turtlenecks, that line the Loring stairs (figure 3.6). Even the name Vanessa could be a play on the word "vanilla," an association emphasized when the character faces the dilemma of whether to paint the baby's nursery "cheesecake" or "custard," two essentially identical shades of off-white. The extreme whiteness of the Loring household

116 • It's All in the Delivery

FIGURE 3.6. Juno *(2007)*. *Corny family photos of the Lorings (Jennifer Garner and Jason Bateman) in matching white turtlenecks play with iconographies of whiteness and conceal the actual cracks in their marriage.*

is class-coded as elevating, but the film uses Juno's ambivalent perspective to make visible the emptiness at its heart.

Juno transgresses the raw economics of her relationship with the Lorings by developing a habit of drop-in visits, enacting a kind of fantasy voyeurism into the life her child will inhabit. In doing so, she accidentally releases the dark id from the basement of the sexless white family home: husband Mark makes a pass at Juno and reveals that he does not actually want children. The film, then, disrupts its own fantasy of adoption as a "clean" solution to the various economic, social, and emotional problems of unwed motherhood and infertility. Class advantage does not, cannot, guarantee the kind of perfection in family life that it is able to achieve in home decor. But even with the fantasy thus disrupted, Juno chooses to place her child with Vanessa, who then becomes a single mother herself, disrupting the paradigm of single = bad/partnered = good that has been so important to the pregnancies detailed in this chapter.

Although Juno immediately and flippantly refuses Vanessa's offer of money in drawing up the adoption contract, the film finds remarkably frank and playful ways to acknowledge the implicit commerce of the adoption process. Juno first finds the Lorings by looking in the *PennySaver* circular, a working-class instrument of commerce. When they offer her money for her medical expenses, she is too frank in replying, "I don't want to sell the thing," accidentally bringing the subtext of the transaction to the surface. She later encounters Vanessa at a mall, the de facto public sphere of modern suburban communities. This scene shows the prospective mother actually kneeling down before the pregnant teen to feel her belly for kicks. Juno becomes a participant in the relationship between her child and the woman who will mother it—she seems to inhabit at the level of fantasy the positions of both loved child (repairing the damage from her own absent mother) and Madonna-like bearer of the gift of family. This is the experience Juno was looking for when she initiated the process of finding adoptive parents for her child, and this scene gives us that reparative experience but qualifies it: we are at the mall. The theme of commerce repeats again at the end of the film, when Juno leaves Vanessa a note written on the back of an old oil-change receipt, renewing her commitment to give the baby to Vanessa, who sacralizes this commercial item, a repurposed piece of rubbish, by framing it and placing it in an alcove above the baby's crib. These reframings do not deny the economic aspects of the adoption process, but they complicate the adoption story as either pure commerce or pure sentiment by putting the two ideas together in ironic combination.

Juno flirts with the classist and coercive history of closed adoption, in which a working-class white pregnant teen is first scolded for her pregnancy and then praised for the redemptive decision to relinquish the child, under the presumption that a middle-class family could offer a better life. But it also takes that ideology apart by making whiteness hypervisible rather than an unremarked subtext to the transaction, and allowing the repressed commercial aspects of the adoptive relationship to show through the film's happy narrative and tidy ending.

CONCLUSION

This chapter has focused on "too early" pregnancies and the ways comedy has pushed back against scolding social and political scripts that use the figure of the unpartnered pregnant woman as a negative exemplar to justify control over women's and girls' sexuality, bodily autonomy, and self-definition. The next two chapters pick up these same regulatory themes in different ways, first by examining the "too late" paradigm of infertility, delayed conception, and miscarriage (chapter 4) and finally by filling in the missing issue of abortion (chapter 5), an option that is aggressively suppressed in *Juno* and many of the other movies and shows covered in this chapter. Placing these three issues in conversation with one another reveals how the tropes and conventions of each orbit around the same set of invisible norms, which limit reproductive choices to a narrow and heavily racialized set of options. Reclaiming reproductive justice from the mediated rhetoric of "bad pregnancies" requires a closer understanding of all forms of stigmatized pregnancy and how these bad examples are used to protect a limited, conservative definition of socially sanctioned childbearing.

Chapter 4

BABY BUST

INFERTILITY AND ITS DISCONTENTS

THE 1963 SCREWBALL COMEDY *The Thrill of It All*, starring James Garner and Doris Day, begins with a series of shots showing a well-dressed, middle-aged woman (played by fifty-five-year-old Arlene Francis) laughing and clowning in the back of her chauffeured car, laughing and skipping as she walks into an office building, then giggling in a crowded elevator full of men in suits (figure 4.1). The businessmen soon start laughing with her, though no words are exchanged—her joy is simply contagious. When she dances into her husband's corporate office, her first words finally reveal the source of her infectious merriment: she's pregnant. Her joy in finding herself pregnant, after many years of trying, launches the film on a thrilling note. Like the biblical Sarah, laughing to learn that she will bear a child late in life, this woman responds to her long-desired pregnancy with an explosion of pent-up desire, anticipation, and disbelief.

Stories of infertility and delayed conception are built around thrilling highs and crushing lows, as they narrativize a set of hopes joyfully fulfilled or cruelly dashed—but the lows outnumber the highs. The unfairness, the randomness, the inability to control the outcome of conception beggars the natural human tendency to find meaning in patterns and experiences. Susan Sontag, in her book *Illness as Metaphor*, reflects on her own cancer and notes that the more poorly understood the physiology of a disease is, the more intensively wrong-headed metaphors are attached to that disease.

FIGURE 4.1. The Thrill of It All *(1963). A woman (Arlene Francis) experiences contagious joy at being pregnant after a long period of infertility.*

Nothing is more punitive than to give a disease a meaning—that meaning being invariably a moralistic one. Any important disease whose causality is murky, and for which treatment is ineffectual, tends to be awash in significance. First, the subjects of deepest dread (corruption, decay, pollution, anomie, weakness) are identified with the disease. The disease itself becomes a metaphor.[1]

It is useful to apply her insights to infertility. The metaphoric understanding of infertility for women is sterility, barrenness, a lack of ripeness or maternalism. For men, it is impotence, effeminacy, and weakness. Let me be clear that these are stereotypes and bear no real relation to the medical causes of infertility and delayed conception. But these stereotypes, these metaphors, these narratives imposed on the incomprehensible, uncontrollable quality of infertility in the human body are irresistible to genre fiction, which requires some kind of cause to animate its effects in order to form a satisfying narrative and resolution.

And sure enough, after *The Thrill of It All* opens with a joyful, almost wordless celebration of a woman's pregnancy, the film goes on to encase that remarkable event in the tedious metaphor of the infertile woman's ability to "relax." Obstetrician Gerald Boyer (James Garner) explains to his wife Beverly (Doris Day) how he effected this miracle: he had instructed the couple to stop trying and instead to take a three-month ocean cruise.

GERALD: It took the pressure off psychologically.

BEVERLY: How did you know it would work?

GERALD: I didn't. But I knew I had three things working for me: they were capable, they love each other, and there is very little to do on a three-month ocean cruise.

This idea that the best cure for infertility is for the prospective parents to relax and stop trying has often been employed to bring infertility out of the realm of medical mystery and into the more manageable space of behavioral metaphor. Genre fiction loves a behavioral metaphor.

The idea that female stress or perfectionism can cause or contribute to infertility dates back to at least the 1870s in the United States. Experts warned that young women who hoped to be mothers someday should avoid "ambitious outreachings" and confine their interests to home and family. "The young woman who failed to heed such advice and who sought a college education—or worse, a career after she earned her degree—would most likely find herself suffering from infertility brought on by 'uterine inflammation.'"[2] Starting in the late 1940s, the popularization of psychoanalytic theory in the United States led to widespread belief that "a considerable amount of female infertility—some estimates placed it as high as 75 percent—resulted from psychological rather than physiological disorders."[3] High on the list of possibilities was careerism, as one member of the medical community explained: "We have all seen a long-desired pregnancy follow the renunciation of a career. This may be the result of the development of 'motherliness' and the consequent hormonal changes."[4] The gradual movement of pregnancy from the feminine authority of family and midwives to the masculine medical domain of doctors and hospitals, documented in chapter 1 of this book, lent institutional authority to these folksy and unverified opinions. Because the causes of infertility and miscarriage are (even still!) poorly understood and difficult to control, sexist notions about women's participation in economic and public life easily rush in to fill the void left by the absence of real medical knowledge.

Though this bald language has largely disappeared, the idea of ambitious female sterility persists in popular culture through narratives that castigate the career woman for allowing her biological clock to tick unheeded, delaying fertility for reasons of ambition or perfectionism, as in the *Idiocracy* vignette that opened the previous chapter. Diane Negra calls this idea a postfeminist "time crisis," in which women experience pressure to shoehorn an expanded set of ideal qualities and experiences (education, career, love, self-discovery, consumption) into their peak reproductive years, leading to a generation of harried, perfectionist contemporary romantic comedy heroines channeling

Baby Bust • 121

these social pressures into popular media.[5] The specific form of this idea has evolved over the years, but both official and popular narratives of infertility in the United States over the course of many decades scapegoated the female partner's mental and emotional state as a leading cause of problems.

Susan Faludi famously showed in 1991 how the stereotypes of the infertile white career woman were an invention of political forces that rallied in a backlash against the gains of the women's movement. Faludi's review of medical studies and public health data showed that nearly every assumption about rising infertility rates among middle-class professional women in their thirties was incorrect:

> In reality, women's quest for economic and educational equality had only improved reproductive health and fertility. Better education and bigger paychecks breed better nutrition, fitness, and health care, all important contributors to higher fecundity. Federal statistics bear out that college-educated and higher-income women have a lower infertility rate than their high-school-educated and low-income counterparts. The "infertility epidemic" among middle-class career women over thirty was a political program . . . not a medical problem.[6]

It is easy to see how a manufactured "infertility epidemic" could be used as a bludgeon against women's economic and educational gains in the late twentieth century, as it placed women's childbearing opportunities in direct (and false) opposition to their education and career ambitions. And yet in the decades since Faludi's warning, popular media have doubled down on the problematic idea. In the sitcom *Friends*, perfectionist Monica (Courteney Cox) is the only member of the group who struggles with infertility. In *Juno*, Vanessa (Jennifer Garner) is an attorney who keeps an immaculate house. In *Private Life*, Rachel (Kathryn Hahn) rants about how she feels "betrayed" by the feminist ideology she encountered in college, which falsely promised that she could have both a career and a family. "I just don't think it's Gloria Steinem's fault that we can't get pregnant," her husband retorts wryly. Rachel becomes defensive: "Whose fault is it, then? I guess it is mine since I was too busy writing my stupid book." While the conversation is satiric, the frustration of infertility treatments brings out these false causalities that seek to make the condition someone's fault, with the woman's career providing a convenient and socially ubiquitous scapegoat.

Film and television have frequently reinforced the idea that female infertility is a symptom of stress, careerism, or frigidity by suggesting that if a woman relaxes enough, has a psychological breakthrough, meets the right man, or has great sex, her fertility will restore itself without further treatment. The offending texts are too numerous to count, but here are a few millennial examples: In *A Smile Like Yours* (1997), the stresses of infertility treatment nearly ruin the happy marriage between Jennifer and Danny (Lauren Holly and Greg Kinnear). When they stop treatment, they spontaneously conceive triplets. In *What to Expect When You're Expecting* (2012), Wendy (Elizabeth Banks) and her husband Gary (Ben Falcone) have spent two years trying to conceive. When they take a break from trying and enjoy a drunken tumble in the bushes in a park, they hit the jackpot. In *Baby Mama* (2008), Kate (Tina Fey) has a fertility specialist put her chances of conceiving at one in a million. After her attempts at artificial insemination and in vitro fertilization fail, she stops trying and hires a surrogate. Shortly thereafter, she finds a new and wonderful boyfriend (Greg Kinnear again, oddly) and falls unexpectedly, miraculously pregnant.

There is also a strong association between cultural notions of whiteness and this portrait of infertility as excessive self-regulation—and not surprisingly, the above examples are all white women. A rare exception is the Black-cast comedy *Girls Trip* (2017), in which the character Ryan (Regina Hall), a lifestyle guru whose career depends on the appearance of "having it all," reveals that she has been undergoing fertility treatments to have a child. She is humiliated when her husband impregnates a younger woman he has been having an affair with, and the breakdown in their marriage is implicitly blamed on Ryan's careerism and ambition, made literal through her inability to conceive a child. The film is a wild and raunchy celebration of Black women's friendships, and while the character of Ryan is an insightful portrait of the pressures of perfectionism for Black women with high-powered careers, its adoption of the myth of overregulated fertility mirrors the problematic assumptions that animate white-cast texts as well.

The linking of whiteness, self-regulation, and infertility also emerges from the eugenic logic that treats upper- and middle-class white fertility as fragile and valuable, in need of expansion, while poor and non-white communities are assumed to be hyperfertile, in need of control. In addition to being racist and classist, these stereotypes misrepresent the raw numbers. Despite demographers' attempts in the early 1990s to put to rest the idea that infertility was on the increase, the myth of growing sterility remains firmly entrenched, as does its corollary that it is a particularly middle- and upper-class problem. In fact, the causes of medical infertility, including toxic environmental exposures, untreated illness, and poor nutrition, are more common among women living in poverty than among those who are wealthier. It follows, then, that contemporary demographic studies show poor and working-class women enduring higher rates of infertility than their middle-class and wealthy counterparts, but this population remains stubbornly invisible because they are unlikely to seek expensive treatments for the condition.[7]

Baby Bust • 123

In a close variant of the "just relax" mantra, popular media have also clung tightly to the myth that if a couple adopt a child, they will often conceive spontaneously. Though there are, of course, anecdotal examples of couples with diagnosed infertility conceiving a child after adopting, some data suggests that couples who pursue fertility treatment and then shift to adoption are in fact *less* likely to experience a spontaneous pregnancy than couples who end treatment but do not adopt.[8] The use of the conception-after-adoption trope in popular media nearly always posits a causal effect between the two.

Television, which has often used infertility as a story arc over the course of one or more seasons, has been particularly committed to the conception-after-adoption trope. The series finales of *King of Queens* ("China Syndrome, Parts 1 and 2," S9E12, May 14, 2007) and *Mike and Molly* ("I See Love," S6E13, May 16, 2016) follow the same formula: each couple's long quest to have a baby ends with a successful adoption that coincides with the woman's unexpected announcement that she is also pregnant. On television, this pattern reaches back at least as far as *The Mary Tyler Moore Show* ("Ted and the Kid," S6E24, March 6, 1976), in which the characters Ted (Ted Knight) and Georgette (Georgia Engel) adopt a son and then immediately learn of Georgette's own pregnancy. *Rules of Engagement* ("100th," S7E13, May 20, 2013) varied the formula by having its central couple receive the results of a positive pregnancy test on the day their surrogate gives birth. In the first *Sex and the City* movie (2008), the character Charlotte (Kristin Davis), whose infertility treatments were a significant part of the series, has a surprise pregnancy after she and her new husband have already given up trying in favor of adoption.

Though infertility diagnoses are rarely absolute, and pregnancy can certainly happen unexpectedly, the persistence of the pregnancy-after-adoption trope reflects and perpetuates the myth that infertility is not a real condition, but rather a temporary physical state brought on by stress or the perfectionist modern woman's tendency to micromanage the process of conception and childbirth. The harmful implications of this myth go far beyond the fertility clinic: the premise that infertility is rooted in stress, anxiety, or incompatibility is taken to an extreme in the pervasive idea, expressed by Senate candidate Todd Akin in 2012, that pregnancies resulting from rape are uncommon, because "if it's a legitimate rape, the female body has ways to try to shut that whole thing down."[9] This concept that a stressed woman is less likely to become pregnant has exceptionally dangerous cultural implications, in addition to its stigmatizing effect on women battling infertility. To be clear, the medical condition of infertility is not a personality flaw. To treat it like one is a misogynist fairy tale.

This chapter explores the terms by which impaired fertility (in both the male and female partners), miscarriage, delayed conception, and adoption have been subject to these metaphors of false causality in American film comedy. Genre film and television narratives often organize story events around the emotional journeys of characters, as if their readiness for an adventure calls that experience into existence. The cause and effect of narrative is far simpler and more satisfying than the reality of squishy statistical predictions that frequently accompany fertility diagnoses. As a result, genre film and television series often time pregnancy and birth around a narrative logic (unexpected twist! season finale!) rather than a medical one. This timing creates a false cause-and-effect logic to conception and birth that is always complicated but is particularly perilous in the ways it misrepresents impediments to fertility.

ORIGIN STORIES

Predictably, early studio-era comedies left a lot of information unspoken in their narratives of infertility, with character-based explanations filling the information void. For instance, the 1939 comedy *Four Wives* chronicles the adventures of the vivacious Lemp sisters as they settle down and begin to start families. At the beginning of the film, Emma (Gale Page) believes she is pregnant, so her sisters joyfully accompany her to the obstetrician's office. She emerges from the appointment looking crestfallen, informing her sisters that she's not going to have a baby after all, "not now, not ever." The doctor explains that Emma is otherwise healthy, but her infertility is "just one of those things."

As a modern spectator, I am frustrated by the lack of gynecological details in this scene. Did Emma think she was pregnant because her periods stopped? Was this related somehow to her diagnosis of infertility? How did the doctor make such a large and definitive diagnosis on the basis of what seemed to be a very short office visit? The Hays-era prohibitions on discussing such particulars made the diagnosis necessarily opaque and definitive, a plot device more than a physical condition. This opacity further renders the medical professional uniquely authoritative: How would you question a diagnosis that is never explained?

The next scene is equally puzzling. Learning that all four sisters have gone to see the obstetrician, Ben (Frank McHugh), a prosperous businessman married to Emma's sister Thea (Lola Lane), mistakenly believes that it's his own wife who is expecting. He greets her joyfully outside the doctor's office, but she scolds him for his enthusiasm. "Have you gone out of your head?" Thea asks her husband. "I'm not going to have a baby."

Again, the scene prompts questions. Why would it be crazy for Ben to assume that his wife might be pregnant? Is she using birth control? Do they have a celibate marriage? In the utopian small-town world of the Lemp sisters, do women just decide these things?

Things get even stranger a few weeks later, when Thea reveals to her husband that she has set up a nursery in their home. "Whoopee!" he shouts, and again she scolds him, "Are you crazy?"—though she never specifies why she finds his reaction "crazy." Assuming she is pregnant, he asks, "How long will it be?," to which she replies, "A couple of weeks." He is puzzled but just assumes his wife has some remarkable powers of gestation beyond his ken, telling her, "You keep a secret better than any woman I ever heard of." A few moments of comic misunderstanding ensue before she reveals to him that she has applied to adopt a child. Ben is disappointed, but his wife consoles him cryptically: "Of course, it's much better that way." Thea never explains exactly why it is better this way or how she plans to prevent a pregnancy in favor of family building through adoption. Though there are many reasons a woman might not want to bear children in her own body, Thea never actually names one, as if such things were simply obvious. Through these odd scenes of euphemism, obfuscation, misunderstanding, and simple ignorance, code-era films like this one create the impression that some women exercise remarkable but mysterious control over childbearing, while men have less than none. The line between character device and biology is confusingly blurred.

Ultimately, whatever system Thea is using to control her own fertility fails, and she discovers that she is pregnant on the same day that she brings new daughter Caroline back from the orphan home. Months later, as Thea gives birth, Emma's husband Ernest (Dick Foran) approaches Ben in the waiting room: "Emma and I were just thinking, well, now that you have another baby . . . uh . . . and we've grown so fond of Caroline, and maybe you might let us take her. Adopt her, I mean." Ben doesn't even answer, as the very next moment a doctor enters the waiting room to inform him that he's the father of twin girls. In the final scene of the movie, Emma is parenting Caroline while Thea tends her twins, some kind of seamless transfer of custody having taken place off-screen. Both the unhappily infertile woman and the one who prevented conception by mysterious choice have been outfitted with babies.

Comedies and dramas dealing with infertility in the years near World War II shared this heedless drive toward a happy (baby-filled) ending, and they tended to focus on adoption rather than medical treatment as a path to family formation. The comedy melodramas *Penny Serenade* (1941), *Journey for Margaret* (1942), and *My Blue Heaven* (1950) feature pregnancy losses early in the story line, accompanied by an immediate diagnosis of infertility. In *Penny Serenade,* the pregnancy loss is caused by the 1923 Tokyo earthquake; in *Journey for Margaret,* by injuries sustained in the London Blitz; and in *My Blue Heaven,* by a car accident. These events provide decisive causality for the characters' infertility, and the affected couples grieve their losses and go on to adopt children to complete their families without further medical attention.

This narrative of infertility as an absolute diagnosis rather than a problem to overcome through physical treatment became less common in comedies of the postwar era. Indeed, *My Blue Heaven* in 1950 already implants a modicum of doubt in the doctor's diagnosis:

> KITTY: Does Jack know?
> DOCTOR: That you lost your baby?
> KITTY: That I can never have another one?
> DOCTOR (correcting her): That *in all probability* you can never have another one. I'm not God; I haven't the last word in these matters.

The film then follows its lead couple's quest to adopt a child. Recovering from their loss, Kitty (Betty Grable) and Jack (Dan Dailey) visit the home of friends Walter and Janet (David Wayne and Jane Wyatt), who have five children, two of whom are adopted. Janet explains that after three years of infertility, "I was afraid I was going to become one of those frustrated women." So "out of desperation," she and her husband adopted their oldest daughter. Her husband interrupts her: "And then, brother—one, two, three in a row! It got so I was afraid to shake hands with her." His wife laughs and explains, "I guess it's 'cause I stopped worrying so much about it." Inspired, Kitty and Jack make note of the adoption agency that their friends have used and arrange to visit it themselves. Sure enough, the film's ending applies the pregnancy-after-adoption trope with baby-boom-era fervor: Kitty and Jack end the film with two pending adoptions plus a pregnancy, though they have undergone no medical treatment. Adoption here is treated not just as an alternate path to family formation, but as a sure-fire cure for the physical problem of impaired fertility.

Although physicians had been prescribing surgeries, tonics, and behavioral treatments for infertility since at least the mid-nineteenth century (and midwives long before), rapid improvements in patient outcomes coinciding with the baby boom after World War II led to a significant jump in the number of fertility treatment centers and specialists. Between 1952 and 1955, the number of infertility clinics in the United States rose from 66 to 119, mostly in urban centers.[10] Popular media advertised new cures for infertility and ran headlines like "Childless Couples Given New Hope" over stories about medical advances in the field.[11]

Yet infertility was still shrouded in euphemism, and attempts to incorporate these social changes into mainstream comedy film often produced bizarre results. The 1958 Broadway adaptation *Tunnel of Love* was billed as "THE BOLD BLUSHING STAGE HIT OF SEX IN THE SUBURBS!"

and indeed, the oxymoron of "bold" and "blushing" together does capture the film's confused tone. The story follows Isolde and Augie Poole (Doris Day and Richard Widmark), who are under a doctor's treatment for infertility. The opening scenes of the film show Isolde taking her temperature and reminding her husband of the need for timed intercourse, familiar rituals in later fertility comedies that do seem quite daring and thoughtful for 1958.

The plot takes a turn for the bizarre, though, when the couple begin to explore the possibility of adoption. First Augie embarrasses himself in front of the adoption agency representative, Miss Novick (Gia Scala), scuttling their chance for a child, so he asks her to dinner to try to redeem his first impression. Augie takes several tranquilizers to calm his nerves before dinner and wakes up in a hotel room with no memory of the evening whatsoever. When Miss Novick later revisits the Pooles, pregnant herself and promising them an expedited infant placement, Augie panics, imagining that the baby he is being invited to adopt is his own illegitimate child. In the Broadway version of this story—horrifyingly—the baby does turn out to be Augie's, intentionally conceived by Miss Novick in service of her doctoral dissertation on the plight of unwed mothers. In the film adaptation—nonsensically—it doesn't, though the film keeps all the original's jokes about how much the adopted baby looks like Augie. Either way, the pregnancy is a joke about masculine sexual guilt, real or imagined, certainly nonconsensual. Augie's sexual trauma and its aftermath eclipse the women's twinned concerns about infertility and stigmatized extramarital fertility, which are rendered threatening and confusing through Augie's infantilized gaze. The crude Freudian title *Tunnel of Love* has no particular referent other than a general wink-wink attitude toward the whole idea that vaginas exist.

ASSISTED REPRODUCTIVE TECHNOLOGY

I am unable to find much in the way of comedies dealing with infertility produced in the 1960s and 1970s, so I pick up this history in the 1980s, when medical interventions for improved fertility, such as timed intercourse and sperm motility testing, became much more visible in popular culture, reflecting a larger treatment market as real-life spending on infertility treatment hit $1 billion in 1988.[12] As these changes were translated to the screen, they were often framed through a male perspective, suggesting that fertility treatment as a process was emasculating to male partners and driven by baby-hungry women.

She's Having a Baby (1988) is a particularly vivid example. It is structured around voice-over complaints from male partner Jake (Kevin Bacon), who is

FIGURE 4.2. She's Having a Baby *(1988)*. *Jake imagines the nurses laughing at the size of his sperm sample.*

ambivalent at best about the medicalization of the conception process. One scene shows wife Kristy (Elizabeth McGovern) sitting in bed, holding a thermometer and surrounded by pamphlets, shouting to her husband, "Jakey, my temperature's just right. Where are you? Hurry! Hurry!" Jake, loitering in the attic, laments the new regime in voice-over: "My love nest had become a stud farm." Sam Cooke's song "Chain Gang" starts playing satirically as Jake enters the bedroom. When timed intercourse fails to produce any result, Kristy undergoes fertility testing off-screen. Only when her tests all come back normal does she ask Jake to see the doctor as well. He imagines visiting the clinic to present his sperm sample and being laughed at by a room full of nurses and medical assistants, who see that there is very little semen in the cup (figure 4.2). Jake's sperm diagnosis results in a recommendation that he begin wearing boxers instead of briefs. His voice-over narration laments, "To go through the hell of a fertility check and discover that my preference in undergarments was to blame seemed as silly and pointless as everything else about my life." Jake's description of delivering a semen sample to a clinic as "hell" rather aptly captures the tone of films from this era, which have little to say about the procedures women undergo to test and increase fertility but fixate to the point of obsession on the indignities of male reproductive medicine.

Similarly, in *Funny About Love* (1990), every indignity of the fertility treatment process is represented through the male partner Duffy (Gene Wilder) as he reluctantly gives a sperm sample, walks home with a therapeutic ice pack in his shorts, and even gives hormone shots to his wife Meg (Christine

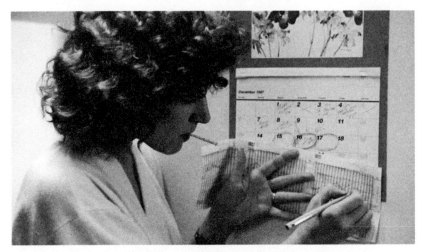

FIGURE 4.3. Funny About Love *(1990)*. *By the late 1980s, images of women taking their temperature and charting their cycles had become common shorthand for a couple's turn from spontaneous sex to a medicalized quest to conceive.*

Lahti). Though Meg is the one who must suffer the pain of the shot and the unknown effects on her body, it is Duffy who announces, "I'm surprised at how calm I am." The implication of this displacement, as in chapter 2, is that women's experiences of infertility treatment are serious business (figure 4.3), while clowning is a masculine prerogative and coping mechanism to alleviate the anxiety and humiliation of the physically invasive process.

Because medically assisted fertility—which reduces the role of spontaneous intercourse in the process of conception—is often treated as both innately bad and an exercise in neurotic feminine control, comic plots employ elaborate contortions to bring women down a peg through the reinstatement of conventional reproductive roles. Kelly Oliver argues that romantic comedies treat assisted reproductive technology (ART) as "an obstacle to overcome for the sake of romance and love."[13] In the sitcom *Living Single*, for instance, Max (Erika Alexander) impregnates herself with purchased donor sperm only to learn that the anonymous donor is actually her ex-boyfriend Kyle (T. C. Carson). The pair reunite when Erika realizes that Kyle does possess all the qualities that had led her to select his profile as a sperm donor ("Let's Stay Together," S5E13, January 1, 1998). *Made in America* (1993) and *The Kids Are All Right* (2010) both explore romances between formerly anonymous sperm donors (Ted Danson and Mark Ruffalo) and the birth mothers who used their sperm (Whoopi Goldberg and Julianne Moore), as if the mothers find something enticing in the idea of connecting with the men who contributed half the DNA to their beloved teenage children. Though each film fractures the restored-family dynamic in a different way, the pull to transform the ART participants into a conventional nuclear family animates these stories.

Donor sperm is often mishandled in comedies, and the terms of that mishandling suggest that there's something wrong with free-range sperm or that it needs to be eliminated to enable a "natural" happy ending. In *Miss Conception* (2008), Georgina (Heather Graham) is desperate to find a sperm donor to impregnate herself during what the doctors have told her is her last ovulation ever (note: not a real medical diagnosis). The donor sperm, stored in an apartment fridge, is spilled all over a cake, but Georgina's boyfriend Zak (Tom Ellis) catches an early flight back from a trip just in time to make a baby the old-fashioned way. In *The Switch* (2010), Kassie (Jennifer Aniston) intends to use donor sperm to conceive, but her best friend Wally (Jason Bateman) drunkenly dumps the cup of semen down a sink. Wally uses his own sperm to compensate, setting off a series of events that lead to their becoming a happy family. In *Jane the Virgin* (2014–2019), Jane Villanueva (Gina Rodriguez) is accidentally inseminated with a stranger's sperm by an intoxicated ob-gyn, but the stranger turns out to be a wealthy, sensitive, and handsome hotel magnate, and the two share an on-again, off-again romance for the remainder of the series. In all three of these texts, there is something close to hostility toward the idea of anonymous donor sperm, which is splattered all over a cake in one text, dumped down the sink in another, and callously mishandled by a drunken doctor in a third. The women's reproductive plans must be thwarted to make room for conventional marriage plots.

Infertility comedies equally revel in the idea that sperm sample production is a sexual humiliation to a male partner. In *A Smile Like Yours*, a nurse leads the way to a room labeled "masturbatorium" and points out the many options for pornographic videos: "Anatomy, nature, soft porn, not-so-soft porn, deviant behavior, women with men, women with women, miscellaneous . . . clean linens here, soiled linens there." The matter-of-fact presentation of pornographic material in the sterile clinical environment is itself a joke. In *Daddy's Home* (2015), Brad (Will Ferrell) pulls down his pants and sits down in the sperm sample room only to realize the blinds are not quite closed. Standing up to adjust them, he accidentally knocks down the entire window blind, fully exposing himself to the room next door, where a large crowd is gathered to celebrate a child's birthday party (figure 4.4, top). In *Private Life* (2018), the would-be father sits in an exam room with his pants around his ankles, watching a pornographic video. Unmoved by the video, he tries to change the channel, accidentally turning up the volume instead. When he tries to fix this, he breaks the remote control and must stand up and hobble across the room, pants still down, to fix the volume manually. The sanitary paper cover from the chair sticks to his rear end, floating behind him as he walks (figure 4.4,

Baby Bust • 131

FIGURE 4.4. Daddy's Home *(2015) (top) and* Private Life *(2018) (bottom). Men experience sperm sample humiliations.*

bottom). These scenes are studies in mortification, as if masculine participation in ART is always and necessarily emasculating, a failure of sexual virility.

In *It's Complicated* (2009), Jake (Alec Baldwin) has already raised three adult children with his first wife, Jane (Meryl Streep), when he divorces her and enters into a midlife marriage with a much younger woman, Agness (Lake Bell). Agness wishes to have a child, but Jake's fertility has decreased with age. At his wife's insistence, Jake makes regular visits to a clinic to improve his fertility, but he clearly finds the whole process humiliating and does not share his wife's strong desire for another child. A pan across the waiting room shows several other gray-haired men with their younger wives, all looking bored or irritable. Jake further undermines his own grudging participation in the process of medically assisted fertility by sneaking a medication to control his frequent urination despite a known side effect of decreasing sperm count. When he confides his frustrations to ex-wife Jane, she replies, "Isn't a baby part of the deal when you marry a woman that age?" Jake's resentment and deceptive behavior reveal his assumption that reproductive medicine is an exercise in female control over her male partner, possibly even his karmic punishment for the crime of leaving his wife for a younger woman.

Because the process of sperm donation is framed as a humiliation for the male partner, most of these comedies can find happy endings only by restoring the man's centrality and virility—releasing him, essentially, from the masturbatorium. In *A Smile Like Yours*, the stresses of fertility treatment nearly end the marriage between Jennifer and Danny, so they simply stop trying. Jennifer makes a romantic dinner for her husband and promises that she will "coach" his "slow swimmers" in lieu of further medical intervention. This is a sexually and medically incoherent concept, but sure enough, a brief epilogue shows the couple taking their triplets to a park for an outing. The fact of triplets conjures the specter of ART (which is more likely than natural conception to result in pregnancies with multiples), but here the idea seems to be that Jennifer has somehow elicited such a powerful sexual response from her formerly subfertile husband that his sperm were healed by the power of their love.

Stories of male-factor infertility show a particular need to restore male virility as part of their drive toward a happy and generative ending. Historically, as long as a male partner was not impotent, the female partner was assumed to be responsible for any impairment in the couple's fertility. Modern estimates postulate something more like a fifty-fifty split between male and female factors in the prevalence of infertility among couples who seek treatment, but the close association between infertility and impotence persists. Two recent films about masculine rivalry, *Game Night* (2018) and *Daddy's Home* (2015), use male infertility as a metaphor for the sensitive male partner's lack of virility in comparison with an unpartnered, dangerous male double. *Game Night* is about Max and Annie (Jason Bateman and Rachel McAdams), a pair of game-loving newlyweds trying to start a family. They consult a fertility specialist, who tells Max, "I'm not loving your semen." Atypically, the doctor immediately frames Max's sluggish sperm in terms of male psychological factors, a reversal of the usual emphasis on female perfectionism. She asks the couple if he is feeling anxious or stressed. Max is humiliated by this turn of the conversation and tries to steer the discussion back toward physiology, while Annie suggests to the doctor that perhaps Max is dreading the visit from his wealthy, tall, and very confident brother Brooks (Kyle Chandler). This description piques the doctor's interest, and she asks if Brooks is single, leading a chagrined Max to ask, "So are we done talking about my semen?"

The rest of the film is an action comedy centered around a game night gone wrong when what is supposed to be a staged crime game turns real, revealing that Brooks has amassed his fortune through criminal means. The game requires Max to show greater courage and confidence than his criminal brother, proving his masculinity, while also having soul-searching conversations with his wife in moments of danger. A key element in the crime involves a stolen Fabergé egg (perfectly on theme), which the characters desperately toss around as they evade assorted criminal henchmen. Though the egg breaks in the course of their getaway, eventually all is put to rights, with Max and Annie working together to defeat the villains, rescue a now-deflated Brooks, and solidify their baby plans. Three months later, Annie announces her pregnancy at a game night by drawing a Pictionary clue for "bun in the oven." By defeating his brother and exposing him as a criminal, Max has resolved the conflicts around his masculinity and desire for children, a process that cures his sluggish sperm.

Another portrait of precarious masculinity, *Daddy's Home*, begins with voice-over from main character Brad (Will Ferrell) explaining that he has always wanted to be a dad but cannot have children of his own because of a medical accident at the dentist's office. A brief explanatory flashback shows a dental assistant aiming the X-ray machine at Brad's face but failing to secure it properly, so the apparatus droops downward until it is pointing at Brad's crotch when the distracted technician shoots the X-rays. This backstory of Brad's infertility is already a loaded visual metaphor for impotence, the phallic X-ray machine becoming a limp mirror of Brad's suspect masculinity.

The rest of the film chronicles Brad's marriage to Sara (Linda Cardellini), whose two adorable kids are just beginning to bond with their new stepfather when their biological father Dusty (Mark Wahlberg) comes for an extended visit, angling to displace his rival and reunite with his ex-wife. The comic rivalry between mild-mannered Brad and alpha male Dusty takes many forms, but Dusty's most insidious gambit is to tell Brad that Sara wants another baby. Pretending to be helpful, Dusty secures an appointment for Brad and Sara with a famous fertility specialist who happens to be Dusty's personal-training client. Dusty accompanies them to the appointment, where Brad is humiliated at every turn, most unsubtly when the doctor asks Dusty to drop his pants so that Brad can see what an ideal specimen of human testicles looks like. Ironically, the plan backfires when the doctor later reveals that Brad's sperm count has risen to normal levels as a result of the stimulating presence of a male rival: "In lab rats, whenever another alpha male comes around, it can spike testosterone, driving up sperm counts." By the end of the film, Sara has a new baby. As in *Game Night*, the man's fertility is directly connected to his competition with a more dominant man. The narrative logic of Brad's masculine restoration is here baldly transformed into a wholly make-believe medical diagnosis.

"NOT MEANT TO BE"

Closely related to the mythology of infertility as character flaw, comedies of impaired fertility and miscarriage also often revert to the platitude that "when the time is right," the couple will bear a healthy child. To take an extended example, season 4 (1995–1996) of the sitcom *Mad About You* deals with the growing frustration of the central couple (Paul Reiser and Helen Hunt) with their attempts to conceive over the course of about a year. The show deals sensitively with topics like the two characters' frustration with timed intercourse (S4E10), weird advice from friends and medical professionals (S4E14), and the divisive quality of the two members of the couple being medically evaluated separately, raising questions of which person is responsible for the lack of a successful pregnancy (S4E18). At the same time, the infertility arc on *Mad About You* very much participates in the logic that says a couple will conceive and bear a child when they are emotionally ready. At one point, Jamie is placed under anesthesia during a procedure to evaluate her reproductive capacity, and she has an out-of-body hallucination in which she stands next to the surgeon as he operates on her ("The Procedure," S4E19, April 14, 1996). He tells her that her reproductive organs are fine.

> JAMIE: So, you're saying I'm all right; I can have children?
> DOCTOR: I'm saying there don't seem to be any medical problems.
> JAMIE: What does that mean?
> DOCTOR: It means when the time is right, one way or another, you'll have children.

This idea that Jamie's attempts to conceive are being stalled not by a physical problem but by the fact that her body is waiting until "the time is right" conventionally conflates reproductive health with marital and emotional health and implicitly suggests that some divine force will determine what is "right" with her body—indeed, the surgeon starts to glow with artificial radiance just after this chat.

The remainder of the show's fourth season bears out this dream-state prediction, as the central couple continue to experience infertility while their marriage deteriorates and they nearly divorce, but then they recommit to the partnership in the final episode of the season. Three diegetic weeks later (or roughly the standard time lapse between fertilization and a missed period),

Jamie pees on a stick and smiles. Unfortunately, it's a satisfying narrative solution to tie fertility to emotional readiness, which creates emotionally complex narrative closure for the sitcom season or family comedy. However, this manufactured causality between characters' emotional development and their fertility stigmatizes the condition and falsely ties the inability to conceive and bear children with negative stereotypes about women or couples with insufficient warmth, maturity, or vitality.

Closely tied to this representation of infertility, film and television comedy's relatively sparse representation of miscarriage tends to imply that a pregnancy loss is "for the best" because of the prospective parents' unreadiness or unfitness. For instance, out of the five prospective mothers in *What to Expect When You're Expecting*, the only one who experiences pregnancy loss is the one whose pregnancy is the result of a one-night stand. Although the character goes through a mourning process, the screenwriters' decision that the loss of an unplanned pregnancy would be less tragic than the loss of a planned one reinforces the idea that miscarriage is a tidy outcome for unplanned pregnancies. Even when the subject has been handled with relative sensitivity, as when Gloria Stivic (Sally Struthers) miscarries a wanted pregnancy in the first season of *All in the Family* ("Gloria Has a Belly Full," S1E6, February 16, 1971), the pregnancy loss serves the too-convenient narrative purpose of ending the Stivics' plans to move into their own apartment to gain some independence from Gloria's parents, Archie and Edith Bunker (Carroll O'Connor and Jean Stapleton). Though the miscarriage is sad, by the end of the episode, diegetic normalcy is restored, with Archie and Edith considering a movie while Mike and Gloria embrace, enjoying the prospect of having the house to themselves. Though no one tells Gloria not to mourn her loss, there is no question that her miscarriage was the "best" path forward for the series, which was not ready to disrupt the two-generations-under-one-roof dynamic that it was still exploring in season 1.

From the 1980s into the present, mainstream film and television have frequently used miscarriage to end narratively inconvenient pregnancies, thus avoiding the taboo subject of abortion (discussed further in chapter 5) while also avoiding the tonal changes that would come with children. Given that popular film and television shows are reluctant to represent miscarriage at all, this trope enjoys outsize influence, wrongly tying unsuccessful pregnancies to maternal guilt, ambivalence, or unfitness. This trope is also understandably hurtful to women who experience pregnancy loss and have to counter the idea that they must have said, done, or thought something to cause their bodies to reject the pregnancy or that they are inherently damaged or unworthy.

Even very recent shows that should know better, like the *Sex and the City*

(1998–2004) reboot *And Just Like That . . .* (2021–), have sidestepped abortion plots with convenient miscarriages. Ambitious Lisa Todd Wexley (Nicole Ari Parker) is already raising three children and is on the brink of an enormous career breakthrough when she learns she is pregnant again. Wexley is appalled by the new pregnancy, noting, "Goddammit, I thought it was finally my time" ("The Last Supper Part One: Appetizer," S2E10, August 17, 2023). But the show doesn't even call abortion by its name. Wexley's husband Herbert (Chris Jackson) asks, "Should we be having the other conversation?," to which she replies cryptically, "I've thought about it, but I can't." True to generations of plot evasions, Wexley then suffers a miscarriage and sits around feeling guilty about it, later wondering, "Did I wish the baby away?" ("The Last Supper Part Two: Entree," S2E11, August 24, 2023). The show bypassed an opportunity to fill some of the representational gaps around either Black professional women seeking abortions or the common experience of miscarriage for women over forty and instead chose to reinforce old and bad ideas about the unmentionability of abortion and the myth that maternal ambivalence causes miscarriage.

The most audacious example of a comic text framing a character's miscarriage as "for the best" comes from the comedy drama *Moonlighting* (1985–1989). The show became famous for the chemistry between the characters of Maddie Hayes (Cybill Shepherd) and David Addison (Bruce Willis), who begin a sexual relationship at the end of season 3. Early in season 4, Maddie discovers she is pregnant ("A Tale in Two Cities," S4E4, November 3, 1987), an accommodation to Shepherd's real and complicated pregnancy with twins, which also required her to pretape several scenes and to be absent from much of the narrative action late in the season. When ratings plummeted, the producers decided they no longer wished to pursue the pregnancy plot or incorporate a baby into the storyline. The first episode of season 5, then, ends the pregnancy in miscarriage ("A Womb with a View," S5E1, December 6, 1988).[14]

Rather than show the miscarriage from Maddie and David's point of view, the episode focuses primarily on Baby Hayes (also played by Bruce Willis) inside Maddie's womb, surreally represented by a clear inflated apparatus isolated on a black-painted set (figure 4.5). The fetus is visited by Jerome (Joseph Maher), an elegant gentleman who introduces himself as "an emissary of the creator" and gives Baby Hayes a glimpse of the world and family he is about to enter. The baby has doubts about David and Maddie's constant bickering but ultimately decides he is ready to be born. At that moment, Jerome receives a phone call telling him to cancel the delivery. In the regular diegesis, Maddie grasps her stomach in pain and panic.

When Baby Hayes asks Jerome why his birth has been canceled, the dapper

FIGURE 4.5. Moonlighting *("A Womb with a View," S5E1, December 6, 1988). The womb set features Baby Hayes (Bruce Willis) being visited by a divine emissary (Joseph Maher).*

emissary replies, "You want an answer and I can't give you one. There are reasons. Perhaps these people weren't quite ready to be parents. Perhaps the world wasn't quite ready for this particular family. Perhaps . . . perhaps . . . there's a greater wisdom at work here than mine." He goes on to assure Baby Hayes that he will still be born ("All souls are born") but to a different family. "You're destined to be either Kirk Cameron's little brother or Bill Cosby's grandchild," he promises, referencing two popular family sitcoms (*Growing Pains* and *The Cosby Show*) that were also pursuing pregnancy plots that season. He also assures Baby Hayes that Maddie and David are going to be "fine." "Time has a way of healing these things. Love grows stronger. There really is a reason." This news cheers up Baby Hayes, who joins Jerome in singing "On the Sunny Side of the Street" as the two dance together up a giant white staircase into an unknown beyond.

Moonlighting was known for these occasional flights of fancy and big production numbers, so the episode's surrealist approach to a lost pregnancy is consistent with its trademark emphasis on both diegetic and extradiegetic play. And yet even within the established rules of *Moonlighting*, this episode is weird. This was a miscarriage of convenience for the writers, who were trying to reset the clock to recapture the magic of seasons 1 through 3, when the chemistry between Maddie and David was based on sexual attraction, not weighed down by impending parenthood. Audio commentary from the director and producer on the DVD edition of season 5 of *Moonlighting* contains more notes about the crisis of the show's declining ratings, excessive budgets, and alienation from critics than it does meditations on the experience of miscarriage/stillbirth or the narrative logic of this episode. The show's creators wanted to stop the financial bleeding, and they sought a painless and low-controversy way to end Maddie's pregnancy and the couple's impending parenthood. The fetus who dances off into eternity (to be born on a more suitable family sitcom) sidesteps either the controversy of an abortion plot or the emotional pain of a conventional miscarriage plot.[15]

In the attempt to make this narrative development into something light and simple, however, the show's creators tapped into a number of lazy and hurtful ideas regarding miscarriage, captured in the emissary's toothless platitudes of reassurance. For all the thought and effort that went into the development of the high-concept episode, particularly its special effects and musical numbers, remarkably little seems to have gone into the dialogue, full of clichés like "there are reasons" and "time has a way of healing these things." More damagingly, this raft of platitudes includes a few speculative ventures into the idea that the couple "were not quite ready to be parents," evoking the idea that miscarriages happen for the best. The through line of film and television representations of miscarriage is this idea that pregnancy loss, like infertility, can be traced back to the unsuitability of the prospective parents.

BABY MAMA

The most commercially successful comedy about infertility to come out of the millennial cycle of pregnancy movies, *Baby Mama* (2008) brings together a number of the problematic ideas of its genre peers. This pregnancy comedy, starring buddy feminists and celebrity moms Tina Fey and Amy Poehler, ties itself into knots to transform a story of two women making their own reproductive decisions into a story of two unplanned pregnancies that restore the centrality of heterosexual coupling and the "happy ending" of partnered births. As Dana Stevens notes in her disappointed review, "For all the methods we've invented of making babies—in test-tubes, with turkey basters, in the wombs of other women or event transmen—Hollywood still prefers its leading ladies to put a rock on their fingers and push one out the old-fashioned way."[16]

The first words of *Baby Mama* are "I did everything that I was supposed to do," the start of an expositional monologue by corporate vice president Kate Holbrook (Tina Fey) on the reasons for her delayed childbearing:

Baby Bust • 139

I did everything that I was supposed to do. I didn't cry in meetings; I didn't wear short skirts; I put up with the weird upper-management guys that kiss you on the mouth at Christmas. Is it fair that to be the youngest VP in my company, I will be the oldest mom at preschool? Not really, but that's part of the deal. I made a choice. Some women got pregnant; I got promotions.

The film thus frames its story fully inside familiar stereotypes of infertile professional women, who put corporate success before family. Kate's job as an executive at the fictional Round Earth foods associates her with unpalatable organic foods, smugly fashionable lifestyle trends, and financial security. She lives in a very pretty beige apartment and doesn't seem to have any friends except her sister.[17]

After several attempts to conceive a child on her own through donor sperm, Kate hires a surrogate, working-class Angie Ostrowiski (Amy Poehler). Though Angie begins the movie living in her own apartment, an argument with deadbeat boyfriend Carl Loomis (Dax Shepard) causes her to move in with Kate, wreaking havoc on the older woman's life through her childish antics and outright deceptions. In a typically supernatalist happy ending, Angie eventually gives birth to Carl's baby, while Kate spontaneously conceives a successful pregnancy with her new boyfriend Rob (Greg Kinnear). Kate's sister (Maura Tierney) and the owner of the surrogacy agency (Sigourney Weaver) have new babies, too, just for good measure.

Built on a central dyad of an infertile professional woman and a fertile working-class surrogate, *Baby Mama* is partly about the politics of class within whiteness. Laura Harrison argues that "Poehler's character is decisively cast as an inappropriate mother—her ethnic last name, poor hygiene, bad manners, greed, lies, and manipulation all categorize her as 'white trash,' a category marked by failed whiteness."[18] Her fertility is also figured as out of control, both in her failure to suppress her own sexuality during the implantation window (she becomes pregnant with Carl's child instead of Kate's) and in her life history. At their first meeting, Kate asks her, "So, have you done this before?," and Angie replies, "No, but I know I'm good at gettin' pregnant." The confession of multiple unplanned pregnancies (presumably aborted, since she does not have any children at the start of the movie and there is no indication of miscarriage) suggests a body unruled by Kate's code of tightly contained self-perfection.

The film is at its best when it lets Angie present a running commentary on the absurdities of bourgeois pregnancy culture, pointing out its cruelties through her refusal to suffer. When Kate brings Angie organic food, she replies, "Eh, that crap's for rich people who hate themselves." When Kate takes her to a birthing class, the sanctimonious teacher tries to shame the women who intend to have medically assisted labors: "How many of you are planning on using toxic Western medications to drug your baby for your own selfish comfort?" Undaunted by this description, Angie raises both hands in the air, points to herself, and makes a honking noise of affirmation. When Kate asks Angie to take giant prenatal vitamins, she is unable to swallow them, even when Kate holds Angie's nose and strokes her throat, scolding, "Come on, cats can do this!" Many of these moments involve Kate's attempt to put things into or keep things out of Angie's body, now that Angie is to be the physical receptacle for Kate's fertilized egg. But Angie is stalwart in her refusal, pointing up the absurdity and excess of these physical impositions that treat the pregnant person's bodily comfort as being in direct competition with (instead of harmony with) the health of the fetus.

The film's interest in class and women's bodies also extends to surrogacy guru Chaffee Bicknell (Sigourney Weaver), a bizarre caricature of effortless privilege who serves as a foil to Kate's striving stuffiness. Despite her advanced age (Weaver was fifty-eight at the time of filming), Bicknell has a young baby when Kate first meets her, and Kate comments on her successful use of surrogacy. Bicknell laughs and says, "My husband and I had our baby the old-fashioned way." The reply suggests that surrogacy is unnatural and less prestigious than Bicknell's uncanny lifelong fertility. But while Bicknell presents her effortless childbearing as a sort of honor, the other characters react to it with alarm. At a surrogacy counseling meeting, Bicknell announces yet another pregnancy, shocking the room.

> BICKNELL: That's right, I'm expecting again.
> ANGIE (whispering): Expecting what? A social security check?
> KATE (whispering): I know—it's gross!

The running joke's final payoff happens when Kate rushes Angie to the delivery room: they peek in the open door of another room, where they see a serenely beaming Chaffee Bicknell holding twins, a pink-wrapped baby in one arm and a blue-wrapped baby in the other (figure 4.6). Kate takes a moment to mutter, "Gross," before resuming the rush to get Angie some pain relief.

Bicknell stands in for a culture of celebrity superwomen who seem able to have babies later and later in life. For example, Janet Jackson had a son at age fifty, Laura Linney and Beverly D'Angelo gave birth at age forty-nine, Kelly Preston and Geena Davis at forty-eight, and Holly Hunter and Halle Berry at forty-seven. Because these celebrities do not always reveal the fertility treatments that may have enabled these pregnancies, the public's impression is likely to be that stars possess some combination of great wealth and genetic

Baby Bust • 141

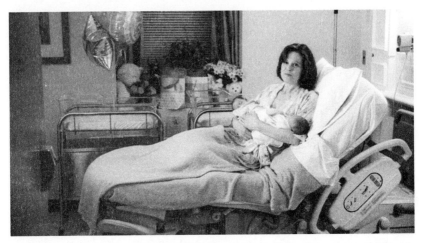

FIGURE 4.6. Baby Mama *(2008). This scene makes a visual joke of the uncanny fertility of Chaffee Bicknell (Sigourney Weaver).*

superiority that makes childbearing possible at any age. Bicknell's infinite fertility also seems to echo the ways large families can be a badge of privilege for those who can afford expensive treatments as well as nannies and other staff to ease the labor of child-rearing.

The repetitions of the label "gross" in the film help push the stigma of ART off Kate, putting her into the solid middle ground between Angie's loose reproductive life and Chaffee Bicknell's truly elite geriatric fertility. But the film is also a bit hard on Kate's decision to use a surrogate, not least in the way the screenplay bends over backward to develop a "better" solution to Kate's infertility by providing her a perfect boyfriend and a conventional pregnancy. Harrison argues that the film's finale undoes the threatening features of surrogacy to arrive at a conservative solution: "The threat of reproduction without men (for Kate) and pregnancy without motherhood (for Angie) is neutralized by the reinstatement of the nuclear family."[19] In this way, the most popular and successful mainstream comedy to deal with infertility treatment in the early twenty-first century did nothing to decrease the stigma of in vitro fertilization (IVF) and surrogacy, settling instead for an ending that invents medically improbable ways to suggest (yet again) that the best cure for infertility comes not from medical treatment but from emotional readiness and good sex.

Baby Mama also struggles with its representation of the racial privileges of each woman's fertility, particularly as reflected by doorman Oscar (Romany Malco), who serves as a confidant to both Angie and Kate and provides a racial subtext to the white women's transactional childbearing. He speaks the line that explains the film's title: "You pay the bills. She have the baby. That's called a baby mama. You ask any black man in Philadelphia." This joke is a nod to the loose ends and unspoken assumptions about race that circulate in the narrative beneath the more visible class struggles. The specter of racial difference lurks around the edges of the film, as when Kate tells her mother (Holland Taylor) that she has applied for an adoption, and her mother implores her, "Don't get a Black baby. I've just had it with all these movie stars showing off," mocking, "'Look at me and my Black baby.'" Though their mother's comments horrify her liberal daughters, *Baby Mama* uses the mother's unfiltered remarks to acknowledge the ways that solutions to infertility frequently incorporate racially heterogeneous family formations through adoption, surrogacy, and donor sperm.

The DVD of *Baby Mama* includes an alternate ending where the adoption application comes through the same day that Kate finds out she is pregnant, culminating in an epilogue that shows her one year later with a Black toddler and a white infant, happily enmeshed in a family celebration. The film's production team may have scrapped this ending, which treats the Black child (on-screen for mere seconds) as a visual joke, but the film remains saturated with unexamined traces of the ways elite modes of family formation are enabled by racial as well as class inequality.

Chaffee Bicknell explains her company's mission in terms of a service economy: "We don't do our own taxes anymore. We don't program our computers. We outsource. And what is surrogacy if not outsourcing?" Kate, acknowledging the reference to global systems of economic inequality, asks, "Wait, you're not saying my baby would be carried by some poor underpaid woman in the third world?" "No," Bicknell replies, pausing to write the idea down, as if it is a new and promising notion she may explore in the future. The moment is played as a joke, but in reality, this kind of international surrogacy arrangement was already booming at the time of the film's production, particularly in India, where international commercial surrogacy generates an estimated $400 million annually.[20] Bicknell goes on to compare surrogacy to nannying, another profession characterized by class and racial differences: "A nanny is a person you trust to take care of your baby after it's born. A surrogate mother is someone you trust to take care of your baby before it's born." Just at this moment, Bicknell's own nanny, played by Filipina American actress Drea Castro, brings her baby into the office for a visit.

These weird, backgrounded, sly acknowledgments of non-white laborers working in support of upper-middle-class family structures point to the whiteness at the core of *Baby Mama* and how (like *Idiocracy*) its focus on intraracial class differences covers for a world of racial privilege that is suppressed as soon as it becomes visible. The casting of good buddies and celebrity mothers Tina

Fey and Amy Poehler further links the two, their off-screen feminist personas covering for the focus on a narrowly white, medically conservative vision of reproductive choice.

PRIVATE LIFE

Tamara Jenkins's 2018 comedy *Private Life* is a story of infertility that foregrounds the alienating and uncontrollable qualities of the treatment process and its outcomes rather than imposing dubious character psychology on the medical void. Rachel and Richard (Kathryn Hahn and Paul Giamatti) are a pair of New York writers in their forties seeking to build their family through either ART or adoption. The film begins with both processes well underway, Rachel and Richard already frustrated and broke from the endless routine of injections, treatments, paperwork, home visits, and payments. Here, the process of adopting or conceiving a child is not presented as a goal that requires romance, maturation, or the resolution of the pair's marital difficulties. Instead, Rachel and Richard are hanging on by a thread, emotionally buffeted by their inability to control either process.

A birth mother strings them along with nightly video calls, even sending ultrasound photos in the mail, before simply abandoning them. They fly to Arkansas to meet her in person only to be left waiting at a roadside restaurant, never to hear from her again. They are left wondering whether the young woman had even been pregnant or simply wanted attention, what the social worker calls an "emotional scam." This experience prompts them to restart the fertility treatments that they had briefly halted, resulting in a painful, expensive, and wearing round of IVF that fails to produce a pregnancy. By pairing the adoption process and medical interventions for infertility together in this way, the film emphasizes how both experiences exact great costs in time and money, emotional investment, frustrating bureaucracy, and heartbreak.

Richard and Rachel pursue both avenues with intensive energy, but there is no evident relationship between their level of effort and the probability of success. They are borrowing money from Richard's brother-in-law, lying to the adoption agency about the fact that they are still pursuing fertility treatment, and growing increasingly irritable with each other as they navigate the stresses of the two demanding processes. As the couple prepare their apartment for a home visit from an adoption agency social worker, Rachel—in the throes of a midtreatment hormonal surge—scrubs the bathroom and storms around the apartment, ranting at her husband while holding a can of abrasive cleanser and wearing nothing but a short T-shirt, the lower half of her body completely exposed. The scene makes visible and literal the sense of vulnerability and exposure she is experiencing, as well as the chaos of their home life, which they are obligated to transform into a tidy portrait of marital stability for the social worker.

Though filmic time is often compressed by editing and montage, *Private Life* makes a motif of the idea of waiting. Richard and Rachel are frequently shown in waiting rooms, always surrounded by a crowd of other patients also waiting for treatment. Rachel takes a lollipop every time she leaves an appointment, a ritual that helps add whimsy to the endless routine. Long, moving camera shots out of car windows represent the slow process of getting from here to there. Time passes in days, meals, seasons, dog walks, and the daily minutiae of the couple's lives as they watch the calendar and the clock. These moments of deferral recall Lauren Berlant's argument that the fraying social fabric of modernity engenders conditions of "cruel optimism," in which "a sustaining inclination to return to the scene of fantasy . . . enables you to expect that *this* time, nearness to *this* thing will help you or a world to become different in just the right way."[21] The desire for a child both animates their optimism and keeps them bound to an immiserating set of rituals oriented toward an uncertain future.

The processes of adoption and infertility treatment also represent a constant process of compromise and brinksmanship, as Richard and Rachel find themselves in sketchy moral and economic territory as the clock runs out on their fertility. Early in the film, Richard's sister-in-law Cynthia (Molly Shannon) tells her husband, "They are like fertility junkies," who will do anything in search of a child. Though Cynthia is portrayed as judgmental and uptight, while Rachel and Richard are warm and human, the film does leave the viewer to ponder the metaphor of addiction as the couple makes one moral, medical, and financial compromise after another in their pursuit of a child. When a doctor recommends that the couple consider another round of IVF using donor eggs, Rachel and Richard reveal that they had previously ruled out this option, disliking the idea of taking genetic material from another person. But another bright line is crossed as they resolve to keep trying.

Deciding that a known egg donor would be preferable to an unknown one, they make the morally dubious decision to ask Richard's step-niece Sadie (Kayli Carter), who is not a blood relation to either of them, to donate her eggs. Sweet and naive, Sadie idolizes her aunt and uncle, still calling Richard "Uncle Cool," a nickname she gave him as a child. Sadie has taken a leave of absence from college, where she does not feel as though she is making progress on her ambition to become a fiction writer, and is seeking mentorship and guidance from her aunt and uncle. She is in a moment of vulnerability, looking for meaning and purpose in her life, and she romanticizes the idea of being a savior to her beloved uncle by providing her eggs. The couple ruminates on

Baby Bust • 145

and recognizes the moral implications of the ask ("She's *so* young," Rachel notes. "That's the point, isn't it?" Richard replies sardonically), but they move forward anyway; Sadie enthusiastically agrees. Sadie's mother Cynthia is enraged, and Rachel tries to placate her: "We're not going through with this without your support." Yet they do go through with it without her support; Sadie and her mother do not reconcile until well into the process, and Cynthia makes it clear that she still does not really approve of the arrangement. The fertility process makes a liar out of Rachel and continually moves past the lines that the couple has drawn, as their need for a child pushes other considerations into the background.

Sadie lives with her aunt and uncle throughout the process of egg donation and transfer, and the home life they establish reveals the greater complexity of their decisions. Sadie, in the throes of a hormonal surge, lays her head in Rachel's lap and begins rambling in ways that uncover her own juvenile fantasy of what she is doing: "And now it's going to be, like, so intense, because a little bit of me mixed with a little bit of him is going to be growing inside of you." The camera tilts upward to reveal Rachel's startled face as she processes this description of the process, which edges uncomfortably toward the incestuous. While Sadie brings a lightness and sweetness to the household—as if in dress rehearsal for the child they hope to have—her presence, her youth, and her candor make it impossible for Richard and Rachel to suppress their own awareness of how asymmetrical and problematic this arrangement is. The film sketches all three characters humanely but does not hide from the moral complexity of the process.

Finally, this donor arrangement culminates in a moment of real medical risk for Sadie. After the egg retrieval, Sadie experiences sudden weight loss, extreme fatigue, and cramping. She confesses to the emergency room doctor that she had increased her dose of follicle-stimulating hormone to improve the chances of a successful donation after being chastised by a clinician for producing a too-small number of eggs. Richard and Rachel are horrified, angry, and guilty over these risks Sadie took on their behalf, but they cannot undo what she did. "It's not their fault," Sadie tells her mother from the hospital bed. "It was me. I was the idiot." The camera pans horizontally past Sadie's worried parents to Richard and Rachel, who look unconvinced that this situation is not in fact their fault. Sadie had taken a foolish risk in a state of emotional agitation, brought on both by the hormones and by her desire to help a beloved aunt and uncle. The process ends in another failed implantation, meaning it has all been for nothing. Not only is Sadie now fully immersed in the feelings of disappointment and self-reproach that often accompany an unsuccessful fertility treatment process, but the kerfuffle over her insufficient

FIGURE 4.7. Private Life *(2018)*. *In the final scene of the film, Richard and Rachel (Paul Giamatti and Kathryn Hahn) wait in a diner, ready to meet a birth mother who is willing to consider them as adoptive parents. The unresolved ending foregrounds the process of waiting, uncertainty, and lack of control central to the experience of infertility rather than resolving the story with a pregnancy or baby.*

eggs also gives her reason to worry about her own future fertility, a new burden with unknown implications.

Moving on from the failed procedure enables a sort of "happy ending" that the procedure itself has failed to produce: Sadie is accepted to a prestigious writing residency at Yaddo, and Richard and Rachel are proud to drop her off there, noting familiar features from Rachel's three residencies at the same estate. Sadie is happy, and it appears that Richard and Rachel's mentorship has helped bring her to this point. They begin to enjoy their lives again, reconnecting to their neighborhood and careers.

A final coda, nine months later, emphasizes the restoration of Richard and Rachel's marriage rather than providing the conventional "happy ending" of a baby (or three). A call comes in from a young woman seeking an adoption arrangement. The film ends with Richard and Rachel waiting to meet the new birth mother in a roadside diner, echoing the site of their earlier disappointment. The only difference is that this time, Richard stands up and joins Rachel on the same side of the table; they hold hands and wait together, facing the door of the restaurant to see if anyone will come through (figure 4.7). The film ends here, the credits rolling over more than a minute of a static shot of Richard and Rachel holding hands and looking toward the door, only diegetic diner noises breaking the uncomfortable silence. This choice to end the film with another wait, not a child, leaves the focus on the characters themselves, their marriage and choices, and counters other film and television comedies of infertility, which nearly always present a new baby as inevitable. The film's emphasis on life in suspension—waiting and hoping and managing expectations—is a particularly vivid representation of how contemporary systems of assisted family formation require total commitment to their means while remaining very uncertain in their ends.

MASTER OF NONE

While *Private Life* represents a step away from an emotional-causality model of infertility, the continued emphasis on coupled, heterosexual white people who have delayed childbearing in favor of career building leaves other aspects of the conventional infertility plot well in place. Few mainstream comedies have filled in greater detail about how fertility issues may be experienced among younger people, non-white communities, queer couples, trans men, or individuals with disabilities.

This chapter concludes with an analysis of a rare exception to this exclusion. Remarkably, the story arc of the little-seen third season of *Master of None* (*Moments in Love*, "Chapters 1–5," S3E1–5, May 23, 2021) follows a difficult fertility journey for a Black lesbian (on-again, off-again) couple, finding observational comedy in all the small details of their experiences.[22] The first two episodes show Denise and Alicia (Lena Waithe and Naomi Ackie) asking Denise's cousin Darius (Anthony Welsh) to serve as their sperm donor and negotiating the terms of that decision. The donation does result in a pregnancy, but Alicia miscarries. The stress of this miscarriage reveals fractures in Denise and Alicia's marriage, and both women have affairs, leading them eventually to divorce.

In episode 4, several years after the divorce, Alicia decides to pursue fertility treatment to become a single mother. This episode is entirely devoted to Alicia's fertility treatments (Waithe does not appear at all) and includes some particularly original insights into how the medical infrastructure of the fertility industry fails single women and queer women. The medical counselor gives Alicia a long monologue on how a woman's fertility declines throughout her thirties, with lower odds of even IVF producing a successful pregnancy for each attempt. The camera remains on Alicia in a long take for the tail end of this conversation, as the two characters share this remarkable exchange:

> COUNSELOR: Your insurance does cover IVF, but it's complicated. We have to prove that you are infertile and that you have been trying to conceive with a partner for six months.
> ALICIA: What does that mean, with regards to me and my sexuality?

148 • It's All in the Delivery

COUNSELOR: The insurance company doesn't have a policy for that.

ALICIA: They don't have a policy for queer people?

COUNSELOR: The insurance company needs a diagnosis code in order to confer benefit. The majority of American insurance companies do not have a code for "gay and desires pregnancy" or "single and desires pregnancy." They have a code for "being attacked by an orca" and they have a code for "being sucked into a jet engine," but they do not have a code for "gay and desires pregnancy."

The counselor goes on to explain the cost of the procedure and the additional costs of using Alicia's preferred sperm donor, Darius, who has to be tested and screened. Alicia notes that if she had a heterosexual partner, there would not be this screening expense, and the counselor confirms that yes, if she had a male sexual partner, it would be understood that she had already taken the risk of exposure, so no screening would be necessary. These granular investigations into how Alicia's lived experience as a single, queer, Black person seeking fertility treatment does not fit within the financial and medical model of American fertility treatment are presented in a way that emphasizes their absurdity and reveals how many assumptions are built into the system about who would or should be seeking medical assistance to bear a child.

Later scenes emphasize how Alicia is going through the process of shots and appointments alone, often isolating her in the frame for long takes. Back in her apartment, loaded up with boxes of syringes and hormonal serums, Alicia must give herself a series of abdominal injections. In other films and shows, it is always a male partner who gives these shots, and Alicia struggles to find the courage to push the needle into her own belly. She calls her mother, who provides moral support: "Thousands upon thousands of women have done these injections, and you're not trying to tell me that you're weaker than all of them, are you? Because I don't believe that, love . . . Furthermore, I have made a down payment on this grandchild, so you can't give up now and lose all my money." Now laughing, Alicia is able to do the shot, marveling, "It's not even that bad!" When she goes to the clinic for a follicle check involving an uncomfortable vaginal ultrasound, the kind technician tells her, "Next time, bring someone to hold your hand." When she comes out of the anesthetic after egg retrieval, the doctor asks if she has a ride home, and Alicia replies that she will just get a car. A quick cut shows her waiting on the curb for an Uber. These moments emphasize the particular challenges of undertaking fertility treatments as an unpartnered person and the simple human need for support through what are often uncomfortable and emotionally difficult medical procedures.

Master of None emphasizes the tedium and uncertainty of the procedure, foregrounding the particular quality of temporal distortion that comes with

FIGURE 4.8. Master of None (Moments in Love, "Chapter 4," S3E4, May 23, 2021). Alicia (Naomi Ackie) tells her mother that her second IVF cycle has succeeded, and she is pregnant.

living one's life by an ovulation clock. When Alicia's first IVF fails to produce a viable embryo to implant, she initiates a second procedure, telling her doctor that it will work this time because she is a "bad bitch" and the doctor is a bad bitch too—using the character development model of infertility for self-support. The show patiently takes the viewer through the entire procedure again, from unpacking the boxes of hormone serum through clandestine abdominal injections in the break room at work, multiple sonograms to assess her follicles, egg retrieval, and this time implantation. The episode's exceptional patience with this process takes the temporal experience of fertility patients seriously, as if the viewer is being invited to sit with the patient through both the banal and the intense moments of the process, as well as the uncanny déjà vu quality of its repetitions. The success rate for IVF is well under 50 percent, so the prospect of a happy outcome, while not impossible, is genuinely uncertain. Presenting every aspect of the procedure twice invites the viewer to consider this uncertainty, as well as the frustration, boredom, and physical discomfort of the long routine.

Episode 4 ends with two phone calls. First, kind nurse Cordelia calls Alicia with good news: the second cycle has succeeded, and she is pregnant. Crying, Alicia proceeds to call her mother. The camera holds her in close-up as she sniffs and says, "Mom?" (figure 4.8). Here the episode cuts to the final credits, a plain lavender screen with white text and a soaring musical score. Alicia's happy ending, like the laughing woman who opened this chapter, is a moment of emotional excess, heightened by the waiting, the struggle, and the uncertainty of the outcome. This final, euphoric image of pregnancy after infertility is earned by the episode's careful attention to the process of wanting and working for a child under conditions that were not built for Alicia and the shape of her life.

CONCLUSION

Private Life and season 3 of *Master of None* make a useful pair of texts to conclude this chapter, because both end on notes of time suspended. Richard and Rachel are left waiting for a child as the credits roll, while Alicia is left rejoicing in a moment that will change everything. Both comedies take pains to show these moments using unconventional temporal techniques, with an uncomfortably long take in the first and a joyfully abrupt cut in the second. This emphasis on how infertility and ART actually bend one's experience of time refocuses the conclusion of each narrative from an earned cause-and-effect outcome to one that is deeply uncertain, a lottery win or loss.

These two texts' interest in the temporal uncanniness of infertility recalls Diane Negra's description of a "postfeminist time crisis," in which women in popular media are increasingly harried, rushed, and stressed by the competing demands of modern life. Negra notes that marital pregnancy is often presented as an antidote to this crisis, as "the pregnant woman is often endowed with cultural permission to slow down and savor time."[23] This idealization of pregnancy as a solution to the temporal crush of modernity is obviously problematic in multiple ways, but it is particularly pernicious in the ways it treats a woman's whole life outside of pregnancy as time that must be optimized amid the crush of modern hustle culture, including optimization for fertility. By finding ways to emphasize instead the temporal distortions, repetitions, ellipses, dead time, and cruel optimism at the affective center of contemporary fertility treatment and adoption practices, *Private Lives* and *Master of None* successfully reframe fertility as a process notable for how little it conforms to generic narrative logics of cause and effect, complication and resolution. The characters may or may not grow as people, they may or may not repair their relationships, they may or may not have great sex; none of this matters to the medical realities of egg fertilization, implantation, and growth. And whether or not each story ends with babies, this separation of character and biology is a good and necessary corrective to a century of bad ideas about infertility.

Baby Bust • 151

Chapter 5

SHMASHMORTION

TERMINATING ABORTION STIGMA THROUGH COMEDY

REPRESENTATIONS OF ABORTION HAVE NEVER exactly been commonplace in mainstream US film or television, but when the subject has appeared at all, it has often appeared in melodramas. The silent film *Where Are My Children* (1916) dramatizes a man's horror upon discovering that his socialite wife has aborted three pregnancies instead of bearing his children. The procedures render her sterile, and they live out their years in loneliness. Another cautionary tale, *The Road to Ruin* (1928), shows a young woman lost to a path of drinking, gambling, sex, and eventually an illegal abortion. As she lies in her deathbed following the botched procedure, "The Wages of Sin Is Death" appears written in fire above her bed. In *Beyond the Forest* (1949), Bette Davis plays an unhappily married character whose illicit lover is not pleased with her pregnancy. Desperate, she throws herself down a hill to terminate the pregnancy, resulting in a fatal case of peritonitis. The daytime soap opera *Another World* featured an abortion plot as early as 1964, when the character of Pat Matthews (Susan Trustman) had an illegal abortion at the urging of her boyfriend Tom Baxter (Nicholas Pryor). The procedure leaves her sterile, and she later shoots the faithless Tom in a fit of rage. In *Valley of the Dolls* (1967), beautiful and fragile Jennifer (Sharon Tate) leaves show business to settle down with lounge singer husband Tony (Tony Scotti), but when she learns he has a debilitating genetic condition, she aborts her wanted pregnancy and begins working in soft-core pornography to support him. Dulling her pain with pills, Jennifer descends into addiction and despair, and she eventually commits suicide.[1]

On the combat medical drama *China Beach* in 1990, Red Cross worker Holly (Ricki Lake) has an abortion and nearly dies from the resulting infection ("Holly's Choice," S3E14, January 31, 1990). On *Grey's Anatomy* in 2011, hardworking doctor Cristina (Sandra Oh) has no ambivalence about aborting an unexpected pregnancy, but her husband disagrees ("Free Falling," S8E1, September 22, 2011). The marriage never recovers and eventually ends in divorce. In *The Ides of March* (2011), a vulnerable young campaign intern (Evan Rachel Wood) aborts a pregnancy that results from her affair with a presidential candidate (George Clooney) and later takes a fatal overdose of pills when the affair and abortion become the subject of political blackmail.

A mode of narrative frequently associated with female audiences, melodrama—whether it takes the form of feature films, soap operas, or TV movies—has provided a useful frame to process the thorny issue of abortion. Melodrama is a genre of moral quandaries and difficult decisions. Peter Brooks traces melodrama's roots to the early Enlightenment and notes its long-standing social role as a secular mode of moral instruction:

> Melodrama is indeed, typically, not only a moralistic drama but the drama of morality: it strives to find, to articulate, to demonstrate, to "prove" the existence of a moral universe which, though put into question, masked by villainy and perversions of judgment, does exist and can be made to assert its presence and its categorical force among men [*sic*].[2]

As a polarizing social issue, abortion suits the melodrama's search for moral coherence in a fallen world. Early melodramas clearly punished abortion with women's death and infertility, while many more recent politically oriented melodramas have flipped this polarity and shown how individual women can experience suffering as a result of regulation, censure, and violence. Suffering is foregrounded either way.

By framing stories about abortion in the generic logic of melodrama, mainstream film and television implicitly capitulate to the idea that abortion is a moral problem to be solved. Gretchen Sisson and Katrina Kimport conducted a content analysis of 310 feature film and narrative fiction television plotlines (1916–2013) in which a character considered abortion. Strikingly, 13.9 percent of these plotlines resulted in the death of the character, either as a result of the procedure itself or because of suicide, an accident, or murder. Although this statistic combines television programs set in the pre-Roe and post-Roe eras, the effect is a generalized sense of risk. Sisson and Kimport report that the actual statistical chance of a woman dying during or after a contemporary medical abortion is "effectively zero." The authors were particularly struck by the fact that if characters even considered abortion, this increased their chances of dying, creating a generalized affective association between abortion and death.[3] Kelly Oliver points out that many of the explicitly feminist melodramas arguing for the importance of abortion rights for women, such as *If These Walls Could Talk* (1996) and *Revolutionary Road* (2008), "have a scary dimension that makes them feel more like cautionary warnings than pro-choice alternatives."[4]

Though these cautionary tales play an important role in educating the public about the history of political struggles for access to abortion care and the fatal consequences of its criminalization, to relegate abortion solely to the realm of melodrama is to cede the point that there is something tragic about the procedure. This dark tone contributes to what Janet Hadley has called the "awfulization" of abortion, a tactic that creates negative emotional associations about abortion to support the movement toward criminalization of the procedure.[5] What would stories of abortion look like if they were freed from this frame? The legacy of forty years of safe and legal abortion could be multiple generations of stories that make visible the ways abortion care is a common procedure that opens up possibilities for women stemming from the right to exercise control over their own bodies and health. To date, this possibility is only beginning to be realized.

In this chapter, I argue that bringing the tool kit of comedy to the subject of abortion provides a necessary alternative to the problems of the melodramatic frame. This tool kit includes a number of key elements that promise new frames for abortion storytelling. These elements, discussed in more detail in the introduction, are as follows:

- Comedy enables satiric critiques that reframe entrenched social and political issues.
- Comedy can activate social bonds, creating a common language of shared experiences cemented by the affective bond of laughter.
- Comedy is a genre of disorder and resists simple or dogmatic ways of thinking.
- Comedy refuses a discourse of shame, providing a frame for breaking social taboos and censures, particularly as regards the body.

Each of these elements is essential to the project of releasing abortion from the melodramatic frame, and this chapter adds a fifth factor that specifically applies to abortion comedies:

Shmashmortion • 155

- Comedy genres seek a happy ending, the absorption of personal or social conflicts into a narrative arc toward reconciliation and community.

The combination of an abortion plot and a happy ending not only reflects the psychological and physiological reality of the procedure for most patients but also fully breaks the myths of danger and misery that have too often defined abortion stories on-screen. Evidence-based research suggests that abortion very much enables "happy endings" for the abortion seeker. A 2013 study conducted by researchers from the University of California San Francisco found that the most common emotion reported by women who had received abortions one week after the procedure was "relief."[6] A longitudinal study found that three years after an abortion, 99 percent of women still felt that they had made the right decision.[7]

Popular media have only rarely reflected these experiences. Instead, from the late 1960s through the present, there have been two significant trends in film and television comedy that function to reinforce an abortion taboo: an emphasis on fetal personhood that treats the fetus as an independent subject, even at very early stages of gestation; and an insincere discourse of "choice" that pays lip service to the option of abortion but implicitly or explicitly stigmatizes the choice to terminate a pregnancy as anathema. This chapter documents the rise and spread of these paired conventions, while weaving in the parallel history of how comedy's tool kit has been used to break these conventions and push back against the visual and verbal rhetoric that maintain the abortion taboo in American popular media.

FETAL PERSONHOOD

Historian Barbara Duden notes that prior to contemporary reproductive technology, the discourse of reproduction relied on a woman's felt experiences of nausea, breast tenderness, and especially "quickening," the fetus's first movements in the womb, for diagnostic information. With modern technology, these felt experiences that invested the woman with authority over her body have been replaced by visual technologies.[8] The woman now knows she is pregnant because she sees a plus sign on a plastic pregnancy test. Fetal development is monitored through ultrasound. These technological changes are not bad in and of themselves, but it is important to recognize that an element of female authority has been ceded here: the regime of feeling has been replaced with a regime of vision, which trumps female authority with medical data that permits greater professional and public surveillance.

In 1965, when *Life* magazine published a series of color fetal photographs by Lennart Nilsson, the idea of the visible fetus immediately caught the public imagination. In the multipage spread, only one photo depicted a live fetus photographed inside the womb. The others were, as the article admitted, "surgically removed for a variety of medical reasons."[9] Careful readers could recognize that this language was a euphemistic reference to abortion, as fetuses cannot survive once they have been "surgically removed" from the womb. And yet, to avoid the grisly impression of obviously dead fetuses, the photos were staged and captioned in a way to suggest that they were still living. Nilsson used unprecedented miniaturized technology to capture the fetus at a scale that was previously impossible and gave the images lighting and color effects to better mimic the appearance of a born baby.[10] Just three years later, Stanley Kubrick's *2001: A Space Odyssey* (1968) cemented the iconicity of the doll-like fetus, here used to represent species futurity at the conclusion of a bleak evolutionary journey. Kubrick's open-eyed fetus floats free in space, erasing the presence of a mother altogether and placing the viewer in direct ethical relationship to the fetus as an impossible independent entity.

This iconicity of fetal personhood has been supported by developments in sonogram technology that similarly lift the image of the fetus out of the mother's body and relocate it to a nearby screen. Lauren Berlant argues that this new 1960s-era concept of the unencumbered fetus, supported particularly by advances in ultrasonography, disrupted earlier understandings of the mother's and fetus's bodies as part of a symbiotic whole: "Prior to the new technology, the mother's expanded body had functioned both as the representation of the fetus's body, and as its armor. The expansion of the fetus to human and even superhuman scale within the frame of the photograph shattered the aura of maternal protection, making the fetus miraculous in a new way, vulnerable in a new way, and human in an unprecedented way."[11] This false impression of fetal independence has underlined a wide-ranging set of social claims about the moral and legal statuses of the fetus that rely on the public's distorted impressions of fetal personhood for their affective power.

Sonogram images still play a medical role in pregnancy care, but they have also taken on a powerful social role for expectant families. Often an ultrasound photo is placed as the first picture in a baby book or used as a pregnancy announcement on social media. Nonmedical boutiques offering higher-resolution 3D ultrasounds that can be transformed into photographs or kept in digital form now exist as a luxury service for expectant parents to get a better look at their future children. This casual social treatment of the ultrasound photo as baby picture has further popularized the visual rhetoric arguing for fetal personhood. There's no question that anti-abortion activists hope ultrasound will play this role. Many recent laws have gone so far as to require a

Shmashmortion • 157

woman to receive a sonogram before she can receive an abortion; these laws clearly hope that seeing the fetal images on-screen will psychologically establish fetal personhood for those who are pregnant, some of whom will then choose not to terminate their pregnancies.

Rosalind Pollack Petchesky has argued that the political movement for reproductive rights has not yet found an icon to counter the iconicity of the independent fetus:

> The strategy of antiabortionists to make fetal personhood a self-fulfilling prophecy by making the fetus a public presence addresses a visually oriented culture. Meanwhile, finding "positive" images and symbols of abortion hard to imagine, feminists and other prochoice advocates have all too readily ceded the visual terrain.[12]

Without obvious ideological intent, pregnancy cinema has followed along with this project of personifying the fetus, in ways subtle and not so subtle. As an extreme example, the mainstream comedies *Look Who's Talking* (1989) and *Look Who's Talking Too* (1990) take the logic of fetal subjectivity literally, using the schtick of wise-cracking adults (Bruce Willis and Roseanne Barr) lending their voices to preverbal babies. Both films begin in the womb, with the drama of sperm meeting egg, and the special effect of a little electrical spark marks the invisible moment when the fertilized egg becomes alive. Both films then give voice to the thoughts of the developing embryos and fetuses, spread out over several scenes that suggest the passage of time (though no specific gestational ages are given for the film's various special-effect fetuses). The intrauterine antics of Mikey and Julie are juxtaposed with the adventures of mother Molly (Kirstie Alley) as she navigates her two pregnancies. The fetuses look like dolls or puppets, cradled in cloudlike pink wombs (figure 5.1).

As visual media, film and television have played a key role in cementing the iconicity of the fetal person and expanding the social role of ultrasound as an essential way of knowing about pregnancy. In pregnancy comedies, ultrasound scenes generally replicate the wider social role of the ultrasound as family-building social enterprise—often literally solving family problems as everyone sets aside their differences to come together for the sake of the expected baby. In comedies of ambivalent fatherhood, they also often serve as the occasion for fathers to recommit to their partners' pregnancies after a period of confusion or ambivalence (as in *Nine Months* [1995], discussed at length in chapter 2). The unfortunate implication is that the pregnant woman does not merit the man's attention, and instead he's forming an intense bond with the independent fetus. The framing of many of these scenes shows the father looking away

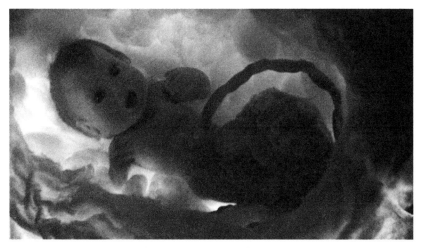

FIGURE 5.1. Look Who's Talking Too *(1990)*. *The fetus as baby doll, complete with hair, and also as speaking subject (voiced by Roseanne Barr), advances the logic of fetal personhood.*

from his pregnant partner as he enters into the sublime and transformative experience of bonding with the ultrasound image (figure 5.2).

It is important to recognize that every one of these fetal images, from the Nilsson photographs to the sonograms, is manufactured, even false. Berlant says, "For although the fetus may be a living thing, it is also, as a representation, always a special effect."[13] These familiar images are now central to our cultural vision of what is happening in the internal space of the pregnant uterus, and that mental concept inherently exaggerates the size, development, and independence of the fetus, which is nearly always pictured at a very late stage of development. The internal, organic embryo and fetus exist only in the context of a woman's body, and the woman must be restored to centrality in this scene for the balance of the representational field to shift.

To counter the logic of the free-range fetus, pregnancy comedies that would support reproductive rights must recontextualize pregnancy as a physical condition that happens within the pregnant person as a social and legal subject. Petchesky calls on advocates for reproductive rights "to image the pregnant woman, not as an abstraction, but within her total framework of relationships, economic and health needs, and desires."[14] Though this work is not as easy to put in bumper-sticker form as the independent fetus, one way to imagine recentering the pregnant person would be to push for more accurate representations of the scale of early pregnancy. In season 6 of *Girls* ("Gummies," S6E5, March 12, 2017), for instance, a pregnant Hannah (Lena

FIGURE 5.2. Fools Rush In *(1997)*. *The father (Matthew Perry) and doctor (Annie Combs) turn away from the pregnant woman (Salma Hayek) to celebrate the fetus on the screen.*

FIGURE 5.3. Girls *("Gummies," S6E5, March 12, 2017)*. *Pregnant Hannah (Lena Dunham) reads a pregnancy website telling her that a six-week embryo is about the size of a lentil, then puts a lentil on her finger to study it.*

Dunham) holds a lentil on one finger after she reads a pregnancy website that tells her that at six weeks' gestation, her embryo is about the size of a lentil (figure 5.3). The camera can barely pick up the tiny lentil, blurring it out in shallow focus, while Hannah's face dominates the frame. This image, which corrects the magnification used in ultrasound technology, helps restore the pregnant individual to a place of centrality in cultural conversations around pregnancy. One challenge to contemporary media producers, then, is to develop more ways of centralizing the pregnant person in the story of early pregnancy and choice.

MAUDE'S LEGACY (1970S AND 1980S)

When film and television comedies have taken on this challenge of broadening the conversation about abortion, they have often done so very successfully. Even before *Roe v. Wade*, the Norman Lear sitcom *Maude* aired a compassionate and biting two-part episode dramatizing Maude's decision to have an abortion ("Maude's Dilemma: Parts 1 and 2," S1E9–10, November 14 and 21, 1972). The first episode begins with Maude returning home from the doctor's office with news of an unplanned pregnancy and mainly consists of her surprisingly frank and funny conversations with family and friends about the choice she will make. Maude's daughter Carol (Adrienne Barbeau) argues unabashedly that her mother should terminate the pregnancy, while her husband Walter (Bill Macy) refuses to take a position, saying he wants whatever Maude wants. Walter regrets his two-year process of waffling about a vasectomy, taking on shared responsibility for their birth control choices and engaging a dilemma of his own. After a period of indecision, Maude has a heart-to-heart with her husband, who confesses over gin rummy, "I think it would be wrong to have a child at our age." Maude responds with relief, embracing him and confessing, "Me too, Walter, me too!" The episode concludes after the two discuss their decision, and the abortion procedure is never dramatized. In the next episode of the series, Maude is no longer pregnant.

There are two main threads to the episode's jokes about Maude's pregnancy, neither of which makes light of abortion itself. Most of the show's humor comes from jokes about Maude's age of forty-seven (actress Bea Arthur was actually fifty at the time of filming) and the incongruity of this elegant, gray-haired matron, already a grandmother, birthing and raising a new baby. When Maude reveals her secret to best friend Vivian (Rue McClanahan), even the words "I'm pregnant" provoke gales of laughter from the studio audience, as Vivian's face registers the shock. Vivian insists that it must be a false pregnancy, and Maude laments, "There's no mistake, Vivian, the rabbit

FIGURE 5.4. Maude ("Maude's Dilemma: Part 1," S1E9, November 14, 1972). Maude (Bea Arthur) asks Vivian (Rue McClanahan) to look away so she can break the news of her pregnancy at age forty-seven. Vivian assumes it is a joke.

died. Laughing, no doubt" (figure 5.4).[15] The other characters gently rib her throughout the episode, using stereotypes of young mothers to point out how incongruous Maude's pregnancy is with her urbane middle age.

A second set of jokes focus more directly on reproductive health and Maude's option to have an abortion. Here the characters' discomfort discussing reproductive health at all creates the tension that amplifies the punch lines.

> VIVIAN: Maude, one thing I don't understand about all this. Weren't you using the pill?
> MAUDE: No, it gives me migraines.
> CAROL: What'd you do, cross your fingers?
> (Maude gives her a wry look.)
> CAROL: Well you're not going to tell me you were using some old-fashioned method.
> MAUDE: Bingo! And the old-fashioned thing happened—I got pregnant.

Maude's daughter Carol serves as the spokesperson for terminating the pregnancy, while Maude uses wry humor to put the brakes on her prodding.

CAROL: You're just scared.
MAUDE: I'm not scared.
CAROL: You are, and it's as simple as going to the dentist.
MAUDE: Now I'm scared.

Maude *is* scared, and the episode shows her using humor as a defense mechanism to force her daughter to back off. When she and Walter finally make the decision, it is in their bedroom, relieved of the pressures of others' expectations.

Norman Lear's particular combination of economic clout and auteur status made room for the risk-taking in this series, though those factors did not protect it from backlash as political forces were just beginning to rally against the legalization of abortion. Initially, CBS asked Lear not to film the episode, but Lear insisted that if this script wasn't approved, the network would have to find something else to fill *Maude*'s time slot, as he refused to develop an alternative script. The network caved. At the time, *Maude* attracted 41 percent of the ratings pie, a formidable share in the era before either cable or home video had begun to siphon off viewers. The first airing of the episodes was carried by all but two CBS affiliates.

Roe v. Wade passed in the span of time between the episodes' original broadcast and the routine schedule of summer reruns, and a new wave of anti-abortion activism, galvanized by the Supreme Court decision, took on *Maude* as its first target. Protesters picketed local stations, and some of them lay down in front of CBS chairman William Paley's car to get his attention.[16] By the time summer reruns came around, thirty-nine CBS affiliates had joined the protest, and all corporate sponsors had withdrawn their support for the rebroadcast of these two episodes. In this half-year span, pressure groups tasted their first success from the new strategy of targeting commercial sponsorship for programming that depicted safe and legal abortion without moral recrimination. This strategy had a powerful effect in shaping the depiction of abortion on the small screen in the decades to come.

For a time, even after anti-abortion activism had all but eliminated abortion from small screens and most movies, a cycle of teen film comedies still incorporated abortion subplots as evidence of their edgy, R-rated status. In the mostly soulless teen sex farce *The Last American Virgin* (1982), abortion creates the conditions for the film's only representation of male tenderness. Nice guy Gary (Lawrence Monoson) loves the angelic new girl in school, Karen (Diane Franklin), but she chooses ladies' man Rick (Steve Antin) instead. When Karen becomes pregnant, Rick cruelly dumps her, but Gary helps her pick up the pieces, telling a tearful Karen, "I'm going to take care of this." He thinks of everything, making an appointment, driving her to the clinic, and arranging for the two of them to spend the weekend at his grandmother's empty house while she recovers. While Gary runs off to pawn his stereo to pay for the abortion, the film uses a montage to link his active, purposeful quest with Karen's passive surgical preparations. The shots include intimate close-ups of Karen's body as she undresses, the camera tilting upward from her panties as she pulls them down, past a full frontal image of her naked breasts, stopping on her tearful face. This camerawork is undeniably exploitative, making Karen into a spectacle of abjection, the provocation for Gary's increasing maturity.

But even with its problematic fetishization of Karen's vulnerability, *The Last American Virgin* is able to imagine abortion as something else besides the occasion for abjection. Karen wakes up from the procedure and immediately begins to laugh out loud, an extraordinary and unexpected moment. Presumably, she is laughing at the fact that Gary is holding a Christmas tree in one hand and a bag of oranges in another, his gifts for her recovery—but her laughter is also an expression of relief that the pregnancy and the procedure are over. The film, then, balances the abortion between tears and laughter, making room for the complexity of Karen's experience, if only for this brief and astonishing moment before rejoining the roller coaster of adolescent male sex farce.

Amy Heckerling's *Fast Times at Ridgemont High* (1987) is a comedy about teenagers behaving like adults, and abortion is treated as just one part of the landscape of their experiences. Heckerling and screenwriter Cameron Crowe develop some of the film's most original insights about 1980s teen culture by emphasizing the economic independence of Ridgemont's young people, who all have jobs at the local mall or side gigs to finance their social lifestyle. The economic independence of these teenagers allows them to be shockingly emancipated from their parents. Even the film's youngest and most naive character, Stacy (Jennifer Jason Leigh), is composed enough to manage the details of an abortion with unmelodramatic precision. When she finds herself pregnant after an awkward sexual encounter with Mike (Robert Romanus), Stacy immediately makes her own appointment at a local clinic. She informs Mike of her decision, and their conversation quickly turns to the $150 cost of the procedure:

> **MIKE:** I suppose you want me to pay for it.
> **STACY:** Half, OK? And a ride to the clinic.
> **MIKE:** Seventy-five dollars and a ride. OK.

Mike then spends an evening calling up all the people who owe him money but is unable to raise the funds and does not show up to give Stacy a ride. Stacy resourcefully persuades her brother to drive her (telling him she is going bowling) and obtains a medically supervised abortion with no immediate emotional or financial support. Her brother figures out the deception and is gallantly waiting for her when she exits the clinic.

When Stacy's friend Linda (Phoebe Cates) learns that Mike has broken his agreement for $75 and a ride, she spray-paints the word "Prick" on his car and "Little Prick" on his locker, shaming him in front of the school. According to the film's teenage moral logic, the only shame and stigma to be assigned in this situation fall to Mike for failing to live up to a financial agreement. Linda's revenge clarifies the film's moral stakes while reestablishing the comic tone.

Although *Fast Times* did not inspire the same level of activism as *Maude*, Heckerling indicates that the film's preview screenings in conservative Orange County shook the studio's already-low confidence in the film: "I got [screening comment] cards where people were just insulting me . . . um . . . for exploiting teenagers and saying that everybody should get abortions."[17] Universal originally gave the film a limited release in August 1982, but it so exceeded expectations that it went nationwide in September, eventually earning $27 million on a $4.5 million production budget even before becoming a classic on video and cable. In 2000, *Fast Times* was included on the American Film Institute's list of one hundred greatest comedies of the twentieth century, not least because of its representational courage. Taken together, these comedies—*Maude*, *The Last American Virgin*, and *Fast Times at Ridgemont High*—modeled how abortion could be worked into narratives that refused the catastrophizing moral logic of melodrama. Abortion is treated as a reasonable medical choice and represents no great threat to the woman's health, her family relationships, her future success, or her past or future identity as a mother.

These early explorations of how abortion might be incorporated in a range of narrative comedies found audiences and modeled some successful strategies for breaking the abortion taboo moving into the legalization era. But later producers for the most part did not build on the groundwork they had laid, instead yielding to the growing pressures from activist groups seeking to reinforce the abortion taboo in service of a political movement for criminalization.

ONLY ONE CHOICE (1990S AND 2000S)

The experience with *Maude* taught religious pressure groups that sponsors were the weak link in the network television ecosystem—they had no aesthetic or ideological commitment to the product, only a profit motive that could be undermined with the threat of controversy. Throughout the 1980s and 1990s, pressure groups like the American Family Association successfully used this tactic to sink television programs that dramatized abortion in any context other than explicit moral condemnation. Broadcast networks generally capitulated to this pressure, leading to showdowns with screenwriters and producers who wanted to dramatize safe and legal choice in programming. CBS forced the producers of *Cagney and Lacey*, for instance, to rewrite a 1984 episode that was to have seen Cagney becoming pregnant and considering an abortion.[18] In the episode based on the revised script, ironically titled "Choices" (S3E7, May 14, 1984), Cagney turns out not to be pregnant, but she still gets a lecture on responsibility from her partner Lacey.[19] A 1989 TV movie about the legalization of abortion, *Roe v. Wade*, purportedly cost NBC $1 million in advertising revenue.[20] In 1990, ABC pulled the abortion-themed episode of *China Beach* from summer reruns after advertiser defections cost the network $780,000 on its first broadcast.[21]

Fox refused to greenlight a 1996 episode of its serial drama *Party of Five* (1994–2000) that would have featured an abortion ("Before and After," S2E18, February 21, 1996). Producer Amy Lippman later remembered:

> We wrote an episode in season two where Julia had an abortion. Then we got a call from John Matoian, "I need to see you." We walked in, and he burst into tears, "I'm so sorry. It's what would happen. It would win awards. We cannot put it on our air." So we had to make an adjustment to the story, that she miscarried, and that was distressing to us because we thought there was real value in showing what a character in that family under those circumstances would do.[22]

The idea that abortion was simply too hot to handle, even in a serial drama, even on the edgy outsider network Fox, had become received wisdom during this time, regardless of the personal convictions of content creators or the real experiences of American women seeking abortion care in these years.

This taboo was durable into the new millennium. In 2009, Fox refused to air an episode of the animated comedy *Family Guy* (1999–) because it depicted responsible mom Lois deciding to have an abortion.[23] Readers familiar with *Family Guy* will know that the show revels in tastelessness, regularly flirting with racist humor, sexual humor, jokes about the degradation of women, and scatology. But an abortion plot was considered too offensive to air.

Television's occasional use of miscarriage as a low-controversy substitute for abortion, as in *Party of Five* and many others, including *Moonlighting* (1985–1989), *Beverly Hills 90210* (1990–2000), *Desperate Housewives* (2004–2012), *Big Love* (2006–2011), and *Girls* (2012–2017), does a disservice both to the real trauma of miscarriage and to the concept of choice.[24] Lauren Rosewarne argues that the trope of the preabortion miscarriage shields characters from the stain of taboo; rather than "becoming 'baby killers,' they were 'gifted' miscarriages which cast them as figures of sympathy."[25] The "gift" of the miscarriage suggests that the woman needs to be relieved from the pressures and consequences of exercising her own choice.[26] (And a gift from whom? Her body? God? The writers' room?) The use of miscarriage as an easy escape valve from the moral question of abortion implies a kind of natural or divine intervention that always resolves things for the best—the same kind of moral logic that abortion opponents use to justify the expectation that all women should carry an unwanted pregnancy to term. Further, the fact that unwanted pregnancies in the movies or TV always seemed to disappear without medical intervention also contributed to the popular misconception that miscarriage can be a natural result of maternal ambivalence or carelessness, a cruel kick in the pants for women who have experienced miscarriages of wanted pregnancies.

When the miscarriage escape valve wasn't activated, the women of 1980s and 1990s film and television nearly always chose to carry unplanned pregnancies to term regardless of extenuating circumstances, such as in *Roseanne* (1988–1997), *Murphy Brown* (1988–1998), *For Keeps* (1988), *Frasier* (1993–2004), *Angie* (1994), and *The Object of My Affection* (1998). While there's nothing inherently wrong with the outcomes of miscarriage or birth—which are part of the spectrum of pregnancy experiences—for any individual narrative, the aggregate effect of their proliferation is to make visible the near-total absence of the third possibility: a safe and legal abortion. This kind of willful avoidance is the very definition of a taboo.

As film and television producers tiptoed around the issue of abortion in these years, a simple desire to appease those on both sides of the issue led to a tepid and misleading discourse of "choice" in comedies of unplanned pregnancy. Kelly Oliver argues that pregnancy romantic comedies have frequently co-opted the language of choice meant to safeguard abortion rights and instead used the word to suggest that there was only one *right* choice: to have the child. "The language of pro-choice is recuperated into the conservative ideals of motherhood as a woman's calling and the fulfillment of her life."[27] Eve Kushner looks back at the end of the 1990s and laments the representational absence: "Abortion exists only as a faux option—something to choose *against*."[28] Many films and television shows of the millennial decades dramatized this idea literally, having characters flee from a scheduled appointment at the abortion clinic, often at a run, as in *For Keeps* (1998), *Sex and the City* (1998–2004), *The Secret Life of the American Teenager* (2008–2013), and *Juno* (2007).

In these years, the political language of choice even became a bit sinister when it was disingenuously channeled into the private dialogue between couples discussing whether to seek abortion. In the 1989 family comedy *Parenthood*, married couple Gil (Steve Martin) and Karen (Mary Steenburgen) learn of their unexpected pregnancy the same day that Gil has quit his soul-crushing corporate job. Overwhelmed, with three children already and now no paycheck coming in, they begin to argue:

KAREN: Why don't you just say what you're really thinking?
GIL: What am I thinking?
KAREN: That I should have an abortion.
GIL: I didn't say that. That's a decision every woman has to make on her own.
KAREN: What are you, running for Congress? Don't give me that. I want your opinion about what we should do. Let's pretend it's your decision, OK? Pretend you're a caveman or your father. What do you want me to do?
GIL: I want . . . I want whatever you want.
KAREN: Well, I want to have the baby.

This dialogue dangerously manipulates the political logic of choice, which exists to preserve women's access to reproductive health services, not to settle disputes within families. When Gil uses political catchphrases as code words for his hope that Karen will have an abortion, she has to call him on his evasions and ask for his opinion. This is not the same as acting like a "caveman" or "your father," figures of patriarchy. The discourse of choice provides a funhouse mirror for this conversation, where the woman appears to be asking for more controlling masculinity but is really trying to ask for her husband to be a responsible agent in a private family decision.

Similarly, in *Fools Rush In* (1997), Isabel (Salma Hayek) tells Alex (Matthew Perry) of her pregnancy, and he immediately seeks out the political discourse of choice to cushion his discomfort:

ISABEL: There's only one thing for me to do . . .
ALEX: Oh, thank God. I understand and I respect your decision. I have always believed in a woman's right to choose.
ISABEL: That's good, because I *choose* to keep this baby.

By parroting the political language of choice, the "sensitive" men in these films are able to preserve their self-image as enlightened liberals who support women. But at a personal level, the viewer can perceive that they are not listening to what their partners want. Having thus paid lip service to the liberal value of choice, the films actually stigmatize abortion as the bad choice, even making it the choice that men would impose on women if they had their way.

Quickly, the absence of stories about abortion became a self-perpetuating cycle, as producers decided not to borrow controversy. *Designing Women* (1986–1993) producer Linda Bloodworth-Thomason was known for her feminist politics, but she steered far clear from the issue of abortion on her hit show, noting, "It's tough when you're doing a comedy and people see that favorite character week after week and remember what happened to her."[29] This desire not to taint a recurring character with a decision that some of the viewing audience will disapprove of led some shows to use a minor character to explore an abortion plot, as in *Beverly Hills 90210*, *China Beach* (1988–1991), and *Friday Night Lights* (2006–2011), or to put a confessed abortion far in a character's past, where it would cause less trouble, as in *21 Jump Street* (1987–1991), *Scrubs* (2001–2010), and *Sex and the City*. When Murphy Brown faced an unplanned pregnancy in 1991, she dreamed of the nine US Supreme Court justices silently wagging their fingers at her in disapproval. This is an odd image of legal ambivalence, given that the court had continued to hold to the precedent of *Roe v. Wade* regarding the constitutionally protected right to abortion. The personification of Murphy's guilt as a panel of black-robed justices suggests the extent to which the procedure still occupied shadowy civic and moral territory in the popular imagination during this era, despite its patent legality.

This taboo held steady for decades. When a saturation cycle of pregnancy comedy movies was released between 2007 and 2015, choice still meant maternity. Many of these films' plots featured unwanted pregnancies, as in *Juno* (2007), *Knocked Up* (2007), *Waitress* (2007), and *What to Expect When You're Expecting* (2012), but as had become typical, the films either ignored the option of abortion or showed characters rejecting it as moral anathema. Famously, the title character of *Juno* (Elliot Page) runs away from the abortion clinic after she has time to consider a protester's remark that her "baby" already has fingernails. *Waitress*'s Jenna (Keri Russell) doesn't explain her decision but just tells the doctor, "I'm having the baby and that's that." This seems to be the general consensus of these movies: that abortion is simply off the table, and the less said the better.

Knocked Up has the courage to discuss the issue at length, but the conversations are full of evasions and assumptions, associating the case for abortion with the worst characters and coldest motives. Ben (Seth Rogen) has a pretty intense marijuana habit, no formal career, and a chaotic social circle, while Alison (Katherine Heigl) has a job but still lives with her sister. While not indigent, both characters are economically vulnerable and have plans for their lives that do not include a baby or each other. When Alison becomes pregnant after a one-night stand, the idea of abortion would seem to be a reasonable one according to the social logic of unwed pregnancy in the context of upwardly mobile, secular Los Angeles residents. And yet the film bends over backward to take abortion off the table, putting the suggestion in the mouths of two amoral and pushy supporting characters. Ben and Alison reject their advice and proceed to form a dubiously happy family. The obvious implication, picked up by every commentator, left and right, is that romantic comedy as a genre simply could not tolerate an abortion. If the film botched the social logic of its characters' worlds, where abortion would have been commonplace, it was adhering to the higher calling of genre logic. Abortions belong in melodramas.

The first mention of abortion comes from Alison's mother (Joanna Kerns), who suggests, rather coldly, that she "take care of" the problem, a scene that makes her, in Ross Douthat's words, "a hissable villain" for suggesting it.[30] She goes on to suggest that Alison follow the model of her stepsister: "She had the same situation as you, and she had it taken care of. And you know what? Now she has a real baby." Alison's mother wears pearls and a starched pastel shirt, communicating class-conscious coldness. As she speaks, Alison leans away from her, physically distancing herself from the idea.

The other suggestion of abortion comes from one of Ben's friends, the abrasive Jonah (Jonah Hill), who offends his friends with his obnoxious remarks, while the more sensitive Jay (Jay Baruchel) responds in horror. *Knocked Up* is a gross-out comedy from Judd Apatow, so the whole point of the movie is for the male characters to say and do taboo things, which they do. The DVD release claims that it's "unrated and unprotected," further boasting of its grossout bona fides. I spent much of the introduction to this book celebrating the movie's pioneering attention to reproductive physiology. These factors make it even more striking that when it comes to abortion, the film clams up, veering off into nervous euphemism. The friends sit around the living room to discuss the problem, while Ben sulks, silently taking hits from a bong.

> JONAH: You know what I think he should do? Take care of it.
> JAY: Tell me you don't want him to get an a-word.
> JONAH: Yes, I do, and I won't say it for little baby-ears over there, but it rhymes with shmashmortion. I'm just saying—hold on, Jay, cover your ears—you should get a shmashmortion at the shmashmortion clinic.
> JAY: Ben, you cannot let these monsters have any part of your child's life, all right? I . . . I . . . I'm gonna be there to rear your child.
> JASON: You hear that, Ben? Don't let him near the kid, he wants to rear your child.

The young men talk as if Ben himself will undergo the procedure: "You should get a shmashmortion"; "You don't want him to get an a-word." The woman is excluded both from the reproductive process and from the comic scene, relegated to a family melodrama with her mother, and she is even excluded from the discussion of her choice, which is instead defined by comically immature homosocial boys. After these alienating-on-purpose meditations on abortion as a choice, the film proceeds to document the now-inevitable coupling of Ben and Alison and the birth of their baby.

Although these two conversations about abortion received most of the attention from critics, nearly every plot event in *Knocked Up* seems framed to suggest that the only appropriate choice is to carry this pregnancy to term. When Ben and Alison go to the ob-gyn for their first prenatal visit, the doctor initially addresses them as Mr. and Mrs. Stone, an outrageous assumption that elicits the barest eye roll from Alison. The doctor asks why they have come in, and Alison responds neutrally, "I took a home pregnancy test and it said that I was pregnant, so here we are." Without inquiring whether she intends to carry the pregnancy to term, the doctor jumps right to the ultrasound, pulling on his gloves and chirping, "OK, let's have a look." He inserts the transvaginal ultrasound probe and interprets the image on the screen for Alison and Ben, pointing out the gray flickers that represent the amniotic sac, the eight- or nine-week embryo, and its flickering heartbeat. Alison looks at the screen: "That . . . that's it?" The doctor again assumes that this young woman will not terminate the pregnancy: "Yeah. Take good care of it. Now the fun part starts. I'll make a picture for ya. That'll be fun." Alison starts crying as the doctor says this, and this seems to be the first time it occurs to him that this is not a planned or wanted pregnancy. He backs away mumbling that he will leave her to get dressed and meet her in his office.

Although the doctor's obliviousness is played for comedy, the film does nothing to condemn the inappropriate and unprofessional healthcare on offer here. The doctor's script for the conversation adheres to the same assumption the rest of the movie makes: that Ben and Alison's coupling and childbearing are inevitable and happy events and will lead to a happy ending.

The "awfulization" of abortion was so overt in *Knocked Up* that what had been a subterranean pattern became explicit. A firestorm of articles targeted the film's manipulative condemnation of abortion as a viable choice. Even the *New York Times*' conservative columnist Ross Douthat seemed a bit perplexed: "No recent movie has made the case for abortion look as self-evidently awful as *Knocked Up*, Apatow's 2007 keep-the-baby farce."[31] *Slate*'s Dana Stevens lamented how decades of political pressure had bent the spines of commercial producers, so that these twisty narrative backflips came to seem not just necessary but reasonable:

> Apatow's reticence on the subject seems to spring less from personal conviction than from the fear of offending his audience's sensibilities.

This kind of Trojan horse moralism is maddeningly common in pop-culture representations of abortion, which seem muzzled, invisibly policed, by either the pro-life lobby or the fear of it.[32]

The phrase "invisibly policed" seems particularly apt in this case. Apatow has commented a number of times on this abortion conversation, and his input often emphasizes abortion's status as a social taboo that will alienate audiences, presumably more so than the jokes about scatological and sexual humor that are at the core of his aesthetic:

> And from the very beginning we knew we wanted to have a moment where Seth and his idiotic stoner friends debate abortion. And we actually improvised for five hours, these guys debating the issue. Some of it you will see on the DVD. And it's very, very funny, but really shocking and disturbing. It may have killed Jerry Falwell. (Laughs.)[33]

Jerry Falwell's death by cardiac arrest was in the news in 2007, so this brief joke is already out of season as a reference to current events, but it still resonates as a bit of a tip to Apatow's discomfort with abortion. Falwell was a founder of the Moral Majority, a conservative organization that lobbied media outlets to promote its evangelical Christian values, including opposition to homosexuality, abortion, and Islam. Most likely, Falwell would not have enjoyed any of Apatow's movies, but this imaginary censure did not particularly impact the films' many jokes about sex, poop, or drug use—and political pressure to stigmatize homosexuality has been more effectively resisted. In 1990, the American Family Association persuaded sponsors to abandon both *China Beach*'s abortion episode and an episode of *Thirtysomething* that showed a gay couple lying in bed together ("Strangers," S3E6, November 7, 1989).[34] Almost thirty years later, *Modern Family* (2009–2020), featuring a married gay couple as part of its central ensemble, regularly drew ten million viewers per episode, and although the fight for full equality is ongoing, mainstream comedy has decisively stopped being scared of backlash around positive representations of gay characters.[35] But long after other taboos have lost their power to frighten skittish executives, abortion has remained a third rail of American commercial comedy, with the ghost of Jerry Falwell still hovering over the proceedings.

I don't mean to argue that Apatow is unique in his aversion to representations of abortion, but the influence of this attitude and his personal influence are far-reaching. As an executive producer on HBO's *Girls*, Apatow advised the series creators not to feature a character's abortion in the pilot. Producer Jenni Konner later explained, "Judd was like, 'Don't lead with it. Like, you

172 • It's All in the Delivery

don't know these characters. You can do any story you want once you know the characters. But you're not gonna' . . . I believe he said, 'It's like having Kramer hold up a puppy and shoot it in the head in the first episode,' or something like that (laughing). It was horrible."[36] This comparison of abortion with puppycide makes explicit the cultural logic that inevitably emerges from film and television's long history of squeamishness about abortion—that it's a terrible thing and will cause audiences to hate a character who chooses it. For at least a generation, commercial film and television have been fetishizing the fetus, treating the subject of abortion as radioactive, banishing it from comedy, and making "choice" a call for childbearing. The cumulative effect of these representational norms, though they may seem tepid on the surface, has been to reinforce the position that abortion is one of the worst things in the world.

PLAYING DUMB

In the years when mainstream narrative comedy had nearly gone dark on the subject of abortion, a number of independently produced texts made audacious interventions into the conversation by skewering the very reverence with which other outlets treated the subject. This cultural work has generally appeared on cable or subscription television or in independent movie theaters, where uncensored material is a prestige branding strategy rather than a commercial liability.

Given the fact that both advocates and opponents of legal abortion cannot agree on the basic terms of the debate (fetus versus baby, pro-choice versus pro-abortion, pro-life versus anti-abortion), it often seems that the debate both reveals and reinforces actual different worldviews, not just different opinions. Simply by choosing a name for each of these concepts, one is taking a side and claiming a set of values. Alexander Payne's *Citizen Ruth* (1996) and Sarah Silverman's *The Sarah Silverman Program* (2007–2010) developed their own interventions into this conversation through the satirical device of the character too naive to understand the codes of each side. Fiction creators have often used "dumb" characters to cut through and reveal the layers of social convention that conceal the mechanisms of political and economic power. The character Lorelei Lee in Anita Loos's *Gentlemen Prefer Blondes* (1925), for instance, speaks openly about the importance of marrying a rich man, her "dumb blonde" candor revealing the transactional nature of traditional gender roles that smart girls are taught to conceal. Similarly, the naive characters of Ruth Stoops in *Citizen Ruth* and Sarah Silverman (the comedian's fictionalized alter ego) ask taboo questions and hold taboo positions simply because they don't know the rules.

Citizen Ruth is a dark comedy telling the story of a young addict (Laura Dern) who has lost custody of four children already and is pregnant yet again. Ruth is a craven, unlikable character; her addiction makes her abrasive, irresponsible, maudlin, acquisitive, and self-centered. She speaks often and earnestly of getting her life together but takes every opportunity to become intoxicated, often just after promising to change her ways. She is not cunning in these deceptions but behaves more like a trapped animal that has learned to cringe and cry and ingratiate to be spared further violence. Though this may sound like the stuff of melodrama, Payne's comedy uses Ruth's feral psychology to pry open the lofty abstractions at the heart of the abortion debate. Ruth has no personal convictions outside her own self-interest, so the discourse of rights, principle, and ethics simply does not compute for her or her situation.

Ruth is a pawn in a political debate not of her choosing, and her lack of interest in playing the role of perfect plaintiff makes her real self an inconvenience to both sides. Ruth's story begins when she is arrested for huffing paint in a parking lot, and when it is revealed that she is pregnant, the judge offers her a reduced sentence if she has an abortion rather than bringing yet another child she cannot care for into the world. A family of anti-abortion activists, led by Norm and Gail Stoney (Kurtwood Smith and Mary Kay Place), immediately seize on her as a symbol, paying her bail and giving her a place to live while they try to persuade her to reject the abortion offer. When Ruth's bad behavior begins to frustrate the socially conservative couple, Ruth is taken in by a pro-choice group led by a lesbian couple who sing to the moon (Swoosie Kurtz and Kelly Preston). The pro-life group, called the Baby Savers, stages a vigil outside the feminist commune where Ruth is staying, trying to get her back to their side, and soon the news media descend, turning Ruth's choice into a public media circus. The national leaders of both movements (an oily preacher played by Burt Reynolds and a pantsuit-clad celebrity spokesperson played by Tippi Hedren) arrive on the scene, and Ruth fields monetary offers from both sides, each hoping to influence her decision.

In the end, Ruth miscarries but tells no one and allows herself to be taken to the abortion clinic on the morning of the scheduled procedure. While the media circus continues outside, Ruth sneaks out of the abortion clinic unobserved, carrying the bribe money in a bag. The final shot of the film shows her walking away down a suburban street, leaving the shouting protesters from both sides of the issue to continue their standoff outside the clinic behind her.

It is something of a standard reading of *Citizen Ruth* that it mocks both sides of the abortion debate equally. Al-Yasha Ilhaam argues that "the film's frankness suggests that because the abortion debate is divided by emotionalism, loaded language, and political rhetoric, the only hope for progress within it might lie in the ability to be of great and deliberate offense to everyone."[37]

According to Janet Maslin at the *New York Times*, the film "has evenhanded fun skewering both sides."[38] The film's ending certainly supports this reading, with Ruth leaving the whole debate behind her, but I do not find the middle section of the film nearly so balanced. While the pro-choice activists are a bit excessive with their self-congratulatory militancy, the pro-life group is subject to a more pointed and political critique. On an individual level, the film ascribes a certain hypocritical sexual perversity to all the men in the Baby Savers: Norm Stoney leers at Ruth through a half-closed bathroom door, mesmerized by the exposed waistband of her thong; Blaine Gibbons, the religious leader played by Burt Reynolds, employs a teenage boy to rub his shoulders and bring him beverages. The film implies that the male group members use their family values discourse to conceal a neurotic and predatory sexuality. On a larger level, the language of the Baby Savers is relentlessly mocked, as their many sentimental rhetorical gestures at fetal personhood fly right over Ruth's head.

The film holds up for scrutiny the rhetoric of the independent fetus, which the fictional Baby Savers employ in their many appeals to Ruth to carry her pregnancy to term. In one scene, they take Ruth to the Tender Care Pregnancy Center, a facility based on real crisis pregnancy centers that exist to steer pregnant women and girls away from abortion services by giving incomplete, incorrect, or sensationalized information.[39] In the fictional clinic, the camera's perspective eschews a traditional shot/reverse shot structure to adopt an unusual angle from Ruth's side of the table, so the viewer sees the two medical providers addressing the camera directly. They look as if they are starring in an infomercial or other highly artificial staged advertisement (figure 5.5). This is all a show.

Ruth informs the nurse that she wants an abortion, but the clinic exists to turn her away from this option, so her perspective is met with multiple redirections. The doctor reverently holds up a plastic fetus and tells her, "At ten weeks, the baby is just about this size." Ruth is not sensitive to the language of reverence: she accepts the model, taps her fingernail against the plastic, says, "Oh, it has a little thing," and tosses it back across the table at the doctor. By handling the model fetus as if it is a toy rather than accepting the clinician's invitation to imagine it as a baby, Ruth undercuts the psychological manipulation of the exercise. The clinicians persist, asking her if she would like a boy or a girl and what she would name it. Ruth is disengaged, giving cursory answers and grudgingly choosing the name Tanya. They seize on this admission and begin to speak with great enthusiasm about baby Tanya, but Ruth does not join in the fantasy. After asking for an abortion three times and being redirected three times, Ruth loses her temper and responds in her candid style, screaming at the clinicians, "What's the matter, are you fucking people deaf?

FIGURE 5.5. Citizen Ruth *(1996)*. *An unusual straight-on camera angle frames the Tender Care clinic workers (Kenneth Mars and Kathleen Noone) as highly artificial and untrustworthy, as if they are starring in an infomercial.*

I want an abortion!" Their pitch thus derailed, the clinicians plant Ruth in front of a video that describes abortions in America as a holocaust comparable to what took place at Auschwitz and Dachau. She leaves the clinic dazed and traumatized.

By refusing to take seriously the political tactics of the pro-life movement, *Citizen Ruth* robs these symbolic gestures of their power. The Baby Savers logo is a cartoonish drawing of a late-stage fetus with overdeveloped face and hair, his hands clasped over his umbilical cord in a way that suggests prayer (figure 5.6). The image alone speaks to the ideology of fetal personhood, with the umbilical cord reaching out to a protective lifesaver, symbolically replacing the mother's womb with the external organization—as if the Baby Savers might reach through the woman's body to save a drowning fetus. The satiric image draws attention to the ways that the woman is erased from the scene of gestation so that the activists can express their mission in terms of a direct ethical relationship to the independent—and distinctly white—fetus. "I love that little Aryan baby," says Payne with a laugh in the DVD director's commentary, tying the anti-abortion political movement to the eugenic valuation of white babies above all others. The both-sides logic of the conclusion is a cover for the fact that the film's most cutting satire is reserved for organized religious opposition to abortion.

Sarah Silverman uses her shock comedy style to take a radically different and more aggressive strategy, rarely seeking the appearance of balance. In an episode of her *Comedy Central* sitcom, *The Sarah Silverman Program*, the

FIGURE 5.6. Citizen Ruth *(1996)*. *The Baby Savers logo features an independent fetus, comically blond, with no reference to the woman or her uterus.*

character Sarah encounters a pro-life group protesting what they describe as the murder of babies. Misunderstanding the group's mission as the salvation of born babies rather than the prevention of abortion, Sarah eagerly joins. The group takes her to the target of their protest, and she is surprised to learn it is an abortion clinic.

> SARAH: I don't get it. So you guys are against abortion? I thought you were just against killing babies.
> PROTESTER: Sarah, abortion *is* killing babies.
> SARAH: I guess I just always thought of babies as, like, little people who cry and poop and sit in cribs. Not like little, like, lumpy things on the side of my uterus.

Silverman uses her character's radical, stubborn illiteracy of cultural norms to cut through the conflation of baby and embryo. With no fear of giving offense, Sarah simply describes the difference between the two. The distortions of development and sentimental language of fetal personhood disappear in her description of "lumpy little things."

Eventually, the trusting Sarah is convinced that abortion is wrong and takes a few minutes to process this shift while sitting on a park bench. The show then cuts to a flashback montage of the character's three previous abortions, audaciously set to the Green Day song "Good Riddance (Time of Your Life)." The lyrics of the song suggest a learning experience but also are positive

Shmashmortion • 177

FIGURE 5.7. The Sarah Silverman Program *("Bored of the Rings," S2E1, October 3, 2007)*. *A flashback montage depicts Sarah visiting the abortion clinic through the years.*

in a way not typically associated with abortion: "It's something unpredictable / But in the end, it's right / I hope you had the time of your life." The montage uses framed photos of presidents on the clinic wall to date Sarah's three abortions, making the political context explicit (figure 5.7). First, as a nervous teenager, she passes by a portrait of Ronald Reagan; then, as a rebellious twenty-something all in black, she takes a moment to plant a kiss on the portrait of Bill Clinton; and finally, as her contemporary self, she strolls past a portrait of George W. Bush. Back on the park bench, Sarah smiles as she remembers the kind clinic staff.

This episode of *The Sarah Silverman Program* willfully rejects the industry norm that says abortion must be handled delicately because some viewers will be upset by the suggestion that it could be an experience defined by support, relief, and care. The abortion debate is so divisive that simply suggesting that clinic visits could be positive experiences has the same potential to shock as many of Silverman's other transgressive jokes about race, sexuality, and the body.[40] Given the ways that mainstream comedies had gone cold on the issue of abortion during the 1990s and early 2000s, these texts' choice to use a dumb protagonist to contest the discursive and affective framing of anti-choice political movements provided a useful rhetorical wedge into the discourse of fetal personhood that was not being challenged in commercial comedy.

OBVIOUS CHILD AND THE COMIC IMPERATIVE

The 2014 Sundance feature *Obvious Child* is exceptionally self-aware of its status as a comedy about an abortion and uses its generic frame quite explicitly to make the argument for why the logic of comedy must be brought to bear on the issue of abortion to banish the formal and informal systems that have conspired to suppress the procedure beneath a culture of taboo and euphemism. *Obvious Child* tells the story of Donna Stern (Jenny Slate), an aspiring stand-up comic in her midtwenties who unexpectedly finds herself pregnant after a one-night stand with a young businessman, Max (Jake Lacy). The setup sounds a great deal like that of *Knocked Up*, and although it seems the producers avoided mentioning *Knocked Up* or Apatow in interviews, it is more than coincidental that *Obvious Child* is nearly a point-by-point reversal of this specific predecessor. Director Gillian Robespierre described her dual intentions for the film in a 2014 interview:

> We really just wanted to combine a lot of things that we felt our culture was suppressing. One is a strong, empowered, funny female lead, and one idea that I feel like has been swept under the carpet is

a realistic abortion that is done safely and with a lot of thought put into it and, you know, has a happy ending.[41]

Though these two items might seem unrelated, they are both specific reversals of *Knocked Up*'s formula, which pairs an unfunny woman with a funny man-child. The asymmetry of their relation to humor helps dehumanize Alison and lock her into the unexplained choice to become a mother. Here Donna is the funny one, while Max is an appreciative audience and straight man, participating endearingly but awkwardly in her jokes. Donna is also the less responsible one, still working a low-wage bookstore job and drinking at night with her comedian friends, though she struggles to get her life together without sacrificing her dreams. Max, we learn, was a star student in business school and now has a steady career.

The comedy is filtered through Donna's point of view, and she speaks often and candidly about bodily functions and other intimate aspects of her life without the kind of rule enforcement associated with highly polished cinematic femininity. And finally, she chooses to terminate her pregnancy and makes this choice public through her stand-up performance. The film explicitly adopts what has been a past romantic comedy plot device, the unintended pregnancy, and then takes it in a direction in which its predecessors were not willing to go. It does so without ceasing to be a comedy and indeed ends with the main characters relaunching their relationship through Max's loving care for Donna on the day of the procedure. In other words, the movie takes precisely the perspectives that *Knocked Up* suppresses and finds that the impregnable female body of its protagonist does not mandate her recusal from the world of humor.

Instead, *Obvious Child* can be understood as being structured around Donna's stand-up monologues, which establish her vulnerability and candor. The film's first words showcase her on-stage comedy:

> I used to hide what my vagina did to my underpants—uh, and by the way, what all vaginas do to all underpants, OK? There is no woman who, like, ends her day with a clean pair of underpants that look like they've ever even come from the store. They look like little bags that have, like, fallen face down in a tub of cream cheese (audience laughs) and then commando crawled their way out.

The movie thus announces that it's going to be about things women aren't supposed to say. The word "vagina" is important here because it is notably direct and also points out through contrast how often women's body parts are referenced by cute euphemisms.

Donna's stand-up is based in mild discomfort, but it doesn't follow the logic of aggressive gross-out humor. She speaks frankly about body parts and sex but does so to amplify her own rawness and exposure rather than to create an impression of toughness. Robespierre revealed that her interest in bodily comedy was not about shocking the audience, but about connecting with them.

> I think that farts are funny, and I think talking about it is not raunchy—I think it's actually quite confessional and vulnerable and makes you a little empathetic too. So I think there's a combination when you talk about what goes in and out of your body that makes it not just really laugh-out-loud funny but also something that other people can connect to you with.[42]

This is something of a thesis statement for the film and perhaps an explanation of how it approaches the challenge of maintaining a comic tone while dealing with the culturally charged topic of abortion. Donna's business professor mother (Polly Draper) does not understand her comedy and sees it as crude triviality: "And now you waste that 780 verbal [SAT score] on telling jokes about having diarrhea in your pants." But her friend Nellie (Gaby Hoffmann) sees both the vulnerability and the boundary breaking in Donna's performances: "What is so great about you is that you are unapologetically yourself on that stage every time, and that's why people love you." The film asks us to understand Donna's stand-up performances as vulnerable and uncensored moments of connection.

Max is straitlaced and kind ("I bet he knows Santa Claus," Donna says) but not completely square. The film frames the relationship with bathroom references and irreverent humor, but unlike the homosocial gross-out humor of *Knocked Up*, which excludes Alison from the male world, the scatology in *Obvious Child* is unisex. Indeed, the first time the audience sees Max, he is in the unisex bathroom of the comedy club, watching Donna put her glass on the sink before disappearing into a stall. It's a brief moment but an important one in that the film is revising the logic of the romantic comedy meet-cute, as it irreverently connects Max's attraction to profane bodily functions. The two get very drunk, then leave the bar together and pee in the street. While he is standing and she is squatting nearby, Max accidentally passes gas, and Donna responds, "Did you just fucking fart in my face?" She collapses against him as he apologizes repeatedly, not knowing if she is laughing or crying. She is laughing, and the two kiss. It is significant that their relationship begins with bathrooms, farts, and crude laughter, mistaken for tears. Women have no responsibility in this film to be clean, maternal, responsible, or emotional, and no responsibility to teach their partners how to grow up.

The replacement of tears with laughter becomes even more significant when Donna discovers she is pregnant and schedules an abortion. The abortion plot is not laugh-out-loud stuff, but the film uses comedy to remove the stigma from the topic of abortion and bring it into the discourse of relational candor established by Donna's stand-up routines. The appointment at a Planned Parenthood clinic is shot and edited to convey a tone of light awkwardness, with the female doctor patiently answering all of Donna's questions and smiling sympathetically at her attempts to make corny jokes. Compared with many predecessors (documented in this volume, particularly in chapters 2 and 3), *Obvious Child* transforms women's healthcare from a site of fear and ignorance of the female body into a wryly normal experience, neither farce nor tragedy nor political rant. When Donna seeks counsel from her mother and Nellie, both women tell her stories of abortions from their own past. Neither woman experienced pain or great fear, and neither regrets her choice. These moments are framed as nurturance, particularly the one where Donna is finally able to bond with her mother, as they are cuddled in bed together, crying and laughing. Because abortion is loaded with cultural shame and secrecy, these moments resonate with the disruptive power of women speaking their own experiences of their healthcare choices, rescued from the realm of taboo, washed in relief.

Donna's final stand-up routine completes the film's argument that comedy must be brought to bear on the subject of abortion, precisely because of comedy's ability to banish taboo. Unless individuals can speak openly about their experiences and own them, craft their stories and invest them with the rebellious energy of comedy, those topics remain shrouded in shame and fear. This routine is a public announcement of both Donna's pregnancy and her impending abortion. The theme of her set is what it means to be an adult woman, including the concept of motherhood. She notes that she's always idealized adult women: "I've always wanted to have just, like, a bra and a blouse and a schedule." Then she transitions to how that vision of adulthood is being complicated by her pregnancy: "The second thing that I would like to say right now out loud, and I'm going to say it out loud right now—out loud right now, I'm fine. Everything's fine. I'm just rolling along with this out loud right now—is that I'm going to have an abortion. OK. OK. Keep breathing— Tomorrow, which is Valentine's Day." The repeated hesitations suggest the significant social barriers to sharing this story in a room full of strangers, even for a professional specializing in confessional comedy. The audience responds to her candor; her admission ramps up the audience's sense of tension, which sets the scene for relief when she provides punch lines.

Some of her statements sound as though they are going to be melodramatic or political but then veer into comedy at the last second, as in this anecdote of telling her mother about the pregnancy and termination: "She actually ended up telling me that she herself had gotten an abortion in the '60s, which is pretty amazing because the bushes were so big then." Just as the opening set was unflinching in its use of the word "vagina," the final set uses the word "abortion" without euphemism—another clear contrast with "smashmortion." What seems like a social risk, a stand-up comedy set about a forthcoming abortion, becomes an opportunity to reject shame, go public, and control the narrative about an experience of the female body.

The final scenes of the film show Max taking Donna to the Planned Parenthood clinic for the procedure. These scenes are simple and quiet, emphasizing the safe and humane qualities of Donna's abortion. Max and Donna joke gently about the medical history forms and about the weather. The camera actually follows Donna into the procedure room and focuses on her face as she receives the sedative and smiles to herself as it takes effect. The scene then cuts to the recovery room, where Donna sits quietly in a pink robe, surrounded by other women in pink robes, all calm but with subtly different facial expressions that acknowledge a complex range of motivations, life stories, and emotions. She makes eye contact with another woman, and they both smile faintly.

The abortion sequence is robbed of all melodrama, demystifying the clinic experience and bearing out Donna's prediction from her stand-up routine that "it's not gonna be the worst Valentine's Day I've ever had." Afterward, Max takes her home, and in this scene, Robespierre takes great care with all the small gestures of nurturing: Max brings her tea, makes some corny jokes with her, tucks a blanket over her, invites her to put her feet up in his lap, and suggests that they watch *Gone with the Wind* (figure 5.8). Donna reminds him, "You know that's like eight hours long, right?" but Max is not deterred.[43] This conversation rather elegantly dramatizes that he has time for her—in fact, the abortion has restored this time for them to get acquainted without the pressure of a ticking pregnancy clock. Recall Petchesky's challenge "to image the pregnant woman, not as an abstraction, but within her total framework of relationships, economic and health needs, and desires." This appealing final image of Donna and Max settled in on the couch—a moment of relief, care, and time restored—models a new way of visualizing an abortion experience, one that centralizes women and the complex networks of their lives—and makes room for happier endings to come.

CONCLUSION

In the evolving US political climate, there seems to be a new urgency and courage among television showrunners and filmmakers interested in telling stories of abortion in the context of comedies. In the first season of Netflix's

FIGURE 5.8. Obvious Child *(2014)*. *In this film, post-abortion care is romance.*

1980s-era wrestling comedy *GLOW*, Ruth (Alison Brie) terminates a pregnancy, and like *Obvious Child*, the show features an extended sequence inside the clinic ("Maybe It's All the Disco," S1E8, June 23, 2017). Ruth's hardboiled manager Sam (Marc Maron) drives her to the clinic and surprises her by posing as her husband during the check-in process, joking with the clinic staff and making Ruth laugh. He offers to wait with her to let her pick out a doughnut after the procedure, adding a note of sweetness to the difficult day. The episode ends with a point-of-view shot from Ruth's position on the procedure table, the camera staring straight up at a ceiling tile painted a calm blue, a signal that someone on the clinic staff has considered the psychological needs of the women who will lie down on this table and has created a little gesture of caring. This final moment similarly asks the viewer to adopt the position of Ruth, to put themselves in those stirrups and consider her vulnerability and her relief.

Several television comedies have similarly taken up the challenge of incorporating abortions into storylines in ways that affect recurring characters, challenging viewers to consider the characters' choices in the context of their multiseason character arcs. In *Crazy Ex-Girlfriend* (2015–2019), the main character's forty-something best friend Paula (Donna Lynne Champlin) has two school-age children already and is studying to advance from paralegal to lawyer. When Paula discovers she is pregnant, her school plans are threatened, but she is surprised when her husband suggests that she has "options" ("When Will Josh and His Friends Leave Me Alone?," S2E4, November 11, 2016). Paula replies, "I'm a married mother of two, OK? Those options are for teenagers the month after winter formal." But she later changes her mind and terminates the pregnancy off-screen. The viewer sees the character recovering in bed, looking tired but untroubled. When the pizza delivery man rings the doorbell, her normally lazy teenage son calls out, "Mom, I'll get it since you just had an abortion." The procedure is not secret or shameful; it is known to her family and supported by them, and it's over in a single episode. That's it.

In *Jane the Virgin* (2014–2019), the main character's mother Xiomara (called Xo, played by Andrea Navedo) does not want any more children and even ended a relationship with Jane's father when she realized that she did not share his desire for a new baby. When Xo unexpectedly becomes pregnant following a one-night stand with a real jerk, she tells her daughter without ambivalence that she intends to terminate the pregnancy ("Chapter Forty-Four," S2E22, May 16, 2016). The abortion happens between episodes, and Xo goes on with her life. When a medical bill arrives at their shared household, Xo's Catholic mother Alba (Ivonne Coll) learns of the procedure and expresses her religious objections to Xo's choice ("Chapter Forty-Six," S3E2, October 24, 2016). The two have a heart-to-heart talk and work it out. In the episodes following the abortion, Xo is not stigmatized, pathologized, or condemned to a life of loneliness and misery. Series creator Jennie Snyder Urman said, "I've seen a lot of the torment and torture of making that choice or considering that choice, but what I hadn't seen is that some women who make that choice are relieved."[44] Indeed, Paula's and Xo's abortions similarly echo the statistical fact that most women who seek abortion care are not teenagers, but women who already have given birth. Like Xo, a majority are also non-white.

Later comic abortion plots in *Shrill* (2019–2021), *Love Life* (2019–2021), *Saint Frances* (2019), *Unpregnant* (2020), and a growing cascade of other examples demonstrate that abortion narratives do not break the comedies they inhabit, but instead invite the viewer to understand the fact of abortion as an aspect of reproductive care, one that enables healthy outcomes for the characters involved. In particular, *Grandma* (2015) and *Unpregnant* are epic comic quest stories that show teenage girls encountering obstacles and condemnation while trying to obtain a legal abortion. In *Grandma*, Lily Tomlin stars as a woman who spends a long day scrounging up the money to pay for her granddaughter's abortion. When they finally arrive at the clinic, the pair encounter a protester who yells, "Your baby has fingernails!"—echoing a line that helped dissuade the title character of *Juno* from her planned abortion in 2007. Tomlin retorts, "Not until twenty-two weeks, genius," as though she is responding to the earlier film and pushing back against the distortions that characterize the movement for fetal personhood.

In *Unpregnant*, Haley Lu Richardson plays Veronica, a Missouri teen who travels with a friend (Barbie Ferreira) all the way to Albuquerque to obtain an abortion without the consent of her Catholic parents. The girls at one point are held against their will by a pair of anti-abortion activists, and when they

Shmashmortion • 185

steal a car to escape, the activists chase them through a Texas field in an RV outfitted as a mobile crisis pregnancy center, the man shouting through a loudspeaker that he wants "to help women make smart, educated decisions."

In both these films, the clinic is a place of safety, refuge, and relief. *Unpregnant*, in particular, makes the clinic a place of warm sunlight and soft voices. A nurse sits patiently with Veronica and explains the procedure in detail, as if also explaining it to viewers at home, paired with visuals showing Veronica going through each step being described. The clinician emphasizes humane elements of the process: how Veronica can choose whether to be sedated or awake, how she doesn't have to look at the ultrasound, and how the procedure will take only ten minutes. As the description ends, a shot of Veronica in the recovery room blurs into a dreamy lens flare and refocuses on the earlier Veronica in the consultation room, where she confesses to the nurse that she is nervous. But in the next shot, the procedure is over, and Veronica steps outside into golden-hour sunlight and hugs her friend. When asked how she is feeling, she answers, "Relieved . . . and hungry." The abortion is the happiest part of the movie, an oasis of calm and care after the girls' perilous and chaotic road trip.

Comic Alison Leiby has said of her stand-up comedy routine about her recent abortion, "I hope that the show helps destigmatize a procedure that should have no stigma. The show has also helped me on a personal level. I needed to laugh through my abortion experience because the alternative—the way my life without the abortion could have turned out—is so upsetting."[45] This canny phrasing draws on the logic that comedy is healing, but it is clear that the trauma from which the comic needs to heal is neither making the decision to have an abortion nor undergoing the procedure. The unplanned pregnancy and the precariousness of abortion rights and abortion access are the real sources of trauma. In a political environment frequently defined by distortion, hyperbole, and shame, these recent interventions present powerful challenges to the limitations of the melodramatic frame. As scholars and activists regroup in the wake of the 2022 Supreme Court decision in *Dobbs v. Jackson*, comedy provides desperately needed tools to reframe abortion experiences through stories of care, community, irreverence, and relief.

Conclusion IT'S ALL IN THE DELIVERY

WHY COMEDY, REVISITED

In the introduction of this book, I explained why I think comedy has been an important lens through which to view pregnancy. Here in the conclusion, I take the reverse shot and explain why I think that a close consideration of pregnancy has an important role to play in social understandings of comedy, specifically comedy created by women. There has long been a perverse connection between the idea that women bear children and the idea that women are not funny. In 1998, Jerry Lewis famously shocked the audience at a retrospective on his life at the Aspen US Comedy Arts Festival when he answered a question about which female comics he admired by noting, "I don't like any female comedians." He followed this up by saying, "A woman doing comedy doesn't offend me but sets me back a bit. I, as a viewer, have trouble with it. I think of her as a producing machine that brings babies into the world."[1] The audience purportedly stood up and left, showing the remark the contempt that it deserved.

Nearly every argument for women's inferiority (intellectual, physical, spiritual) turns on the womb as an inarguable marker of biological difference, so it is perhaps unsurprising that a remarkably similar argument materialized in Christopher Hitchens's notorious 2007 *Vanity Fair* op-ed, bluntly titled "Why Women Aren't Funny," in which he argued, like Lewis, that women are rarely funny unless they are "hefty or dykey or Jewish." (One might be forgiven for being astonished that the editors of *Vanity Fair* saw fit to print this offensive twaddle.) Also like Lewis, Hitchens attributed women's deficit of funniness to the fact that they can bear children: "For women, reproduction is, if not the only thing, certainly the main thing. Apart from giving them a very different attitude to filth and embarrassment, it also imbues them with the kind of seriousness and solemnity at which men can only goggle." He sticks with the childbearing theme for quite a large chunk of the essay, opining purply, "Those who risk agony and death to bring children into this fiasco simply can't afford to be too frivolous. (And there just aren't that many episiotomy jokes, even in the male repertoire.) . . . One tiny snuffle that turns into a wheeze, one little cut that goes septic, one pathetically small coffin, and the woman's universe is left in ashes and ruin."[2]

The idea that women must always be defined by their reproductive capacity is threaded through the essay in this narrowly essentialist way, ignoring trans women, the voluntarily and involuntarily childless, and women who reproduce but also do other things—human women, in other words. Further, the idea that the emotional burden of a child's death falls entirely on the mother is an appalling erasure of fatherhood. Fathers raise children, too, and take on the emotional risk of loving them. To treat this risk as exclusively and biologically female is shockingly reductionist and patently stupid.

But what strikes me most about this analysis is that even when taken in the narrowest possible terms—applied to women telling jokes while visibly engaged in the process of gestating—Lewis and Hitchens remain completely wrong. Pregnancy is both sublime and ridiculous, which is to say a perfect opportunity for comedy. And this idea that pregnancy must always be relegated to the realm of seriousness, sentiment, and even morbidity is shorthand for a certain kind of misogyny that has always sought biological causes to justify the exclusion of women, gestating or not.

While these may seem to be a pair of particularly out-of-touch hot takes from commentators best ignored, Lewis's and Hitchens's attitudes are symptomatic of a particular kind of taboo about women in comedy that centers around pregnancy in a way that is both specific and little recognized. For most of the twentieth century, examples of pregnant women doing stand-up comedy were vanishingly few. In 1967, Joan Rivers appeared on *The Ed Sullivan Show* while visibly pregnant (figure C.1) and made a few mild jokes about how unattractive she felt: "At night when I'm undressed, my husband looks at me and mentally dresses me." Some thirty years later, Sandra Bernhard recorded a stand-up special, *I'm Still Here . . . Damn It!* (1998), wearing a semisheer mesh sheath dress over her pregnant body (figure C.2). She does not mention the pregnancy in the act, though during a break, when an audience member shouts, "How pregnant are you?," she replies, "How pregnant am I?

FIGURE C.1. The Ed Sullivan Show *(1967)*. *Joan Rivers performs stand-up while pregnant.*

FIGURE C.2. I'm Still Here . . . Damn It! *(1999). Sandra Bernhard does not joke about her pregnancy during this special, an adaptation of an off-Broadway show she wrote and began performing before becoming pregnant.*

. . . Just as pregnant as I want to be." This restraint about incorporating the pregnancy into her jokes seems to represent a kind of firewall between Bernhard's comic persona and her personal life as an expectant parent. Her bump, while on display, is off-limits to the content of the act.

It took until the 2010s for pregnancy to become more common among performing stand-up comics and for these performers to incorporate the condition into their material with greater candor and regularity. Earlier generations of stand-up comics were often forced to choose between families and careers, as the travel conditions and social norms of stand-up centered a mobile, isolated, default-masculine laborer and comic persona who could travel the country, work late hours, and spend most nights in smoke-filled rooms telling jokes to drinking people, then sleeping in communal apartments with other itinerant comics. As more women join the stand-up workforce, they have slowly forced changes to these conditions.[3] Christina Pazsitzky (who performs under the name Christina P) explained her own reasoning for continuing to tour in her third trimester in pragmatic rather than ideological terms: "I can't take a year off to have a baby."[4] Josie Long indicated that she worried for her job when she became pregnant: "I don't feel secure enough in my position in the industry to be having a child. No matter how established you are, nothing is a guarantee."[5]

FIGURE C.3. Baby Cobra *(2016)*. Ali Wong uses mobile, aggressive, uninhibited body language in her stand-up routine, countering the idea of pregnant women as fragile or sacred.

Visible pregnancy also changes the way audiences perceive women onstage and amplifies existing sexist ideas about women and comedy. Kara Klenk explained that her pregnancy influenced how the audience received her jokes: "Throughout the entire pregnancy, but in stand-up too, people treat you like you're very fragile. I could feel the audience going like 'Oooh, is she O.K., this precious glass figurine?'"[6] By challenging this understanding of pregnancy as a vulnerable and sentimental condition, stand-up performed by pregnant persons has the potential to alter these fundamentally limiting perspectives on the gestating body—or about the female body as always potentially gestating.

Against this background of misogyny and history of exclusion, Ali Wong's 2016 special, *Baby Cobra*, is a milestone in pregnant stand-up. The comic, seven and a half months pregnant with her first child at the time of taping, uses her body as a performance prop throughout the special (figure C.3). Dressed in a form-fitting knit dress that emphasizes the outline of her pregnant belly, Wong paces the stage in red flats, bending forward to emphasize particular punch lines and sometimes using her body to mime the actions described in her anecdotes.

Most of Wong's jokes are about sex, and on this subject, she is remarkably filthy, taking advantage of the seeming incongruity between her pregnant body and her graphic descriptions of sexual experience. Individual bits cover accidental sex with homeless people, human papillomavirus (HPV), how cunnilingus with white men makes her feel powerful ("I could just crush your head at any moment, white man!"), stimulating a partner's prostate during sex, the relative wetness of her vagina at various ages ("You could just blow a bubble wand with it"), and anal sex. Many of these bits are punctuated with physical movements, as when she tells this story:

> I was very sexually active in my twenties, and as a result, I'm a little bit . . . stretched out down there, OK? So when I finally did anal, I just felt like I got a second chance at life, you know? I was like, "Oh my God! It's like going back in time!" (singing) *A whole new world!* It was magical.

Wong leans forward as she's describing this, mimicking the posture of having anal sex. In a later bit, she talks about how her vagina used to be much wetter when she was younger, an idea that she illustrates by holding her fingers in a V shape in front of her crotch, pretending to flick mucus in different directions at the audience, and announcing gleefully, "I slime you! I slime you! Ghostbusters!" The juxtaposition of her visibly pregnant body and her gleefully profane jokes creates a powerful tension that amplifies the impact of the comedy and challenges the idea of pregnancy as a sentimental condition that somehow overtakes other aspects of her identity.

Wong also addresses the potential losses involved in pregnancy in similarly unsentimental ways. Here is her extended story about miscarriage:

> I'm very grateful to be pregnant and to be this far along, to be seven and a half months pregnant, because last year I had a miscarriage, which is very common—and a lot of women who are in their twenties flip out when they hear that. They're like, "Oh my God, that's so dark and terrible. I can't believe that."
>
> I'm thirty-three. Girl, when you're thirty-three, you'll know plenty of women who have had a miscarriage. It's super common, and I wish more women would talk about it so they wouldn't feel so bad when they go through it. When I told my mom—she's from a third-world country—and when I told her I had one, she was like, "Uh yeah, where I'm from, that's like losing a pair of shoes. It's whatevs, OK?"
>
> And everything happens for a reason. I found out at my six-week sonogram, which is very early. And the doctor says to me, "Oh my God, I see two sacs, which means you're having twins," and I was like "Nooooo!" And then she said, "But what I don't see is a heartbeat." And I was like, "Yeeeees! The Lord is mysterious!"
>
> (audience groans) Don't feel bad, OK? They were the size of poppyseeds. I've picked boogers larger than the twins that I lost.

There's a lot to unpack here, but the material harks back to several of the themes covered earlier in this book: the demystification of miscarriage as a common experience that is relieved of some of its burden when shared, the playfully grotesque repurposing of "everything happens for a reason" that intentionally distorts the familiar saying to transform the doctor's bad news into a shocking celebration, and finally, the use of the poppyseed metaphor to restore perspective so audiences stop thinking of a six-week embryo as morally equivalent to a born baby. Everything about this section of the show challenges viewers to reexamine their sentimental assumptions about miscarriage as a tragic feminine secret.

Wong specifically notes the absence of role models for pregnant women stand-ups: "It's very rare and unusual to see a female comic perform pregnant, because female comics . . . don't get pregnant. Just try to think of one. I dare you. There's . . . none of them." But after her special aired, several other comics had pregnant stand-up specials go into wide distribution, including Natasha Leggero's *The Honeymoon Stand-Up Special* (2018), Wong's own *Hard Knock Wife* (2018), Amy Schumer's *Growing* (2019), and Jena Friedman's *Ladykiller* (2022).

Schumer also plays with the incongruity between sentimental framings of marital pregnancy and explicit displays of sexuality. She jokes about how pregnant women always cup their baby bumps with their hands in photos and says, "I cup the bump . . . in pictures, but I just do it a little bit lower," grabbing her crotch. "'Cause this is the area that got me in trouble in the first place." She notes that others ask her what she's craving and then shouts, "Cock!" with a slightly deranged facial expression. Schumer is candid about the discomforts and embarrassments of pregnancy, lifting her dress to show the audience the two Band-Aids she uses to hold in her distended navel so it doesn't show through her clothes (figure C.4). She explains that she has had hyperemesis (extreme nausea and vomiting) for all five months of the pregnancy, puncturing cultural and legislative ideas that pregnancy is easy or simple, "a miracle." She then connects her physical misery to the labor of stand-up, noting, "I'm contractually obligated to be out here, guys. I'm not like 'I don't care, the show must go on!' I'm like, 'I will be sued by Live Nation.'" This reminder that comedy is work speaks to the ways comedy has only begun to enable women to combine family building with successful careers.

Schumer's most daring joke toys with the idea of abortion on demand:

My husband is a really great sport, he really is. I keep messing with him. Like, I've had a tough pregnancy, so the other day I was like, "Babe, this is kind of too hard for me. I don't think I can do it." And

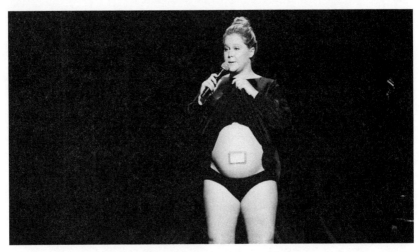

FIGURE C.4. Growing *(2019)*. *Comedian Amy Schumer lifts her dress to show the audience the double Band-Aid that holds in her newly protuberant belly button.*

he's like, "What do you mean?" and I was like, "What do you think I mean? I think I need to get an abortion."

And this was his response, he went (head tilt, disappointed), "Really?"

I was like, "No. What?!" (sarcastically) "I'm going to announce it on Instagram and then I'm gonna be like, 'Actually, forget it, I don't like it.'"

The idea that Schumer might abort her visible pregnancy seems rooted in a new generation of political activism around reproductive rights following the end of *Roe v. Wade*. Comedy writers and performers are showing greater willingness to address abortion in their work, in defiance of long-standing taboos and commercial concerns. Natasha Leggero makes a similar joke in *The Honeymoon Stand-Up Special* when she says, "I'm pregnant! Please hold your applause—I'm still in the abortion zone. I'm gonna decide after this set." Jena Friedman turns to the side to show the audience her belly in profile and says, "I'm twenty-seven weeks pregnant, and I think I'm gonna keep it." These comics are making a point that wanted pregnancy and abortion are not opposites, but part of the spectrum of reproductive experiences that must be connected and protected as essential human rights. These are "good" pregnancies precisely because they are occurring under the conditions of choice in the United States, imperiled though they may be. I take these jokes to indicate that the performers do not want their pregnancies to be co-opted under the logic of "good" sentimental womanhood that is often used as a bludgeon against abortion rights.

Friedman, in particular, uses her pregnant belly to punctuate a ferocious assault on anti-abortion ideas of all kinds. Unlike Wong or Schumer, who use the top-heavy posture of pregnancy as broad physical comedy, Friedman performs her set in a dark room, wearing dark clothing, so that her belly is almost invisible in many of the camera's angles (figure C.5). In this way, she brings the belly forward as a prop only in specific moments, usually to joke about the absurdities of fetal personhood or maternity culture. She jokes, "I feel guilty not getting an abortion while I still had the chance. Sorry, while *we* still had the chance." Here Friedman rubs her belly, then kisses her hand and touches her bump, imitating the gestures and corny sentimentality of pregnancy within a certain kind of online maternity culture. "I feel guilty not getting an abortion while the two of us fully formed humans still had the chance." Though she began writing and performing the material before becoming pregnant, some of Friedman's jokes are possible only when using her belly as a prop, "As I said, I'm twenty-seven weeks pregnant, so I'm right on the cusp. In some states, abortion is totally legal. In others, I could walk into a bank and be like, 'Nobody move!' (holds finger gun to belly) 'Nobody move! I've got a hostage with more constitutional rights than me. Hand over the money.'" It's remarkable that the belly prop here is almost exclusively used for jokes about reproductive justice rather than for body humor or to punctuate jokes about sex or beauty culture.

Like Wong, Friedman also uses her stand-up set to break down social stigmas about miscarriage: "I'm at that age where a lot of my friends are having kids—sorry, miscarriages. A lot of my friends are having miscarriages, because they're cool, hahaha. They spent their twenties traveling, taking improv classes (aside: Zip! Zap! Zop!) they waited to have kids—miscarriages—same thing after thirty-eight." Here Friedman makes her voice high and squeaky: "Girls have kids—bleh, boring." She then flexes her arm muscles and deepens her voice: "WOMEN MISCARRY." The idea that miscarriage is a badge of strength and maturity is both ludicrous and weirdly comforting for the ways it runs counter to either the tragic or not-ready framings that have historically animated the subject.

Finally, Friedman connects the issues of miscarriage and abortion as common reproductive experiences made worse by stigma, secrecy, and legislative overreach:

You guys are so scared. You guys are so scared. What you need to realize is that everybody miscarries. That is a children's book that hasn't

Conclusion • 195

FIGURE C.5. Ladykiller *(2022)*. *Jena Friedman's black clothing and background make her bump invisible from certain angles, so she has the option to feature it as a prop or not over the course of the special.*

been written yet: *Everybody Miscarries*. We just don't talk about it because you guys react like this.

But while we're not talking about it, they are legislating it. They are criminalizing it. In Indiana, there is a law where they want women who miscarry to have to bury the goop—and there's no words for the by-products of conception, so let's just call it Gwyneth Paltrow's lifestyle brand.

I don't know. We just have to talk about this stuff, but it's hard to talk about. It's hard for female comics to talk about our period onstage, let alone one with an elbow.

Yeah, that's one of the worst jokes I ever wrote. There's one worse one coming up. It was so funny for about seven weeks and then it died.

The audience's discomfort, their groans and awkward silences, are essential to the structure of this string of jokes. The tension of this subject is further amplified by the comic's own pregnant body, a condition by which she anchors her authority on reproductive politics. Friedman uses that tension to evoke laughter, opening up the idea that miscarriage, abortion, and pregnancy do not need to be occasions for ghastly seriousness.

I left the subject of pregnant stand-up for the end of this book because the work of these comics provides such rich and incisive examples of why comedy must be brought to bear on the subject of pregnancy that they bring the analysis forcefully home. *It's All in the Delivery* has traced a history of mostly bad ideas about the gestating body over the course of more than a century, from Hays-era prohibitions against even mentioning the subject through more recent but equally foolish musings about the incompatibility of wombs and punch lines. What these bad ideas have in common is precisely the solemn sanction of anti-feminist cultural norms, which impose meanings on the process of gestation that emerge from fear, ignorance, and rank misogyny and then legislate those ideas into reality.

The funny pregnant woman, speaking for herself, is kryptonite to these bad ideas, simply by virtue of her physical and subjective coherence on the stand-up stage. She is self-evidently not a sacred vessel, not a talking fetus, not a projection of a male partner's needs or fears, not a cautionary tale, not a sentimental ideal. With an hour's worth of jokes, some of them about pregnancy and some of them not, these pregnant stand-up comics remind audiences of the subjective experience of the gestating person, their undiminished wit and intelligence, and the ways that pregnancy does not eliminate other elements of a person's identity, such as audacity, sexuality, or political activism. Most importantly, these shows use the asymmetrical power dynamics of stand-up comedy to ask audiences to sit passively and listen to the stories of a pregnant person, something rare indeed in narrative media. Finally, the rise and reign of the pregnant stand-up provides models for bolder, more inclusive, more irreverent, and more humane ways to represent pregnancy and reproductive justice in popular media. These strategies are (pardon the final pun) long overdue.

ACKNOWLEDGMENTS

Many thanks to the brilliant and patient editorial team at the University of Texas Press, especially Jim Burr, Mia Uribe Kozlovsky, Sarah McGavick, Laura Gauggel, and Joyce Bond, as well as two anonymous readers for their generous, insightful, and incredibly useful comments.

I am grateful to have benefited from institutional support and research leave to focus on this project, thanks to the Dodge Family College of Arts and Sciences at the University of Oklahoma (OU). This book was also supported by my wonderful colleagues in the Department of Film and Media Studies, particularly Chairs Joshua Nelson and Man-Fung Yip. Financial support was provided by the University of Oklahoma's Office of the Vice President for Research and Partnerships and the Office of the Provost.

I send warm thanks to Scott McGee and Alfred Martin for helping me screen some hard-to-find materials. Krista Kurlinkus was a wonderful coach and consultant in the early stages of writing and helped get the project launched with joyous momentum. Liorah Golomb was always quick to help me find library resources. I am also grateful for the writers and facilitators of the London Writers' Salon, which has been the supportive community I needed in the last few years of writing and revising coming out of the pandemic.

It was a stroke of tremendous good fortune that this project was supported by a manuscript development workshop sponsored by the OU Arts and Humanities Forum. Thanks to Forum Director Kimberly Marshall, external reviewers Linda Mizejewski and Kathleen Rowe Karlyn, and my OU colleagues Joanna Hearne and Jennifer Holland for the generous gift of their time, expertise, and incredible kindness in providing their feedback on the manuscript, all of which helped give the work exactly the glow-up it needed.

I thank my remarkable mother, Rosalie Sturtevant, for basically everything. My cherished emerita colleague Joanna Rapf gave me excellent feedback on chapter drafts for this project, on top of two decades of support, mentorship, and inspiration. And my dear friend Amanda Cobb Greetham reminded me to celebrate every step along the way to completion.

Finally, I appreciate the love and support of my family, especially my husband Jim and our amazing kids, who have been part of this work since its inception. I love you boundlessly.

NOTES

Introduction. What to Expect When You're Expecting (to Read This Book)

1. Associated Press, "'Doonesbury' Strip Rankles Some Papers," *New York Times*, March 12, 2012, http://www.nytimes.com/2012/03/12/business/doonesbury-strip-on-abortion-rankles-some-newspapers.html.

2. Eyder Peralta, "Michigan State Rep Barred from Speaking after 'Vagina' Comments," NPR, June 14, 2017, http://www.npr.org/sections/thetwo-way/2012/06/14/155059849/michigan-state-rep-barred-from-speaking-after-vagina-comments.

3. This incident inspired the name of Lady Parts Justice League, a reproductive rights comedy group founded by *Daily Show* cocreator Lizz Winstead. The organization has since changed its name to Abortion Access Front to be inclusive of trans and nonbinary people who can become pregnant. https://www.aafront.org/lady-parts-justice-league-name-change/.

4. Amy Biancolli, "'The Back-Up Plan': Chick Flick Nirvana," *Houston Chronicle*, April 22, 2010, http://www.chron.com/entertainment/movies/article/The-Back-Up-Plan-1712759.php.

5. Kathleen Rowe Karlyn, "Comedy, Melodrama, and Gender: Theorizing the Genres of Laughter," in *Screening Genders*, ed. Krin Gabbard and William Luhr (New Brunswick, NJ: Rutgers University Press, 2008), 161.

6. E.g., E. Ann Kaplan, *Motherhood and Representation: The Mother in Popular Culture and Melodrama* (New York: Routledge, 1992); Mary Ann Doane, *The Desire to Desire: The Woman's Film of the 1940s* (Bloomington: Indiana University Press, 1987); Tania Modleski, "Time and Desire in the Woman's Film," *Cinema Journal* 23, no. 3 (1984): 19–30.

7. Linda Williams, "'Something Else Besides a Mother': *Stella Dallas* and the Maternal Melodrama," *Cinema Journal* 24, no. 1 (1984): 3.

8. Molly Haskell, *From Reverence to Rape: The Treatment of Women in the Movies* (New York: Holt, Rinehart and Winston, 1974), 66.

9. Lucy Fisher, *Cinematernity: Film, Motherhood, Genre* (Princeton, NJ: Princeton University Press, 1996), 115.

10. "Fictional pregnancy is almost never funny," notes Parley Ann Boswell. Though the whole logic of this book obviously runs counter to Boswell's observation, I do understand what she is getting at here, as generations of filmmakers and showrunners have struggled with how to manage the tone of pregnancy comedy and often find humor in other

things, such as fatherhood or consumerism rather than the experiences of pregnancy itself. Boswell, *Pregnancy in Literature and Film* (Jefferson, NC: McFarland, 2014), 14.

11. Henri Bergson, *Laughter: An Essay on the Meaning of the Comic* (New York: Macmillan, 1911), 6.

12. Sara Ahmed, "Affective Economies," *Social Text* 22, no. 2 (2004): 117–139, https://doi.org/10.1215/01642472-22-2_79-117; Raul Perez, *The Souls of White Jokes: How Racist Humor Fuels White Supremacy* (Stanford, CA: Stanford University Press, 2022), 10.

13. Sara Ahmed, *Living a Feminist Life* (Durham, NC: Duke University Press, 2017), 246.

14. Arthur Koestler, *The Act of Creation* (London: Hutchinson, 1964), 35.

15. Luce Irigaray, *Sexes and Genealogies* (New York: Columbia University Press, 1993), 85.

16. Angela Carter, *The Sadeian Women: An Exercise in Cultural History* (London: Virago, 2000), 109.

17. Mikhail Bakhtin, *Rabelais and His World*, trans. Helene Iswolsky (Bloomington: Indiana University Press, 1984), 4–15. Originally published as *Tvorchestvo Fransua Rable* (Moscow: Khudozhestvennia literatura, 1965).

18. Bakhtin, *Rabelais and His World*, 21.

19. Kathleen Rowe, *The Unruly Woman: Gender and the Genres of Laughter* (Austin: University of Texas Press, 1995), 33.

20. Mary Russo, *The Female Grotesque: Risk, Excess and Modernity* (New York: Routledge, 1994), 1.

21. Rowe, *Unruly Woman*, 30.

22. Rowe, *Unruly Woman*, 30.

23. Dorothy E. Roberts, *Killing the Black Body: Race, Reproduction, and the Meaning of Liberty* (New York: Vintage Books, 2017), 9.

24. Susan E. Klepp, *Revolutionary Conceptions: Women, Fertility and Family Limitation in America, 1760–1820* (Chapel Hill: University of North Carolina Press, 2009), 107.

25. Jennifer Ellis West, "Technology Knows Best: The Cultural Work of Hospital Birth in 21st Century Film," *Literature and Medicine* 29, no. 1 (2011): 113, https://doi.org/10.1353/lm.2011.0307.

26. Sen. James Lankford (@SenatorLankford), X (formerly Twitter), August 12, 2022, 1:00 p.m., https://twitter.com/SenatorLankford/status/1558181535181709312.

27. Jennifer L. Holland, *Tiny You: A Western History of the Anti-abortion Movement* (Oakland: University of California Press, 2020), 7.

28. E.g., Richard Corliss, "Not Knocked Out by 'Knocked Up,'" *Time*, June 7, 2007, http://content.time.com/time/arts/article/0,8599,1630498,00.html; Dana Stevens, "Unplanned Parenthood: What 'Knocked Up' Gets Wrong about Women," *Slate*, May 31, 2007, http://www.slate.com/articles/arts/movies/2007/05/unplanned_parenthood.html; Ross Douthat, "*Knocked Up*, Again," *Atlantic*, June 9, 2007, https://www.theatlantic.com/personal/archive/2007/06/-i-knocked-up-i-again/54457/.

29. "Katherine Heigl Talks about Marriage, Ratings Ploys, and Why She Thinks *Knocked Up* Is Sexist," *Vanity Fair*, January 1, 2008, http://www.vanityfair.com/news/2000/01/katherine-heigl200801.

30. Stephen Rodrick, "Judd Apatow's Family Values," *New York Times Magazine*, May 5, 2007, http://www.nytimes.com/2007/05/27/magazine/27apatow-t.html.

31. Tania Modleski, "An Affair to Forget: Melancholia in Bromantic Comedy," *Camera Obscura* 29, no. 2 (86) (2014): 143, https://doi.org/10.1215/02705346-2704652.

32. The blurring effect is likely because *Knocked-Up*'s production company had not secured copyright or fair use rights to the video that was not used in the final film. Nevertheless, the blurring has the effect of rendering the video content taboo and unwatchable for the viewer.

33. Ian Caddell, "Birth Scene Crowns Saucy 'Knocked Up,'" *Straight*, May 23, 2007, http://www.straight.com/article-92214/birth-scene-crowns-saucy-knocked-up.

34. Inbar Maayan, "The Miracle of Life (1983), by NOVA," *Embryo Project Encyclopedia*, November 19, 2010, https://embryo.asu.edu/pages/miracle-life-1983-nova.

35. Daniel Robert Epstein, "Spike Lee Believes 'She Hate Me,'" *Screenwriter's Utopia*, August 3, 2004, https://www.screenwritersutopia.com/article/d1902168.

36. *Knocked Up*, IMDb, 2007, http://www.imdb.com/title/tt0478311/business?ref_=tt_dt_bus.

37. "What to Expect and the Pregnancy Bible" featurette included with *What to Expect When You're Expecting*, directed by Kirk Jones (Santa Monica, CA: Lions Gate Entertainment, 2012), DVD.

38. The too early/too late contrast is also used by Kelly Oliver, *Knock Me Up, Knock Me Down: Images of Pregnancy in Hollywood Films* (New York: Columbia University Press, 2012), 18.

Chapter 1. Confinements

1. Jane M. Gaines, "First Fictions," *Signs: Journal of Women in Culture and Society* 30, no. 1 (2004): 1293–1317, https://doi.org/10.1086/421882, 1313.

2. Guy-Blaché did interesting work in representing the appearance of pregnant bodies, even beyond these examples. The 1898 "trick" film, *L'Utilité des Rayons X* (*The Usefulness of X-Rays*), shows what appears to be a pregnant woman being stopped at a customs station and inspected. An X-ray contraption reveals contraband in "her" belly, and the station agents remove the smuggler's costume, revealing a guilty man in disguise.

3. Ignaz Semmelweis, *The Etiology, Concept, and Prophylaxis of Childbed Fever*, trans. and ed. K. Codell Carter (Madison: University of Wisconsin Press, 1983).

4. Judith Walzer Leavitt, *Brought to Bed: Childbearing in America, 1750 to 1950* (New York: Oxford University Press, 1986), 38.

5. Richard W. Wertz and Dorothy C. Wertz, *Lying-In: A History of Childbirth in America* (New Haven, CT: Yale University Press, 1989), 79.

6. Wertz and Wertz, *Lying-In*, 80.

7. Dressmaker Bryant's name was Lena, but she chose to name her business Lane Bryant after a bank officer made the spelling error on an account application. https://www.jewishvirtuallibrary.org/lena-bryant-malsin.

8. "They Sell to Bashful Customers," *Changing Times: The Kiplinger Magazine*, May 1951, 16.

9. Wertz and Wertz, *Lying-In*, 149.

10. The pre-code melodramas that turn on unwed pregnancy (or technically wed but somehow tragic and socially condemned pregnancy), on the other hand, are too numerous to count, including *The Sin of Madelon Claudet* (1931), *Born to Love* (1931), *Mary Stevens, M.D.* (1933), *Torch Singer* (1933), *Christopher Strong* (1933), *Only Yesterday* (1933), *The Secret of Madame Blanche* (1933), *Finishing School* (1934), and *Dr. Monica* (1934). For a comprehensive treatment of the "fallen woman" film, see Lea Jacobs, *The Wages of Sin: Censorship and the Fallen Woman Film, 1928–1942* (Madison: University of Wisconsin Press, 1991).

11. Olga J. Martin, *Hollywood's Movie Commandments: A Handbook for Motion Picture Writers and Reviewers* (New York: H. W. Wilson, 1937), 178. Martin was Production Code Association chief Joseph Breen's former secretary at the time of the book's publication.

12. Jennifer Ellis West, "Technology Knows Best: The Cultural Work of Hospital Birth in 21st Century Film," *Literature and Medicine* 29, no. 1 (2011): 106, https://doi.org/10.1353/lm.2011.0307.

13. Leavitt, *Brought to Bed*, 140.

14. Andrea Tone, *Devices and Desires: A History of Contraceptives in America* (New York: Hill and Wang, 2001), 178.

15. Rickie Solinger, *Pregnancy and Power: A Short History of Reproductive Politics in America* (New York: New York University Press, 2005), 124.

16. The descriptions here are based on the 1929 film version (directed by Frank Craven and Richard Rosson), as the 1920 adaptation is considered lost.

17. For a thorough and fascinating archival account of Sturges's back-and-forth with studio and PCA authorities during the making of *The Miracle of Morgan's Creek*, see Preston Sturges, *Four More Screenplays*, ed. Brian Henderson (Berkeley: University of California Press, 1995).

18. Diane Jacobs has argued that the film's satire uses the figure of the crowd to dramatize the mob mentality that can overrun state institutions: "For in Morgan's Creek, private and public space are indistinguishable. Crowds swell not only on the streets and in the meeting halls, but in homes and yards with gates around them. Crowds are America's majority. Myths to the contrary, they're not noble or kind or understanding—merely susceptible." Diane Jacobs, *Christmas in July: The Life and Art of Preston Sturges* (Berkeley: University of California Press, 1992), 297.

19. "'People Will Talk' with Cary Grant and Jeanne Crain," *Harrison's Reports*, August 18, 1951, 150.

20. "People Will Talk," *Modern Screen*, November 1951, 24.

21. Philip K. Scheuer, "'People Will Talk' Laughter Uneasy but Cast Scores; 'Francis' Returns," *Los Angeles Times*, August 30, 1951, A8.

22. "The Screen in Review: 'Not Wanted,' The First Independent Film Produced by Ida Lupino and Anson Bond, Opens at Globe," *New York Times*, July 25, 1949, 11.

23. The first visible sitcom pregnancy predates *I Love Lucy*. Perhaps because television was so very young, another program about a young married couple called *Mary Kay and Johnny*, which aired during the 1948–1949 season on NBC, proceeded with its shooting schedule despite the visible pregnancy of its star, Mary Kay Stearns. Network notes indicate, "References are kept within bounds and camera treatment has so far been acceptable with no squawks from anybody." Robert Pondillo, *America's First Network TV Censor: The Work of NBC's Stockton Helffrich* (Carbondale: Southern Illinois University Press, 2010), 109.

24. This pilot was shot but did not air in the original run of the series. The recovered episode first aired on CBS in 1990 as a special presentation.

25. Jess Oppenheimer, *Laughs, Luck . . . and Lucy: How I Came to Create the Most Popular Sitcom of All Time*, with Gregg Oppenheimer (Syracuse, NY: Syracuse University Press, 1999), 199.

26. Michael McClay, *I Love Lucy: The Complete Picture History of the Most Popular TV Show Ever* (New York: Barnes and Noble, 2001), 70.

27. Larry Wolters, "44 Million See Lucy Show Day Her Son Is Born," *Chicago Tribune*, January 24, 1953.

28. Arthur L. Charles, "'Now We Have Everything,'" *Modern Screen*, April 1953, 32, 84.

29. *The Opposite Sex* is a remake of George Cukor's *The Women* (1939). The 1939 version, per convention, reduces Edith's pregnancy to a reference to a doctor appointment and another character asking her, "How's the little mother?," followed by a letter announcing the baby's birth. The original play by Clare Boothe Luce (1936) is far more graphic than either film version, with a breastfeeding scene and talk of cesarean scars.

30. Bosley Crowther, "Screen: Father-in-Law; Family Comedy, 'Full of Life,' at Astor," *New York Times*, February 13, 1957.

Chapter 2. Hysterical Fatherhood

1. In this chapter, I use the binary designations male/female and mother/father to describe identity categories that privilege some bodies over others, within a system that bases social gender identity on phenotypical sex assignment. When I talk about male "appropriations" of pregnancy, I am referring exclusively to cishet men, not trans men who can become pregnant. It is my hope that by examining the ways pregnancy has long been understood as an asymmetrical and binary experience, this study can help pave the way for more expansive and inclusive ways of understanding pregnancy as something other than an occasion for heteromasculine panic.

2. For more on this critical convention, please see Linda Mizejewski and Victoria Sturtevant, introduction to *Hysterical! Women in American Comedy* (Austin: University of Texas Press, 2017).

3. Scott Donathan, "'VF' Covers Up outside N.Y.," *Advertising Age*, July 15, 1991, 8.

4. William Marsiglio, *Procreative Man* (New York: New York University Press, 1998), 113; Sherry Velasco, *Male Delivery: Reproduction, Effeminacy, and Pregnant Men in Early Modern Spain* (Nashville: Vanderbilt University Press, 2006), 8.

5. Velasco, *Male Delivery*, 9.

6. K. Horney, "The Flight from Womanhood," *International Journal of Psychoanalysis* 7 (1926): 324–329, reprinted in Karen Horney, *Feminine Psychology*, ed. Harold Kelman (New York: W. W. Norton, 1973), 60–61. Horney herself did not use the term "womb envy" but is credited with originating the idea.

7. See Velasco, *Male Delivery*.

8. Paul M. Levitt, ed., *Vaudeville Humor: The Collected Jokes, Routines, and Skits of Ed Lowry* (Carbondale: Southern Illinois University Press, 2006), 401.

9. Richard W. Wertz and Dorothy C. Wertz, *Lying-In* (New Haven, CT: Yale University Press, 1989), 182.

10. Brittney Cooper and Bambi Haggins offer thoughtful meditations on what the "loss" of Bill Cosby's reputation has meant for generations of African American audiences. Cooper argues that the myth of respectability politics was never going to save Black communities but nevertheless mourns, "And while most have resolved that we must let Bill Cosby go, the letting go feels like letting go of a little bit more of our hope." Brittney Cooper, "Black America's Bill Cosby Nightmare: Why It's So Painful to Abandon the Lies That He Told," *Salon*, July 9, 2015, https://www.salon.com/2015/07/09/black_americas_bill_cosby _nightmare_why_its_so_painful_to_abandon_the_lies_that_he_told/. Haggins recalls a childhood immersed in Cosby's work, consumed by eight-track tapes, *I Spy*, and *Fat Albert*, and carefully traces the generational meanings of Cosby's particular brand of respectability politics and how its reception had already changed in the years leading up

to his public disgrace. Bambi Haggins, "Losing Cosby," *Flow*, October 26, 2015, https://www.flowjournal.org/2015/10/losing-cosby/.

11. [Daniel Patrick Moynihan], *The Negro Family: The Case for National Action* (Washington, DC: Office of Policy Planning and Research, US Department of Labor, 1965), commonly known as the Moynihan Report, https://www.dol.gov/general/aboutdol/history/webid-moynihan.

12. Sarah Arnold, *Maternal Horror Film: Melodrama and Motherhood* (New York: Palgrave Macmillan, 2013), 162.

13. The sex of the child is further marked in the film by the fretting of a boorish supporting character played by Tom Arnold, desperate for a boy after his wife has already given birth to three girls.

14. This quotation is sometimes attributed to Steinem and sometimes to fellow feminist and frequent speaking partner Florynce Kennedy. In a 2012 interview with the *Humanist*, Steinem attributes the joke to an Irish taxi driver in Boston, who heard Steinem and Kennedy in the back of the car discussing the book Kennedy coauthored with Diane Schulder, *Abortion Rap*, and offered the quip as a spontaneous aside. Per the subject of the book, the saying stuck because it was funny. Jennifer Bardi, "*The Humanist* Interview with Gloria Steinem," *Humanist*, August 14, 2012, https://thehumanist.com/september-october-2012/the-humanist-interview-with-gloria-steinem/.

15. *Saturday Night Live*, "Weekend Update," October 13, 2012.

16. The 1984 comedy *All of Me* plays with a similar theme in the supernatural joining of characters played by Lily Tomlin and Steve Martin. At one point, the possessed Martin muses, "What if I got pregnant?" The uncanny physical experience of having one's body either possessed or impregnated is an intolerable assault on the bodily autonomy of the male subject.

17. Beverly J. Camhe, "How I Got Arnold Schwarzenegger Pregnant in 'Junior,'" *Fatherly*, September 15, 2015, https://www.fatherly.com/play/how-i-got-arnold-schwarzenegger-to-star-in-my-movie-about-a-pregnant-guy.

18. Ivan Reitman, *Charlie Rose*, November 22, 1994, https://charlierose.com/videos/18278.

19. Julia Cooper, "No Vagina in Sight: The Queer Case of *Junior*," *cléo: A Journal of Film and Feminism* 2, no. 2 (2017), http://cleojournal.com/2014/08/21/no-vaginas-in-sight-the-queer-case-of-junior/.

20. Emily Martin, "The Egg and the Sperm: How Science Has Constructed a Romance Based on Stereotypical Male-Female Roles," *Signs* 16, no. 3 (Spring 1991): 489.

21. Martin, "Egg and the Sperm," 493.

Chapter 3. Bad Pregnancies

1. Adam Johnson, "'Idiocracy' Is One of the Most Elitist and Anti-social Movies Ever—Why Do Liberals Love Referencing It?," *AlterNet*, March 3, 2016, https://www.alternet.org/2016/03/idiocracy-has-one-cruelest-and-anti-social-plotlines-youll-find-hollywood-movie-why-do.

2. Examples of Black men with this name include *Blazing Saddles* star Cleavon Little and Cleavon Barris, the character James's real name on the sitcom *Everybody Hates Chris* (2005–2009). I can find no prominent white men named Clevon or Cleavon.

3. John Hartigan Jr., *Odd Tribes: Toward a Cultural Analysis of White People* (Durham, NC: Duke University Press, 2005), 115. Precarious or failed whiteness is also a particularly

fraught category in an era when the far right has capitalized on the resentments of a white underclass by promising to restore their sense of racial superiority while failing to address the material conditions of poverty and underemployment in economically precarious communities, white or nonwhite.

4. See Stephen Jay Gould, *The Mismeasure of Man* (London: Penguin, 1997). Alfred Binet's IQ test was originally designed to help identify opportunities for special education of students who would otherwise have been labeled "backward" or "moron." Later proponents of a hereditarian theory of IQ perverted this intention by treating the score as heritable and fixed, an "objective" way to measure the value of individuals and classes of people. Tests were also designed in ways that privileged dominant cultural knowledge, effectively loading the dice against the out-groups whose low scores were then taken as definitive proof of genetic inferiority. Public policies, including immigration restrictions, were frequently based on this pseudo-scientific proof of genetic blight.

5. Richard J. Herrnstein and Charles Murray, *The Bell Curve: Intelligence and Class Structure in American Life* (New York: Free Press, 1994).

6. Herrnstein and Murray, *Bell Curve*, xxi.

7. See Bernie Devlin, Stephen E. Fienberg, Daniel P. Resnick, and Kathryn Roeder, eds., *Intelligence, Genes, and Success: Scientists Respond to "The Bell Curve"* (New York: Springer-Verlag, 1997).

8. Dorothy Roberts, *Killing the Black Body: Race, Reproduction, and the Meaning of Liberty* (New York: Vintage Books, 2017), 157.

9. "Crack Babies Overwhelm Child Welfare System, Senate Says," *Brown University Child Behavior and Development Letter* 6 (April 1990): 6, quoted in Roberts, *Killing the Black Body*, 157.

10. Laura E. Gómez, *Misconceiving Mothers: Legislators, Prosecutors, and the Politics of Prenatal Drug Exposure* (Philadelphia: Temple University Press, 1997), 24.

11. Alfred C. Kinsey, Wardell B. Pomeroy, and Clyde E. Martin, *Sexual Behavior in the Human Male* (Philadelphia: W. B. Saunders, 1948); Alfred C. Kinsey, Wardell B. Pomeroy, Clyde E. Martin, and Paul H. Gebhard, *Sexual Behavior in the Human Female* (Philadelphia: W. B. Saunders, 1953).

12. Frank F. Furstenberg, *Destinies of the Disadvantaged: The Politics of Teen Childbearing* (New York: Russell Sage Foundation, 2007), 12.

13. Although this scene is set in the 1920s, the joke is very much linked to a later era. The historical Fanny Brice never spoofed pregnancy this way, and the scene was fabricated for the Broadway production and later this film.

14. Kelly Oliver, *Knock Me Up, Knock Me Down: Images of Pregnancy in Hollywood Films* (New York: Columbia University Press, 2012), 103.

15. Appallingly, Harris has been virtually shut out of the industry in the subsequent years and, as of this writing, has not directed another feature following this remarkable debut.

16. Richard Brody, "The Still Astonishing 'Just Another Girl on the I.R.T.,'" *New Yorker*, January 24, 2020, https://www.newyorker.com/culture/the-front-row/the-still-astonishing -just-another-girl-on-the-irt.

17. Jamal Batts points out the significance of Tyrone's Jeep, which promises Chantel a way off the I.R.T. (public transportation) and out of the crowded neighborhoods that comprise her world. Jamal Batts, "Just Another Girl on the I.R.T.: Queer Takes on Another Girl," SFMOMA, July 2018, https://www.sfmoma.org/read/just-another-girl-irt/.

18. Beth Coleman, "Subway Rider: Leslie Harris's Low-Budget Trip," *Filmmaker*, Winter 1993, https://filmmakermagazine.com/archives/issues/winter1993/subway_rider.php.

Notes to Pages 96–104 ⁕ 207

19. Julie Phillips, "Growing Up Black and Female: Leslie Harris's 'Just Another Girl on the IRT,'" *Cinéaste* 19, no. 4 (1993): 87.

20. Dan Quayle, "Address to the Commonwealth Club of California," May 19, 1992, http://www.vicepresidentdanquayle.com/speeches_StandingFirm_CCC_1.html.

21. Quayle, "Address to the Commonwealth Club."

22. Jimmie L. Reeves and Richard Campbell, *Cracked Coverage: Television News, the Anti-cocaine Crusade, and the Reagan Legacy* (Durham, NC: Duke University Press, 1994), 217.

23. Bonnie J. Dow, *Prime-Time Feminism: Television, Media Culture, and the Women's Movement since 1970* (Philadelphia: University of Pennsylvania Press, 1996), 153.

24. Jacey Fortin, "That Time 'Murphy Brown' and Dan Quayle Topped the Front Page," *New York Times*, January 26, 2018.

25. Carla Rivera, "Talk of 'Family Values' Termed Veiled Racism," *Los Angeles Times*, July 27, 1992, WB3.

26. Michael Wines, "Views on Single Motherhood Are Multiple at White House," *New York Times*, May 21, 1992, 1.

27. As Bonnie Dow points out, the show takes pains to represent Murphy as sexually restrained, as when Murphy tells her friend Frank, "I have sex about as often as we get a Democrat for President" ("Uh Oh: Part 2," S4E1, September 16, 1991). Dow, *Prime-Time Feminism*, 151.

28. Gillian Brockell, "How 'Murphy Brown' Became a Target for Dan Quayle's Moralizing," *Washington Post*, September 27, 2018, https://www.washingtonpost.com/history/2018/09/27/how-dan-quayles-speech-about-black-poverty-became-murphy-brown-speech.

29. Fortin, "That Time."

30. Brockell, "How 'Murphy Brown' Became a Target."

31. Brockell, "How 'Murphy Brown' Became a Target."

32. Bill Clinton, "State of the Union Address," January 24, 1995, https://millercenter.org/the-presidency/presidential-speeches/january-24–1995-state-union-address.

33. "In the wake of the Columbine shootings, the theme *gun-toting high school kids* is highly questionable." Jeff Strickler, "'Sugar and Spice' and Nothing Nice," *Minneapolis Star Tribune*, January 26, 2001.

34. Kathleen Kingsbury, "Pregnancy Boom at Gloucester High," *Time*, June 18, 2008, http://content.time.com/time/magazine/article/0,9171,1816486,00.html.

35. Jane Brown, "In Cluster of Teen Pregnancies, 'Juno' Comes to Life," interview by Mike Pesca, *The Bryant Park Project*, NPR, June 26, 2008, https://www.npr.org/transcripts/91906103?storyId=91906103.

36. B. E. Hamilton, L. Rossen, L. Lu, and Y. Chong, "U.S. and State Trends on Teen Births, 1990–2019," National Center for Health Statistics, July 8, 2021, https://www.cdc.gov/nchs/data-visualization/teen-births.

37. Transcript of Oral Argument at 56, Dobbs v. Jackson Women's Health, 597 U.S. 215 (2021) (No. 19-1392), https://www.supremecourt.gov/oral_arguments/audio/2021/19-1392.

38. Dobbs v. Jackson Women's Health, 597 U.S. 215, 42n46 (2022) (No. 19-1392), https://www.supremecourt.gov/opinions/21pdf/19-1392_6j37.pdf.

39. Rickie Solinger, *Wake Up Little Susie: Single Pregnancy and Race before Roe v. Wade* (New York: Routledge, 1992), 164–177.

40. Solinger, *Wake Up Little Susie*, 164–177.

41. The United States has many other parallel histories of forced child relinquishment, particularly the separation of Indigenous babies and children from their parents. Native children were forced into abusive government-run boarding schools in the 1800s, a practice that gave way in the 1950s to the so-called Indian Adoption Project, which targeted Native American families with charges of neglect or abuse in order to transfer children to non-Native custody. The 1978 Indian Child Welfare Act was put in place to halt these abuses, but high-profile controversies in recent years have highlighted how parental resources often trump family or tribal claims in family court. See Elizabeth Hidalgo Reese, "The Long History of Native American Adoptions," *Harper's Bazaar*, November 30, 2022, https://www.harpersbazaar.com/culture/features/a42097413/native-americans-scotus-adoption/.

42. Rickie Solinger, *Beggars and Choosers: How the Politics of Choice Shapes Adoption, Abortion, and Welfare in the United States* (New York: Hill and Wang, 2002), 70–80.

43. Margaret Atwood, *The Handmaid's Tale* (Toronto: McClelland and Stewart, 1985).

44. Solinger, *Wake Up Little Susie*, 9.

45. [Daniel Patrick Moynihan], *The Negro Family: The Case for National Action* (Washington, DC: Office of Policy Planning and Research, US Department of Labor, 1965), https://www.dol.gov/general/aboutdol/history/webid-moynihan.

46. Jean Strauss, "In *Juno*, Adoption Pain Is Left on the Cutting Room Floor," *USA Today*, March 19, 2008.

47. Strauss, "In *Juno*."

48. Richard Dyer, *White: Essays on Race and Culture* (London: Taylor and Francis, 2013), 21.

Chapter 4. Baby Bust

1. Susan Sontag, *Illness as Metaphor* (New York: Farrar, Straus and Giroux, 1978), 57–58.

2. Margaret Marsh and Wanda Ronner, *The Empty Cradle: Infertility in America from Colonial Times to the Present* (Baltimore: Johns Hopkins University Press, 1996), 81–82.

3. Marsh and Ronner, *Empty Cradle*, 196.

4. Elaine Tyler May, *Barren in the Promised Land: Childless Americans and the Pursuit of Happiness* (Cambridge, MA: Harvard University Press, 1997), 173.

5. Diane Negra, *What a Girl Wants? Fantasizing the Reclamation of Self in Postfeminism* (London: Routledge, 2009), 48. See also Yvonne Tasker and Diane Negra, "Introduction: Feminist Politics and Postfeminist Culture," in *Interrogating Postfeminism: Gender and the Politics of Popular Culture*, ed. Yvonne Tasker and Diane Negra (Durham, NC: Duke University Press, 2007), 1–26.

6. Susan Faludi, *Backlash: The Undeclared War against American Women* (New York: Crown, 1991), 30.

7. Marsh and Ronner, *Empty Cradle*, 246.

8. Emmet J. Lamb and Sue Leurgans, "Does Adoption Affect Subsequent Fertility?," *American Journal of Obstetrics and Gynecology* 134, no. 2 (May 15, 1979): 138–144.

9. Charlotte Alter, "Todd Akin Still Doesn't Get What's Wrong with Saying 'Legitimate Rape,'" *Time*, July 17, 2014, https://time.com/3001785/todd-akin-legitimate-rape-msnbc-child-of-rape/.

10. Marsh and Ronner, *Empty Cradle*, 182.

11. Barton S. Williams, "Childless Couples Given New Hope," *Los Angeles Times*, June 3, 1953, 23.

12. "50% Success Rate in $1 Billion Infertility Fight," *New York Times*, May 18, 1988, 25, https://www.nytimes.com/1988/05/18/us/50-success-rate-in-1-billion-infertility-fight.html.

13. Kelly Oliver, *Knock Me Up, Knock Me Down: Images of Pregnancy in Hollywood Films* (New York: Columbia University Press, 2012), 154.

14. The loss of a pregnancy after twenty weeks is more appropriately termed stillbirth rather than miscarriage, and Maddie appears to be beyond this stage in this episode. Narrative time is fuzzy, however, and there is no way to pin down the exact progression of the pregnancy. The producers use "miscarriage" to describe this event, so I will follow that lead.

15. Again, though television chronology can be fuzzy in general, Maddie's pregnancy seems too advanced for a plausible elective abortion by the end of season 4 anyway, but the creators do mention this possibility on the DVD commentary.

16. Dana Stevens, "Womb Service: Tina Fey and Amy Poehler in the Surrogate-Mother Comedy Baby Mama," *Slate*, April 24, 2008, https://slate.com/culture/2008/04/baby-mama-reviewed.html.

17. The opening monologue suggests that Kate has waited too long to have a child, but Kate's infertility is later diagnosed as the result of her having a T-shaped uterus, a real condition that affects women whose mothers took the anti-miscarriage drug diethylstilbestrol (DES) during their own pregnancies. This condition is not a function of age but would lead to complications whether Kate was trying to conceive at twenty or fifty. Blaming Kate's age and careerism for her failure to conceive does not even make sense within the movie's medical story.

18. Laura Harrison, *Brown Bodies, White Babies: The Politics of Cross-racial Surrogacy* (New York: New York University Press, 2016), 58.

19. Harrison, *Brown Bodies, White Babies*, 58.

20. Raywat Deonandan, "Recent Trends in Reproductive Tourism and International Surrogacy: Ethical Considerations and Challenges for Policy," *Risk Management and Healthcare Policy* 8 (August 17, 2015): 111, https://doi.org/10.2147/rmhp.s63862.

21. Lauren Berlant, *Cruel Optimism* (Durham, NC: Duke University Press, 2011), 2.

22. *Master of None* was, for a time, a critically acclaimed slice-of-life comedy series cocreated by and starring comedian Aziz Ansari. Season 2 premiered in 2017 and attracted particularly positive attention for an episode focused on his character Dev's close lifelong friendship with Denise (Lena Waithe, the episode's cowriter) (S2E8, May 12, 2017). Because Dev's family does not celebrate Thanksgiving, he had a tradition from childhood of joining Denise's family for the holiday. The episode jumps forward through multiple holidays to show Denise's process of coming out to her family and their growing acceptance of her sexuality, ending with a warm holiday meal. That episode, "Thanksgiving," earned an Emmy for Outstanding Writing for a Comedy Series, and headlines noted that Waithe was the first Black woman to win this category. This backstory is important, because shortly after the Emmy win, Ansari was accused of sexual misconduct, an incident that sparked a significant reevaluation of his earlier sensitive, feminist creative persona. The allegations against Ansari, followed by the COVID pandemic, affected the development and release of season 3. With the series now titled *Master of None Presents: Moments in Love*, the season comprises just five episodes tracing a difficult relationship between Denise and her now-wife Alicia (Naomi Ackie). Ansari cowrote and directed all episodes but barely appears on the screen, relegating himself to a small supporting role. One could read the whole season

as a process by which Ansari seeks to recapture the success of "Thanksgiving" by building up Waithe's role in the series and tapping into what was groundbreaking about that episode: the way it centered Denise's experience (based on Waithe's own life) and found comedy in the details of family life.

23. Negra, *What a Girl Wants?*, 62.

Chapter 5. Shmashmortion

1. Jennifer's suicide also follows on her diagnosis with breast cancer, another catastrophizing outcome erroneously linked with abortion.

2. Peter Brooks, *The Melodramatic Imagination* (New Haven, CT: Yale University Press, 1996), 20.

3. Gretchen Sisson and Katrina Kimport, "Telling Stories about Abortion: Abortion-Related Plots in American Film and Television, 1916–2013," *Contraception* 89, no. 5 (May 2014): 417, https://doi.org/10.1016/j.contraception.2013.12.015.

4. Kelly Oliver, *Knock Me Up, Knock Me Down: Images of Pregnancy in Hollywood Films* (New York: Columbia University Press, 2012), 87.

5. Janet Hadley, *Abortion: Between Freedom and Necessity* (London: Virago, 1997).

6. Corinne H. Rocca, Katrina Kimport, Heather Gould, and Diana G. Foster, "Women's Emotions One Week after Receiving or Being Denied an Abortion in the United States," *Perspectives on Sexual and Reproductive Health* 45, no. 3 (2013): 122–131, https://doi.org/10.1363/4512213.

7. Corinne H. Rocca, Goleen Samari, Diana G. Foster, Heather Gould, and Katrina Kimport, "Emotions and Decision Rightness over Five Years following an Abortion: An Examination of Decision Difficulty and Abortion Stigma," *Social Science & Medicine* 248 (2020), https://www.sciencedirect.com/science/article/pii/S0277953619306999?via%3Dihub.

8. Barbara Duden, *Disembodying Women: Perspectives on Pregnancy and the Unborn* (Cambridge, MA: Harvard University Press, 1993), 81.

9. Lennart Nilsson, "Drama of Life before Birth," *Life*, April 30, 1965.

10. Karen Newman, *Fetal Positions: Individualism, Science, Visuality* (Stanford, CA: Stanford University Press, 1996), 11–15.

11. Lauren Berlant, "America, 'Fat,' the Fetus," *Boundary 2* 21, no. 3 (1994): 154, https://doi.org/10.2307/303603.

12. Rosalind Pollack Petchesky, "Fetal Images: The Power of Visual Culture in the Politics of Reproduction," *Feminist Studies* 13, no. 2 (1987): 264, https://doi.org/10.2307/3177802.

13. Berlant, "America, 'Fat,' the Fetus," 173.

14. Petchesky, "Fetal Images," 288.

15. "The rabbit died" was a common midcentury euphemism for a positive pregnancy test. Before drugstore pregnancy tests were widely available, testing required that a woman's urine be injected into a lab rabbit. The rabbit was later euthanized, and its ovaries were examined for follicular growth that would indicate the presence of pregnancy hormones in the sample urine. The rabbit died one way or the other, unfortunately.

16. Norman Lear, *Even This I Get to Experience* (New York: Penguin, 2014), 265.

17. UT Women in Cinema, "2012 WIC Master Class with Amy Heckerling Part 2," YouTube video, July 9, 2012, https://www.youtube.com/watch?v=3KC5LmwNYjE.

18. For more on how *Cagney and Lacey* navigated feminism in general and abortion in

particular, see Julie D'Acci, *Defining Women: Television and the Case of Cagney and Lacey* (Chapel Hill: University of North Carolina Press, 1994).

19. Susan Faludi, *Backlash: The Undeclared War against American Women* (New York: Crown, 2017), 151.

20. Lewis Beale, "Maude's Abortion Fades into History," *Chicago Tribune*, November 13, 1992, http://articles.chicagotribune.com/1992–11–13/features/9204130017_1_mothers-as-donna-reed-messy-family-life-maude-findlay/2.

21. Howard Rosenberg, "Advertisers Cooling Off to Hot Topics," *Los Angeles Times*, July 26, 1990, http://articles.latimes.com/1990–07–26/entertainment/ca-1054_1_summer-rerun.

22. Jennifer Vineyard, "'Everybody Wants to Live': An Oral History of *Party of Five*'s First Season," Vulture, September 3, 2014, https://www.vulture.com/2014/09/party-of-five-oral-history-1994-1995-week.html.

23. Wikipedia, s.v., "Partial Terms of Endearment," last modified December 1, 2023, https://en.wikipedia.org/wiki/Partial_Terms_of_Endearment.

24. The website http://tvtropes.org keeps an excellent crowdsourced list of film and television plots that employ the trope "Good Girls Avoid Abortion."

25. Lauren Rosewarne, *Periods in Pop Culture: Menstruation in Film and Television* (Lanham, MD: Lexington Books, 2012), 182.

26. This discourse of miscarriage reflecting a character's unreadiness to bear a child has been discussed at greater length in chapter 4.

27. Oliver, *Knock Me Up*, 108.

28. Eve Kushner, "Go Forth and Multiply: Abortion in Hollywood Movies of the '90s," *Bright Lights Film Journal*, July 1, 2000, http://brightlightsfilm.com/go-forth-multiply-abortion-hollywood-movies-90s/#.WOUNPxiZPxt.

29. Jan Hoffman, "TV Shouts 'Baby' (and Barely Whispers 'Abortion')," *New York Times*, May 31, 1992, http://www.nytimes.com/1992/05/31/arts/television-tv-shouts-baby-and-barely-whispers-abortion.html?pagewanted=1.

30. Ross Douthat, "Choosing Life," *Atlantic*, June 2, 2007, https://www.theatlantic.com/amp/article/54427/.

31. Ross Douthat, "The Unfunny Truth," Opinion, *New York Times*, August 10, 2009, http://www.nytimes.com/2009/08/10/opinion/10douthat.html.

32. Dana Stevens, "The Politics of Shmashmortion: 'Knocked Up' as a Litmus Test," Culturebox, *Slate*, June 8, 2007, http://www.slate.com/articles/arts/culturebox/2007/06/the_politics_of_shmashmortion.html.

33. Steve Weintraub, "Judd Apatow Interview: 'Knocked Up,'" *Collider*, May 22, 2007, http://collider.com/judd-apatow-interview-knocked-up/.

34. Rosenberg, "Advertisers Cooling Off."

35. Steven Zeitchik, "*Modern Family* Has an Incredible Legacy: There May Never Be Another Show like It," *Washington Post*, February 5, 2019, https://www.washingtonpost.com/business/2019/02/06/modern-family-has-an-incredible-legacy-there-may-never-ever-be-another-show-like-it-again/.

36. Alison Rosen, "Jenni Konner," February 12, 2017, in *Alison Rosen Is Your New Best Friend*, podcast, 55:40, http://www.alisonrosen.com/2017/02/jenni-konner/.

37. Al-Yasha Ilhaam, "Reading *Citizen Ruth* Her Rights: Satire and Moral Realism in the Abortion Debate," in *Bioethics at the Movies*, ed. Sandra Shapshay (Baltimore: Johns Hopkins University Press, 2009), 32.

38. Janet Maslin, "To Abort, Not to Abort: A Comedy," *New York Times*, December

13, 1996, http://www.nytimes.com/1996/12/13/movies/to-abort-not-to-abort-a-comedy.html.

39. Amy G. Bryant and Jonas J. Swartz, "Why Crisis Pregnancy Centers Are Legal but Unethical," *AMA Journal of Ethics* 20, no. 3 (March 2018): 269–277.

40. For an extended consideration of Silverman's stand-up comedy, see Linda Mizejewski, *Pretty/Funny: Women Comedians and Body Politics* (Austin: University of Texas Press, 2014).

41. Gillian Robespierre and Jenny Slate, "The Women behind 'Obvious Child' Talk Farts, Abortion and Stage Fright," interview by Terry Gross, *Fresh Air*, June 26, 2014, https://www.npr.org/2014/06/26/325508208/the-women-behind-obvious-child-talk-farts-abortion-and-stage-fright.

42. Robespierre and Slate, "Women behind 'Obvious Child.'"

43. *Gone with the Wind* is actually 3 hours and 54 minutes with intermission.

44. Laura Bradley, "How *Jane the Virgin* Crafted the Perfect Abortion Storyline," *Vanity Fair*, October 24, 2016, http://www.vanityfair.com/hollywood/2016/10/jane-the-virgin-abortion-interview-jennie-snyder-urman.

45. Alison Leiby, "Please Laugh about My Abortion with Me," Opinion, *New York Times*, July 13, 2022, https://www.nytimes.com/2022/07/13/opinion/alison-leiby-abortion-comedy-show.html.

Conclusion. It's All in the Delivery

1. "Jerry Lewis: Not Funny," *People*, October 29, 1998, https://people.com/celebrity/jerry-lewis-not-funny/.

2. Christopher Hitchens, "Why Women Aren't Funny," *Vanity Fair*, January 1, 2007, https://www.vanityfair.com/culture/2007/01/hitchens200701.

3. The 2000s were also the years in which anti-smoking campaigns succeeded in eliminating cigarette smoking from most bars and clubs, making the air safer for pregnant women and everyone else within these spaces.

4. Elizabeth A. Harris, "Amy Schumer, Ali Wong and the Rise of Pregnant Stand-Up," *New York Times*, April 19, 2019, https://www.nytimes.com/2019/04/19/arts/pregnant-comedians-amy-schumer-ali-wong.html.

5. Rachael Healy, "'I Did Standup with My Baby Strapped to Me': The Comics Motherhood Can't Stop," *Guardian*, March 14, 2023, https://www.theguardian.com/stage/2023/mar/14/comics-motherhood-josie-long-mothers-day-taboos.

6. Harris, "Amy Schumer, Ali Wong."

INDEX

Pages numbers in *italics* refer to figures.

abortion, 3–4, 6; "awfulization," 155, 171; comedy's tool kit brought to, 155–156; *Dobbs v. Jackson Women's Health Organization,* 3, 113–114, 186; fetal personhood and, 156–161; male pregnancy satire and, 77–78, 91; melodrama and, 153–155, 164, 165, 170–171, 174, 183, 186; miscarriage as narrative substitute for, 136–137, 139, 166–167; in 1990s and 2000s film and television, 165–173; in 1970s and 1980s film and television, 161–165; *Roe v. Wade,* 113, 154, 161, 163, 166, 169, 194; stand-up comics on, 186, 193–195; ultrasound technology in anti-abortion argument, 20–21. See also *Citizen Ruth; Just Another Girl on the I.R.T.; Maude; Obvious Child; Sarah Silverman Program*

Ackie, Naomi, 148, *150*

adoption: coercive, 95–96; conception-after-adoption trope, 124–125; infertility and, 124–128, 143–147, 151; "social problem" framings of, 113–118; stork narrative and, 19, 46–47; teenage pregnancy and, 111–113, 115–118

adulterous pregnancy, 34–35

After the Thin Man (film), 33

Ahmed, Sara, 11, 12

Akin, Todd, 124

Albert, Eddie, 37

Alexander, Erika, 130

Ali Wong: Baby Cobra (stand-up special), 10, *191,* 191–193

All in the Family (television series), 136

Allen, Tim, 9

Allen, Woody, 85, *86,* 90

Alley, Kirstie, 158

All's Fair at the Fair (animated short film), 44

Allyson, June, 40

American Family Association, 165–166, 172

Anderson, Anthony, 9

And Just Like That . . . (television series), 136–137

Angie (film), 167

animated film, 43–47

Aniston, Jennifer, 89, 131

announcement, pregnancy: absence as, 36–37; for "bad" pregnancies, 94; conflated with illness, 37, 38–39; drawings and ultrasound photos as, 134, 157; fainting as, 38; knitting as, 20, 33–34, 61; nonverbal and coded, 20, 32–34, *33,* 33–34, 36–37, 57, 61; songs as, 54–55; stand-up comedy routine as, 182; surrogacy and, 141

Another World (soap opera), 153

Anthony, Susan B., 31

Antin, Steve, 163

Apatow, Judd, 21, 22, 26, 170, 172

Apes of Wrath (animated short film), 46

Are We Done Yet? (film), 19

Arnaz, Desi, 54

Arnett, Will, 88

Arnold, Sarah, 75

Arnold, Tom, 76–77

Arthur, Bea, 161, *162*

assisted reproductive technology, 3, 4, 128–135; donor eggs, 145–146; donor sperm, 130–131, 140, 143, 148–149; in vitro fertilization (IVF), 123, 142, 144–145, 148, 150

Atwood, Margaret, 115
Auntie Mame (film), 99
Averill, David, 4
Away We Go (film), *16,* 16–17

baby boom, 3, 34, 45–46, 51, 57–58, 114, 127
Baby Bottleneck (animated short film), 46
Babymakers, The (film), 89–90
Baby Mama (film), 123, 139–144, *142*
Back-Up Plan, The (film), 5–7, *6,* 18, 21
Bacon, Kevin, 128
Bad Moms (film), 11–12
"bad" pregnancies, 27, 95, 98, 118. *See also* nonmarital pregnancy; teenage pregnancy
Bakhtin, Mikhail, 14
Ball, Lucille, 10, 54–57
Banks, Elizabeth, *2,* 123
Barbeau, Adrienne, 161
Barr, Roseanne, 158, *159*
Barrett, Amy Coney, 113–114
Baruchel, Jay, 25, 170
Bateman, Jason, 89, 116, *117,* 131, 133
Batinkoff, Randall, 103
Bearse, Amanda, 15
Beau Ties (animated short film), 43
Bell Curve, The (Herrnstein and Murray), 96–97
Bergen, Candice, 105, 109
Bergson, Henri, 11
Berlant, Lauren, 145, 157, 159
Bernhard, Sandra, 188, 190, *190*
Berry, Halle, 141
Beverly Hills 90210 (television series), 166, 169
Bewitched (television series), 78–79
Beyond the Forest (film), 153
Biancolli, Amy, 7
Big Love (television series), 166
biological clocks, 3, 73, 121, 145
birth control. *See* contraception
Birth Control (film), 40
bisociation, 12
Bisset, Jacqueline, 101
Black teen pregnancy, 103–105
Blessed Event (film), 34, 35, 53
Blondell, Joan, 57

Blondie's Blessed Event (film), 1–2, 32, 53
Bloodworth-Thomason, Linda, 169
Boardman, Eleanor, 32, *33*
Boy Meets Girl (film), 38, *38*
Bracken, Eddie, 47
Bridget Jones's Baby (film), 67
Brie, Alison, 184
Brody, Richard, 104
Brooks, Peter, 154
Brother Rat (film), 37
Brothers Solomon, The (film), 88, 90
Brown, Jane, 112
Brown, Lisa, 6
Bryan, Jane, 37
Bryant, Lena, 31
Burnett, Carol, 69–70, 71
Bush, George H. W., 78, 106–109
Bush, George W., 179

Cabbage Fairy, The. See La Fée aux Choux
Cagney, James, 38
Cagney and Lacey (television series), 166
Cameron, JoAnna, 100
Camhe, Beverly, 83
Campbell, Richard, 106
Cantor, Eddie, 45
carnival and carnivalesque, 14–15, 22, 77
Carol Burnett Show, The (television series), 69–70
Carrie (film), 26
Carson, T. C., 130
Carter, Angela, 13
Carter, Kayli, 145
Casanova Brown (film), 36–37
Casey Bats Again (animated short film), *62*
Cass, Peggy, 99
Cates, Phoebe, 165
Champlin, Donna Lynne, 184
Chandrasekhar, Jay, 89–90
Cheaper by the Dozen (film), 53, *53*
China Beach (television series), 154, 166, 169, 172
Citizen Ruth (film), 10, 173–176, *176, 177*
"clinical," use of the term, 4
Clinton, Bill, 109, 179
Clooney, George, 154
clothing: child-like, *76;* padded bumps,

52–53, *53,* 57–58, *102*; smocks, 52–53, *53*; stand-up comics and, 193, *194,* 195, *196*
Cody, Diablo, 116
Coll, Ivonne, 185
Columbus, Chris, 77
Combs, Annie, *160*
comedy, genre of, 7–15; abortion and, 155–156; social bonds and, 11–12; women excluded from, 63, 187–188
commodification, 23, 32, 64
Comstock Act, 40, 42
confinement, home, 30–32, 39, 55, 57
consumption and consumerism, 32, 73–74, 114, 115
contraception, 3, 4, 10, 16, 36; eugenics and, 40–43; euphemisms for, 43–47; sabotaging, 75; vasectomies, 161
Cooper, Brittney, 70
Cooper, Gary, 36
Cooper, Julie, 84
Cosby, Bill, 9, 70–73
Cosby Show, The (television series), 68, 71–72, 77, 138; "The Birth," 72, 81, 82; "Calling Dr. Huxtable," 72; "Father's Day," 72; "Rudy's Sick," 72; "The Day the Spores Landed," 81–82
couvade syndrome, 64–65, 74, 78
Cox, Courteney, 122
Crain, Jeanne, 39, 51
Crazy Ex-Girlfriend (television series), 184–185
Creed, Barbara, 75
Crowd, The (film), 32, *33,* 61, 67
Crowther, Bosley, 58
Crystal, Billy, 79, *80*
Cusack, Joan, 76, *76,* 77

Daddy's Home (film), 131, *132,* 133, 134–135
Dailey, Dan, 127
D'Angelo, Beverly, 141
Daniels, Jeff, 16
Danson, Ted, 130
Davis, Bette, 42, 67, 153
Davis, Geena, 141
Davis, Kristin, 124
Day, Doris, 99, 119, 120, 128

Decker, Brooklyn, *2*
Dee, Sandra, 99
Delivery Man (film), 89
Demarest, William, 47
depression, postpartum, 103
Dern, Laura, 174
Designing Women (television series), 169
Desperate Housewives (television series), 166
DeVito, Danny, 83
Diaz, Cameron, *2*
Dick Van Dyke Show, The (television series), 68
divorce, 99, 100, 132, 135, 148, 154
Doane, Mary Ann, 8
Dobbs v. Jackson Women's Health Organization, 3, 113–114, 186
Doctor, You've Got to Be Kidding! (film), 99–100, *100*
Doctor Bull (film), 34
Doonesbury (comic strip), 4, *5*
double entendres, 47
Douthat, Ross, 170, 171
Dow, Bonnie, 105
Downey, Robert, Jr., 89
Draper, Polly, 181
Duden, Barbara, 156
Due Date (film), 89
Dumbo (film), 43
Dunham, Lena, 159, *160,* 161
Dyer, Richard, 116

Ellis, Tom, 131
Employees' Entrance (film), 43
Engel, Georgia, 124
English, Diane, 106–107
essentialism, 188
eugenics, 17, 18, 114; birth control and, 40–43; *Idiocracy* and, 93–94, 96–97; race and, 18, 93–94, 96–98, 123, 176
euphemisms, abortion, 157, 170, 179
euphemisms, body-part, 180–181
euphemisms, infertility, 127–128
euphemisms, pregnancy, 6, 20, 32–35; "blessed event," 20, 35–36, 55; cabbage patch, 20, 29–30, *30,* 43; fainting, 34, 38–39, 51–52; "in trouble," 34–35; knitted items, 20, 33–34, 61;

Index • 217

misreadings of, 32–34; stork, 1, 2, 30, 43–47, *45, 46*; whispers, 61–63

Everything You Always Wanted to Know about Sex* (*But Were Afraid to Ask) (film), 85, *86,* 90

Ex-Lady (film), 42

fainting, men, 67, 72, 76–77, 78
fainting, women, 34, *38,* 38–39, 51–52
Falcone, Ben, 123
"fallen woman" trope, 49–50, *50,* 98
false-alarm pregnancies, 34
Faludi, Susan, 122
Falwell, Jerry, 172
Family Guy (animated television series), 166
Farm of Tomorrow, The (animated short film), 45–46
Fast Times at Ridgemont High (film), 164–165
Father of the Bride (film), 73–74
Father of the Bride Part II (film), 62, 68, 73–74
fatherhood: appropriations of female role in pregnancy and childbirth, 66–77; couvade syndrome, 64–65, 74, 78; male pregnancy depictions, 77–84; Bruce Willis *Spy* cover, 64, *64*; sperm comedies, 85–90; whisper codes and, 61–63; womb envy, 65–66, 82, 83
Father's Little Dividend (film), 53, 63, 68
Father Takes a Wife (film), 33
Faust, Chad, 110
feminism, 20, 101–102, 122, 139, 144, 155, 158, 169, 174
feminist critiques and anti-feminism, 11, 21, 79, 197
feminist film scholarship, 8–9
Ferrell, Will, 131, 134
fertility and infertility, 3, 119–125; assisted reproductive technology, 3, 4, 128–135; "character flaw" stereotypes, 119–123; conception-after-adoption trope, 124–125; in early films, 125–128; as "for the best," 135–139; "just relax" mantra and, 121–124; stigma of, 12; in vitro fertilization (IVF), 123, 142, 144–145, 148, 150. *See also Baby Mama; Master of None; Private Life*

fertilization process, 85–86
Fey, Tina, 123, 139, 143–144
Fields, W. C., 42
Fischer, Jenna, 90
Fischer, Lucy, 8–9
Fischler, Patrick, 93, *94*
Flintstones, The (television series), 68
Fools Rush In (film), *62,* 68–69, *69, 160,* 168
Foran, Dick, 126
For Keeps (film), 103, 167
Forte, Will, 88
Four Wives (film), 38, *39,* 125–126
Foxx, Jamie, 89
Francis, Arlene, 119, *120*
Franklin, Diane, 163
Frasier (television series), 167
free-range fetus, 19–21
Friday Night Lights (television series), 169
Friedman, Jena, 28, 193, 194–196, *196*
Friends (television series), 122
Full of Life (film), 57–58, *58*
Funny About Love (film), 73, 129–130, *130*
Funny Girl (film), 101, *102*

Galifianakis, Zach, 89
Game Night (film), 133–134
Garcia, Jesse, 111
Garner, James, 119, 120
Garner, Jennifer, 113, 116, *117*, 122
Generation (film), 99
Gentlemen Prefer Blondes (film), 173
Giamatti, Paul, 144, *147*
Girls (television series), 159, *160,* 161, 172–173
Girls Trip (film), 123
Gleason, Jackie, 34
GLOW (television series), 184
Goldberg, Whoopi, 130
Goldblum, Jeff, 74
González, Chalo, 111
Goo Goo Goliath (animated short film), 46
Grable, Betty, 51, 53, 127
Graham, Heather, 131
Grandma (film), 185
Grant, Cary, 51
Grant, Hugh, 74, 76–77

Great Depression, 51, 114
Great Lie, The (film), 67
Grey's Anatomy (television series), 154
grotesque, 5, 13–15, 21–26, 67, 74, 84, 193. See also *Knocked Up*
Growing (stand-up special), 193, *194*
Growing Pains (television series), 138
Guy-Blaché, Alice, 29–30, *30*, 36, 56
Gyllenhaal, Maggie, 17

Hader, Bill, 23
Hadley, Janet, 155
Haggins, Bambi, 70
Hahn, Kathryn, 122, 144, 147
Hall, Regina, 123
Hand That Rocks the Cradle, The (film), 40
Hangover, The (film), 22
Hard Knock Wife (stand-up special), 193
Harlan, Otis, 42
Harris, Leslie, 103–104
Harrison, Laura, 140, 142
Haskell, Molly, 8
Hatch, Heather, 27
Hathaway, Anne, 26
Hayek, Salma, 68–69, *69, 160,* 168
healthcare system, 90–91, 95, 171, 182
Heckerling, Amy, 164–165
Hedren, Tippi, 174
Heigl, Katherine, 21, 24, 169
Herrnstein, Richard, 96
Hill, Jonah, 26, 170
Hitchens, Christopher, 187–188
Hoffmann, Gaby, 181
Holland, Jennifer, 20–21
Holliday, Judy, 57–58, *58*
Holly, Lauren, 123
Honeymooners, The (television series), 34
Honeymooners Second Honeymoon, The (television special), 34
Honeymoon Stand-Up Special, The (stand-up special), 193, *194*
Hope, Bob, 100–101
Horney, Karen, 65–66
How to Commit Marriage (film), 100–101
Hubbard, John, 78
Hudson, Rochelle, 34
Hudson, Rock, 99
Hughes, John, 103

Human Comedy, The (film), 51
Hunt, Darlene, 93, *94*
Hunt, Helen, 135
Hunter, Holly, 141
Hunter, Kim, 52
Hutton, Betty, 47, *50*

Ice Cube, 19
Ides of March, The (film), 154
Idiocracy (film), 93–97, *95,* 98, 113, 121, 143
If These Walls Could Talk (film), 155
Ilhaam, Al-Yasha, 174
illness and pathology, pregnancy as, 37–40, 102–103
I Love Lucy (television series), 10, 34, 54–57; "Lucy Goes to the Hospital," 56; "Lucy Is Enceinte," 54; "Lucy's Show-Biz Swan Song," 55; "Pregnant Women Are Unpredictable," 54; "Ricky Has Labor Pains," 55, *56, 63*
I'm Still Here . . . Damn It! (stand-up special), 188, 190, *190*
IMDb, 8
Imitation of Life (1934 film), 8
Imitation of Life (1959 film), 8
infant mortality, 31
Inside Amy Schumer (television series), 10
International House (film), 42
in vitro fertilization (IVF), 123, 142, 144–145, 148, 150. See also assisted reproductive technology
Irigaray, Luce, 12
Irma la Douce (film), 99
Irving, Amy, 73
It's a Wise Child (film), 34

Jackie Gleason Show, The (television series), 34
Jackson, Chris, 137
Jackson, Janet, 141
Jacob, John E., 106
Jane the Virgin (television series), 19, 131, 185
Janney, Allison, 17, 112
Jenkins, Tamara, 144
Joey Bishop Show, The (television series), 63, 67

Index • 219

Johansson, Scarlett, 105
Johnson, Adam, 95
Johnson, Ariyan A., 104
Joke Show (stand-up special), 6–7
Journey for Margaret (film), 126
Judge, Mike, 93
Junior (film), 10, 82–84, 91
Juno (film), 111–118, 122, 167, 169, 185
"*Juno* Effect," 110–113
Just Another Girl on the I.R.T. (film), 103–105

Kaplan, Ann, 8
Keaton, Diane, 75
Kids Are All Right, The (film), 130–131
Kimport, Katrina, 154–155
King of Jazz (film), 42
King of Queens (television series), 124
Kinnear, Greg, 123
Kinsey Reports, 98–99
Klein, Robert, *6, 7*
Klenk, Kara, 191
Klepp, Susan, 19
Knight, Ted, 124
knitting, 20, 33–34, 61
Knocked Up (film), 21–27, *25,* 112, 169–171, 179–181
Koestler, Arthur, 12
Konner, Jenni, 172–173
Kotch (film), 102
Krasinski, John, 16, 90
Kruger, Barbara, 78
Kubrick, Stanley, 157
Kurtz, Swoosie, 174
Kushner, Eve, 167

Lacy, Jake, 179
Ladykiller (stand-up special), 193, 194–196, *196*
La Fée aux Choux (*The Cabbage Fairy*) (film), 29, *30*
Lahti, Christine, 129–130
Lambert the Sheepish Lion (animated short film), 46
Landis, Carole, 78
Lane, Lola, 125
Lane, Priscilla, 38, *39*
Lane Bryant, 31

Lankford, James, 20
Last American Virgin, The (film), 163–164, 165
Lavin, Linda, 18
Lear, Norman, 161, 163
Leavitt, Judith Walzer, 31, 37
Le Beauf, Sabrina, 72
Lee, Spike, 26, 87–88
Leggero, Natasha, 193, 194
Leiby, Alison, 186
Leigh, Jennifer Jason, 164
Lewis, Jerry, 187–188
Life of Riley, The (television series), 61, 68
Linney, Laura, 141
Lippman, Amy, 166
Living Single (television series), 130
Long, Josie, 190
Long, Nia, 19
Look Who's Talking (film), 158
Look Who's Talking Too (film), 158, *159*
Loos, Anita, 173
Lopez, Jennifer, 5, 18
Louise, Anita, 36
Love Life (television series), 185
Lover Come Back (film), 99
Lowery, Marcella, 72
Loy, Myrna, 33, 53, *53*
Lynn, Diana, 48

Ma and Pa Kettle Back on the Farm (film), 53
Mackie, Anthony, 87, *88*
Macy, Bill, 161
Mad About You (television series), 135–136
Madame a des Envies (*Madame's Fancies*) (film), 29–30
Made in America (film), 130–131
Madonna trope, 12–13, 118
Malco, Romany, 142
male pregnancy. *See* fatherhood
Malone, Jena, 110
Mama's Family (television series), 9
Mann, Earl, 93
Mann, Leslie, 24
Manny and Lo (film), 105
Many a Slip (film), 34
Maron, Marc, 184
Married . . . with Children (television series), 15

Marsden, James, 110

Marsiglio, William, 65

Martin, Emily, 85–86

Martin, Olga J., 36

Martin, Steve, 73–75, 167

Mary Tyler Moore Show, The (television series), 124

masculine appropriations, 66–77, 79, 82–83, 91

masculinity: assisted reproductive technology and, 132; clowning and, 130; gender identity and, 82; hypermasculinity, 84, 86; infertility and, 132, 133–135; toxic masculinity, 22; womb envy and, 65–66, 82, 83. *See also* masculine appropriations

Maslin, Janet, 175

Master of None (television series), 148–151, *150*

maternal melodrama, 8

maternal mortality, 31

Matthau, Walter, 102

Maude (television series), 10, 161–163, *162*, 165

McBride, Chi, 88

McClanahan, Rue, 161, *162*

McGinley, John C., 19

McGovern, Elizabeth, 129

McHugh, Frank, 125

Meadows, Audrey, 34

melodrama, 8–9; abortion and, 153–155, 164, 165, 170–171, 174, 183, 186; production codes and, 34, 35, 49, 52; "social problem" framings and, 102–103

Mickey's Nightmare (animated short film), 43

Micki & Maude (film), 73

midwives, 31–32, 66, 121, 127

Mike and Molly (television series), 124

Mildred Pierce (film), 8

Miracle of Life, The (television special), 26

Miracle of Morgan's Creek, The (film), 10, 47–51, *50*, *62*, 99

miscarriage, 148, 174; as "for the best," 135, 136–139; as narrative substitute for abortion, 136–137, 139, 166–167; stand-up comics on, 192–196

Mitchell, Thomas, 39

Mo' Better Blues (film), 26

Modleski, Tania, 8, 24

Monoson, Lawrence, 163

Moonlighting (television series), 137–139, *138*, 166

Moore, Demi, 64; *Vanity Fair* cover, *64*

Moore, Dudley, 73

Moore, Julianne, 74, *76*, 77, 130

Moorehead, Agnes, 79

Motherhood: Life's Greatest Miracle (film), 40

Motion Picture Production Code, 1, 27, 34–40, 47, 51–52, 63, 66

Mouse Divided, A (animated short film), 46

Moynihan Report, 72, 115

Mulroney, Brian, 106

multiple births: quintuplets, 49; sextuplets, 49; triplets, 90, 123, 133; twins, 18, 19, *46*, 72, 81, 110, 126, 137, 192

Munn, Olivia, 89

Murphy Brown (television series), 10, 105–109, 167, 169; "I'm as Much of a Man as I Ever Was," 107–108; "Send in the Clowns," 108; "Uh Oh: Part 2," 107; "You Say Potatoe, I Say Potato: Parts 1 and 2," 108–109

Murray, Charles, 96

Murray, James, 32, *33*

Murray, Ken, 39

Music for Millions (film), 39–40, 51

My Baby's Daddy (film), 62

My Blue Heaven (film), 51, 53, 126–127

Navedo, Andrea, 185

Nazism, 41

Negra, Diane, 121, 151

Nilsson, Lennart, 157, 159

Nine Months (film), *62*, 74, 75–76, *76*, 158

Nobody's Baby (film), 36

nonmarital mothers and motherhood, 52, 102, 108, 112–117, 128

nonmarital pregnancy, 3, 27, 34, 35, 49–52, 98–108, 112–116, 169

Object of My Affection, The (film), 167

O'Brien, Margaret, 40

O'Brien, Pat, 38
Obvious Child (film), 10, 179–183, 184, *184*
O'Connor, Carroll, 136
Odd Couple, The (television series), 68
Office, The (television series), 90–91
Oh, Sandra, 154
O'Hara, Catherine, 16, *16*
Oliver, Kelly, 102–103, 130, 155, 167
O'Loughlin, Alex, 5
One Hundred and One Dalmatians (film), 67
Oppenheimer, Jess, 54
Opposite Sex, The (film), 57
Owens, Geoffrey, 72

padded bumps, 52–53, *53, 57*–58, *102*
Page, Elliot, 111, 169
Page, Gale, 125
Palladino, Aleksa, 105
Parenthood (film), 167–168
Parker, Nicole Ari, 137
Party of Five (television series), 166
Paternity (film), 62, 73
pathology. *See* illness and pathology, pregnancy as
Payne, Alexander, 173, 174, 176
Pazsitzky, Christina (Christina P), 190
Penny Serenade (film), 126
People Will Talk (film), 39, 51–52
Perez, Raul, 11
Perry, Matthew, 68, *69, 160,* 168
Pesca, Mike, 112
Petchesky, Rosalind Pollack, 158, 159, 183
Phillips, Joseph C., 81
Pidgeon, Walter, 101
Place, Mary Kay, 105, 174
Planned Parenthood, 104, 183
Poehler, Amy, 139, 140, 143–144
postfeminism, 121, 151
Powell, William, 33
Prather, Joan, 80
Pregnancy Pact, The (TV movie), 113
pregnancy rates, 51
Preston, Kelly, 171, 174
Private Life (film), 122, 131–132, *132,* 144–148, *147,* 151
Private Number (film), 36

privilege, class and racial, 18, 96, 141–143
production code. *See* Motion Picture Production Code
Production Code Administration (PCA), 47
Purcell, Lee, 101
Puzzled Pals (animated short film), 43–44, *45*

Quayle, Dan, 105–106, 108–109
Quinceañera (film), 18–19, 111

Rabbit Test (film), 79–80, *80*
racism, 11, 28, 71–72, 85–86, 106, 115, 166
Ramirez, Dania, 87
Randall, Meg, 53
Randall, Tony, 68
Ransdell, Ryan, 94
rape, 4, 36, 115, 124
Reagan, Ronald, 73, 96, 97, 179
Reducing (film), 34
Reeves, Jimmie L., 106
Reinking, Ann, 73
Reiser, Paul, 135
Reitman, Ivan, 83
respectability politics, 70
Revolutionary Road (film), 155
Reynolds, Burt, 73, 174, 175
Richardson, Haley Lu, 185
Ringwald, Molly, 103
Rios, Emily, 18–19, 111
Rivers, Joan, 79, *80,* 188, *189*
Road to Ruin, The (film), 153
Roberts, Doris, 80
Roberts, Dorothy, 18, 97
Robespierre, Gillian, 179–180, 181, 183
Rock, Chris, 18
Rodriguez, Gina, 19, 131
Roe v. Wade, 113, 154, 161, 163, 166, 169, 194
Rogen, Seth, 21, 22, 169
Rogers, Ginger, 34
Romano, Ray, 9
Romanus, Robert, 164
Roseanne (television series), 9, 167
Rosewarne, Lauren, 166–167
Rowe Karlyn, Kathleen, 8, 14–15
Rudolph, Maya, 16, *16*

Ruffalo, Mark, 130
Rules of Engagement (television series), 124
Russell, Keri, 13, 169
Russo, Mary, 14, 15

Sagal, Katey, 15
Sagher, Tami, 23
Saint Frances (film), 185
Sanford and Son (television series), 63
Sanger, Margaret, 40
Santoro, Rodrigo, 18
Sarah Silverman Program, The (television series), 173, 176–177, *178*, 179
Saturday Night Live (television variety show), 10, 77–78
Saved! (film), 10, 110–111
Scala, Gia, 128
Schneider, Paul, 89
Schumer, Amy, 10, 28, 193–195, *194*
Schwarzenegger, Arnold, 10, 82–84
Scotti, Tony, 153
Scrubs (television series), 169
Secret Life of the American Teenager, The (television series), 167
sentimentalization, 6–7
Seven Brides for Seven Brothers (film), 67
Sex and the City (film), 124
Sex and the City (television series), 136–137, 167, 169
sexual revolution, 98–109
Shall We Dance? (film), 34
shame, 12–15, 34–35, 37, 155, 182–183, 185–186
Shannon, Molly, 145
Shaud, Grant, 107
Shawn, Wallace, 82
She Done Him Wrong (film), 34–35
She Hate Me (film), 26, 87–88, *88*
Shelton, Marley, 110
Shepard, Dax, 140
Shepherd, Cybill, 137
She's Having a Baby (film), 128–129, *129*
Short, Martin, 74
Shrill (television series), 185
Shuffle Off to Buffalo (animated short film), 44–45, *46*
silent film, 33, 61, 153
Silverman, Sarah, 173, 176–177, *178*, 179

Simmons, J. K., 116
Sisson, Gretchen, 154–155
16 and Pregnant (television reality series), 103
Slate, Jenny, 179
Smile Like Yours, A (film), 123, 131, 133
Smith, Kurtwood, 174
smocks, 52–53, *53*
Smulders, Cobie, 89
Snyder Urman, Jennie, 185
social problem films, 40, 52
"social problem" framings, 93–98; of adoption, 113–118; of nonmarital pregnancy, 98–109; of teenage pregnancy, 110–113
Solinger, Rickie, 41, 114, 115
Sontag, Susan, 119
So You're Going to Be a Father (film), 62
sperm comedies, 66, 85–90
Stand Up and Be Counted (film), 101–102
stand-up comics, 187–197; on abortion, 186, 193–195; clothing and, 193, *194,* 195, *196*; on miscarriage, 192–196; pregnant, 187–197; routine of, as pregnancy announcement, 182
Stapleton, Jean, 136
Steenburgen, Mary, 167
Steinem, Gloria, 77, 122
Stella Dallas (film), 8
Stevens, Dana, 139, 171–172
Stork Bites Man (film), 62
stork euphemisms and narratives, 1, 2, 30, 43–47, *45, 46*
Stork Naked (animated short film), 47
Strauss, Jean, 116
Streetcar Named Desire, A (film), 52
Streisand, Barbra, 101, *102*
Struthers, Gloria, 136
studio films, 99–101
Sturges, Preston, 47–48, 50
Sugar and Spice (film), 110, *111*
Sunny Side Up (film), 42
surveillance culture, 16–17
Swanson, Gloria, 33
Swing It Soldier (film), 39
Switch, The (film), 89, 131

Tate, Sharon, 153

Taylor, Clarice, 72–73
Taylor, Elizabeth, 53
Taylor, Holland, 143
teenage mothers and motherhood, 102, 103, 111–113, 165
teenage pregnancy, 27, 98–99, 102–105, 109–113, 115–118
Teen Mom (television reality series), 103
Tender Comrade (film), 51
Theron, Charlize, 11
Thigpen, Kevin, 104
Thompson, Emma, 83, 84
Three Cheers for the Irish (film), 38–39
Thrill of It All, The (film), 119, *120, 120*–121
Tierney, Maura, 140
Tomlin, Lily, 185
"too early" pregnancy, 113, 118
"too late" pregnancy, 28, 113, 118
Tracy, Lee, 35
transvaginal ultrasound, 4, *6,* 149, 171
Tudyk, Alan, 23
Tully (film), 11
Tunnel of Love (play and film), 127–128
Turnabout (film), 78
21 Jump Street (television series), 169
twilight sleep movement, 37
2001: A Space Odyssey (film), 157

ultrasound, 4–6, 20–21, 75–76, 144, 149, 156–159, 171
United States v. One Package of Japanese Pessaries, 40
unmarried mothers. *See* nonmarital mothers and motherhood; nonmarital pregnancy
unpartnered pregnancy, 12, 18, 102, 105–107, 113, 118, 149
unplanned pregnancy, 13, 98, 103, 136, 139–140, 161, 167, 169, 186
Unpregnant (film), 185–186
Unwed Mother (film), 52
unwed pregnancy and motherhood. *See* nonmarital mothers and motherhood; nonmarital pregnancy

vagina, 5–6, 23–24, 26, 128, 180, 183, 191–192

Valley of the Dolls (film), 153
Vaughn, Vince, 89
Very Idea, The (play and films), 41–42, 114
Vidor, King, 32, *33*

Wahlberg, Mark, 134
Waithe, Lena, 148
Waitress (film), 13, 169
Warner, Malcolm-Jamal, 81
Washington, Kerry, 87
Wayne, David, 127
Weaver, Sigourney, 140, 141, *142*
Welsh, Anthony, 148
Wertz, Dorothy, 31
Wertz, Richard, 31
West, Jennifer Ellis, 20, 37
West, Mae, 34–35
What to Expect When You're Expecting (film), 18, 27, 123, 136, 169; publicity posters, 1–2, *2*
Where Are My Children? (film), 40, 153
whispers as code and euphemism, 61–63
whiteness, 17–19, 96, 115–118, 123, 140
Widmark, Richard, 128
Wiig, Kristen, 23, 88
Wilder, Gene, 73, 129
Williams, Linda, 8
Williams, Robin, 76–77
Willis, Bruce, 64, 137, *138,* 158; *Spy* cover, *64*
Wilson, Alex, 101
Wilson, Marie, 38, *38*
Winters, Deborah, 102
Wolf, Michelle, 6–7
womb envy, 65–66, 82, 83
Wong, Ali, 10, 28, 191, *191*
Wood, Evan Rachel, 154
World War II, 51, 126. *See also* baby boom
Wright, Teresa, 37
Wyatt, Jane, 127
Wyman, Jane, 100–101

Yi, Charlyne, 23
You for Me (film), 57